Deschutes

PENGUIN BOOKS

Legendary Children

Tom Fitzgerald and Lorenzo Marquez are a married couple who have been together for more than two decades. In 2006, they launched their first blog, *Project Rungay*, and were shocked that it gained an audience of some size. In 2010, they quit their jobs in advertising and academia and launched their eponymous site, *Tom + Lorenzo*, where they have been offering fashion, television, film, and cultural criticism to a readership in the millions ever since. They are the authors of *Everyone Wants to Be Me or Do Me* (2014) and the hosts of the weekly *Pop Style Opinionfest* podcast on the Cadence13 network. Whenever the press or the public needs an explanation or some context in the areas of fashion, celebrity, TV and film, pop culture, or LGBTQ life, they have turned to T Lo to get their take.

CHILDREN ·

The First Decade

of

RuPaul's Drag Race

and the

Last Century of Queer Life

TOM FITZGERALD AND LORENZO MARQUEZ

PENGUIN BOOKS

PENGUIN BOOKS
An imprint of Penguin Random House LLC
penguinrandomhouse.com

Copyright © 2020 by Tom Fitzgerald and Lorenzo Marquez

Penguin supports copyright. Copyright fuels creativity, encourages di-
verse voices, promotes free speech, and creates a vibrant culture. Thank
you for buying an authorized edition of this book and for complying with
copyright laws by not reproducing, scanning, or distributing any part of it
in any form without permission. You are supporting writers and allowing
Penguin to continue to publish books for every reader.

LIBRARY OF CONGRESS CATALOGING-IN-PUBLICATION DATA
Names: Fitzgerald, Tom (Thomas), 1966– author. |
Marquez, Lorenzo, author.
Title: Legendary children : the first decade of RuPaul's drag race and
the last century of queer life / Tom Fitzgerald and Lorenzo Marquez.
Description: [New York] : Penguin Books, [2020] |
Includes bibliographical references and index.
Identifiers: LCCN 2019025257 (print) | LCCN 2019025258 (ebook) |
ISBN 9780143134626 (paperback) | ISBN 9780525506430 (ebook)
Subjects: LCSH: RuPaul's drag race (Television program : 2009–)—
Influence. | Drag shows—Social aspects. | Female impersonators—
History. | Male impersonators—History. | Gays in popular culture.
Classification: LCC PN1969.D73 F58 2020 (print) |
LCC PN1969.D73 (ebook) | DDC 791.45/75—dc23
LC record available at https://lccn.loc.gov/2019025257
LC ebook record available at https://lccn.loc.gov/2019025258

Printed in the United States of America
1 3 5 7 9 10 8 6 4 2

Set in Georgia
Designed by Cassandra Garruzzo

Dedicated to all those

fierce and ferocious warrior-goddesses

who stomped and marched and danced in their

platform shoes and stiletto heels

so that we could walk freely and with pride

Contents

Introduction

This book is meant to be read one-handed.

No, you didn't accidentally pick up the wrong book or get a defective copy with the wrong cover on it. What we mean is that this book was devised, from its inception, to spur the reader on to look up more about the people highlighted and spotlighted in it. We want you to become so curious about what Julian Eltinge looked like or how Charles Pierce sounded or whether we're doing Tandi Iman Dupree justice when we describe her legendary lip sync that you can't help but want to see it for yourself. We want you to grab your phone and look up a video or blog post or wiki entry about any of the people or events mentioned in this book whenever the curiosity strikes you. There is an Alexandria-size library of spectacular queer history and cultural essays literally at your fingertips, and this book was written not only with that in mind but in a way that encourages you to look someone up because you read about them in these pages. Practically every performer mentioned in this book has some aspect of their work preserved online, which means you can look up Jackie Shane singing "Walking the Dog" on Canadian television in 1965 or Sylvia Rivera's legendary speech at the Christopher Street parade in 1973 as easily as you can look up Manila Luzon's latest music video.

RuPaul's Drag Race started out as the purest representation of gay male social culture that television had ever seen, and eventually morphed into a celebration of LGBTQ life and culture in general, encompassing all the work and lives of countless queer people who came before it. Every aspect and feature of the show can be traced to some long-standing tradition, event, or practice in queer life, queer communities, and queer culture. RuPaul and company devised a show that serves as an actual museum of queer cultural and social history, drawing on queer traditions and the work of legendary figures going back nearly a century. In doing so, *Drag Race* became not only a repository of queer history and culture but an examination and illustration of queer life in the modern age. It is a series of snapshots illustrating how LGBTQ folks live, struggle, work, and reach out to each other—and how they always have.

The point of this book isn't to reveal all the secrets and hidden meanings behind *Drag Race*—the show isn't that deliberate in its intentions; and besides, that's not how culture works. The point is to show that *Drag Race* exists smack on the continuum of queer culture and history and naturally pulls references from up and down its timeline, sometimes deliberately and sometimes as a result of a cultural osmosis.

The history of the show itself is something of a queer Cinderella story, a nearly perfect metaphor for drag: A dirty little smeared-lens, poorly lit, low-def, rough-looking drag revue sandwiched between HIV meds and leather gear ads on an extremely niche cable network went on to become a worldwide glamour extravaganza. The journey of the show perfectly mimics the journey of drag as an underground form of expression that eventually found its way to the highest arenas of media and entertainment. The first season of *Drag Race* looks like it was shot in the dimly lit back room of a bar somewhere, but by the tenth season, it looked exactly like what it was at that point: a massive hit variety show loaded with sparkle and glamour, populated by impossibly beautiful beings with sickeningly flawless makeup. We're going to show how queer culture generally and drag culture specifically made a very similar journey. When we say "queer culture," that's not necessarily the same thing as queer equality or legal protections, nor does it encompass the broad spectrum of queer existence. It's the shared culture created or curated *by* queer people *for* queer people arising out of our experiences *as* queer people.

The story of *RuPaul's Drag Race* is the same as the story of the LGBTQ political and cultural movement of the past half century; it's impossible to separate one from the other. You can't talk about *RuPaul's Drag Race* in any depth without talking a bit about the history of drag as a form of expression and a part of pop culture. And you can't talk about drag as a form of expression without talking about its place in queer life. And you can't talk about queer life over time without having some idea of what LGBTQ folks faced in the past and how their lives played out.

For the majority of the twentieth century, it was illegal for a man to appear in public wearing women's clothing. It was illegal for men to have sex with other men, and the mere act of flirting could land a man in jail or a mental institution, or have him medicated against his will (a practice known as "chemical castration"). It was illegal to produce or distribute any work that depicted same-sex desires, and it was illegal for bars and restaurants to serve alcohol to gay or lesbian patrons. Same-sex desire and gender nonconformity were considered mental illnesses by the American Psychiatric Association and the majority of the medical community. It's important to know these things in order to understand just how brave and fuck-you fierce our queer forebears actually were. They didn't just declare themselves in the face of societal disapproval; they did so in the face of attempted social genocide. And they just kept on going, surviving and then thriving, creating art, communities, and families—and redefining all three in the process. These people were criminals and outlaws, punks and badass bitches. Maybe they didn't always feel like it at the time, but they were revolutionaries. More important, they won the revolution. It just took some time for everyone else to notice.

But we would never want to claim that those queens and queers of the past lived lives of misery or tragedy. We think a good deal of our LGBTQ forebears would have summed up their lives as ones filled to the brim with a kind of ragingly defiant beauty—gorgeous weeds breaking fabulously through the cracks in the pavement. We choose to see them that way because we feel it pays tribute to their struggles without depicting them as tragic. They were too beautiful, too strong, too brave for us to see them any other way. We hope we've done them justice, and we hope you see them the same way by the time you've read all their stories. They were, every one of them, without question, legends.

Now, put your face on. We've got a show to do.

Legendary

· CHILDREN ·

Chapter 1

In the Werk Room
with Marsha and Sylvia

Waiting at the entrance to the *RuPaul's Drag Race* Werk Room set, inches away from the set lighting and just outside the camera range, a queen with a dream waits for her cue. Tucked and contoured, corseted and wigged, she's got a lewk sure to make those other bitches gag and a catchphrase just waiting to spring forth from her lips that she's hoping will brand her to the fan base for the rest of her career. Maybe she'll drop to the floor or maybe she'll pop out of a box or maybe she'll introduce Ornacia to the world. She might simply announce that she farted or that she came here to fight; but whatever it is she's got planned—and no matter who she is, she will *definitely* have something planned—whether it be shocking, fierce, or hilarious, the one thing she wants her entrance to be above all else is *memorable*. This is the moment she's planned and worked for, the moment when she steps into *Drag Race* herstory, plants her sequined flag, and announces her arrival. If she's lucky and smart, if she demonstrates the required charisma-uniqueness-nerve-talent cocktail of qualities, this won't be the last time she walks through that entrance.

In fact, despite the runway and performance challenges that make up the judging criteria that will decide her fate, her work in the Werk Room will be the single biggest determinant of how long she gets to stay in the competition. How she gets along with the other girls, how well she sticks to the tasks assigned her, and how much camera time she can snag from the producers will be major factors in deciding how long she'll make it in the competition. She's got to strike a balance here, come out strong and hard enough to get plenty of camera time but not make too many enemies or else one of them will throw her under that ever-present reality television bus the second they get the chance.

"This is when the world gets to meet *me*," our queen is thinking. Then: "Are the other girls prettier than me? Are the other girls *shady bitches*?"

From its bright pink pillars to its endlessly repeating shrines to Ru, the *Drag Race* Werk Room has become something of a modern-day temple or senate of drag. Inside the confines of its faux brick walls, dreams are made, friendships die, wigs get literally snatched, and yes, lives even change forever. The Werk Room contains the worktables, the individual queens' corners, and the makeup mirrors, as well as the space where Ru introduces guests and conducts the mini-challenges. It's pretty safe to say it's the heart of the show, but it goes further than that. The main stage is for performing and the Untucked lounge is for family bickering time, but the Werk Room is for doing the work, both mental and physical, of being a queen in the world. It's the focal point of the queens' existence for their time on the show. It's where they make their first grand entrances and their final sign-offs on the makeup mirror. It's where they receive dignitaries ranging from Nancy Pelosi to Lady Gaga. It's where these queens will wind up sniffing each other out or dressing each other down.

It's the space where the queens all retire to the couch to discuss the most recent elimination and the current state of their thoughts, fears, and rivalries. It's where they gather around the table to do a little light reading of each other as they await news for the next challenge. The Werk Room is the social and work-based epicenter of *Drag Race*. It's Miz Cracker at the makeup mirror talking about the empty lunchboxes of her poverty-stricken childhood, or Roxxxy Andrews talking about her childhood abandonment. It's Asia O'Hara sitting down with the Vixen to get her to talk about her feelings of anger over the racism in the LGBTQ community. It's Katya and Miss Fame reaching out under the stress of the competition to hang on to each other for a second and reinforce their sobriety.

The Werk Room is also where we see all the queens in their "boy drag." This was considered a controversial thing to do at the time of the show's launch because drag queens are sort of like puppeteers. They never want you to see the hand up Kermit's butt, so to speak. There was a time when the idea of drag queens appearing on camera out of drag was considered akin to a magician giving away his secrets. Many notable and accomplished drag queens have refused to compete on the show for this very reason. But stripping away the drag is very much of a piece with the show's commitment to showing its full art, which you truly can't appreciate fully without seeing the transformation in process. It's also a way of peeling away any emotional barriers or protections. Ru knows all too well that drag can be a person's way of dealing with the world; and in true reality show fashion, that coping mechanism side of drag is removed in the Werk Room, leaving the queens without the crutches of their wigs and corsets. It's a place of safety where they can take off their armor.

In the beginning, it was a largely undefined space of brightly colored walls, random bits of neon flair, work tables, and makeup mirrors. It would take some time for it to codify and solidify into the sort of backroom Barbie's Playhouse aesthetic of later seasons. In the first few seasons, Ru's suits didn't burn quite so brightly, and everyone looked orange under the lighting. But in the grand tradition of all queer-only spaces, it evolved over time, with improved lighting and spruced-up digs, and it became just a bit more formalized as a space for both gathering and doing the work (or werk).

Historically, queer folks have always created their own spaces, where they could maintain a community, forge alliances, break bread, or just hang out, far from the judgment of people who don't quite understand or who actively want to harm them. It would be nice if we could call them all safe spaces, but for a long time, and up until comparatively recently, there was no such thing as a totally safe space for a queen. Not even if a queen wanted to go out and have a birthday drink. Not even in their own homes.

Marsha P. Johnson's Epic Birthday Party

> "Marsha and I, we were the liberators.
> The street people and the drag queens, they were
> the vanguard of the movement."
>
> *Sylvia Rivera*

In June 1969, a drag queen named Marsha P. Johnson went out to the Stonewall Inn to celebrate her birthday. The Stonewall was a little gay bar in New York where Marsha and her fellow queens, as well as gay men, lesbians, and other queer folks, felt like they could gather, if not safely, then as safely as life was going to allow them at that time. Like all queer-only gathering spaces of this time, it was as underground and hidden as a street-level bar in the West Village could possibly be. Gathering spaces that were known to be or perceived to be gay-only were illegal to operate—meaning people of the same gender were not allowed to dance together, openly flirt with each other, or display any physical desire or affection with each other while on the premises, or in any other public spaces, for that matter. Also strictly illegal: any form of public cross-dressing or dressing in a manner that doesn't conform to social gender expectations. In cities like New York, the places catering to queer patrons were likely to be managed by people who had some experience running illegal businesses—the Mob, in other words. Like all places of business run by organized crime, the continued existence of any gay, lesbian, or generally queer bar was subject to dirty cops receiving payouts to ensure that they would turn a blind eye to any illegal activities. When dirty cops have a steady line of illegal income and that income is generated by disenfranchised people with little to no political power, the results are always harassing and exploitive. On the night of Marsha's birthday celebration, June 28, 1969, the cops showed up at the Stonewall to do what they tended to do with some regularity: harass the patrons and workers there, either to get some payout or to round up a few for arrests. On this night, the queer folks at the Stonewall weren't having it. On this night, Marsha P. Johnson *definitely* wasn't having it.

Marsha was a colorful and well-known figure in the neighborhood. Like so many "street queens," as they tended to be referred to at the time, she was known to get up onstage to perform when someone would let her, but she mostly tended to support herself through sex work. She once appeared in court for soliciting and told the judge the middle initial of her name stood for "Pay it no mind." The judge was so amused by this, he let her go. Everyone seemed to adore her, and even though she spent most of her adult life struggling, those who knew her—both well and casually—described her as a light or even a holy person. A beaming, beatific figure walking the streets of the West Village in New York with a wig made of feathers or Christmas tinsel, and a happy word for every person who crossed her path.

That night at the Stonewall, which has passed into legend, the queens and queers of the place decided they'd had enough. When the crowd started getting angry, the cops tried rounding people up. At that point, two things were said to have happened. A butch lesbian who was struggling against the cops as they tried to arrest her turned to the crowd and asked, "Why don't you do something?" And Marsha P. Johnson, beatific light of the West Village, picked up her shot glass, threw it at the bar mirror, and screamed in an uncharacteristic fury, "I WANT MY CIVIL RIGHTS!"

When the rowdiness of the crowd started blossoming into a full-blown demonstration against the police, word got out quickly in the neighborhood. One of the first people to rush down and join in was another street queen, a close friend of Marsha's named Sylvia Rivera, who said upon hearing of the riot, "It's the revolution!" She had absolutely no intention of missing out on it. Like so many other queer folks who'd been holding their rage in for too long, Marsha and Sylvia gleefully joined in on the brick-throwing and trouble-making of what became known as the Stonewall Riots, screaming their rage into the midsummer New York night. They were not only there at the birth of the modern gay rights movement, they were mothers to it.

Space Queens

A year later, at a time when the just-birthed "gay liberation" movement was figuring itself out and in the process largely shunning the drag queens and transgender folks who'd been active in—if not at the forefront of—the movement, Sylvia and Marsha looked around, saw that the community wasn't going to make space for them, and formed STAR, the Street Transvestite Action Revolutionaries, a group dedicated to protecting the lives and interests of queens and transgender women living on the streets. Seeing the desperate need to provide their sisters a space of relative safety, Sylvia and Marsha set up the first STAR house: a trailer in a parking lot, where queens could hole up for a while to get away from the cold and potential violence of 1970s New York. When the cops had the trailer towed (while twenty people were still inside it), Marsha and Sylvia knew they needed to find a more permanent space for the women they were trying to protect. They managed, against all odds, to secure enough money to rent a building for them. They paid the rent by turning tricks on the streets, using their bodies and their savvy to carve out a space for their community to thrive. If that's not showing a devastating combination of charisma, uniqueness, nerve, and talent, then girl, we don't know what is.

Sylvia Rivera spent her life and career fighting the system, the culture, and even members of the LGBTQ community who couldn't get on board with what she was trying to do. She was considered a loudmouth and a troublemaker when she wasn't being dismissed as an embarrassment to an LGBTQ community desperately focused on a respectful, assimilative approach to gaining equality. Sylvia essentially spent decades of her life screaming "Fuck *that!*" to a gay rights plan that actively sought to exclude her and people like her. When she finally got the chance to speak at the Christopher Street Liberation Day rally in 1973, one of the earliest organized LGBTQ Pride events—and after being ignored or pushed aside most of the day—she did what she became known for doing her whole life: She tore into the gay community for its complacency and narrow-mindedness. "Y'all better quiet down," she said to their boos and catcalls. "I've been trying to get up here all day for your gay brothers and your gay sisters in jail that write me every motherfucking week and ask for your help and you all don't do a goddamn thing for them." After calling out the movement for being a "middle-class white club," she ended her speech by screaming, "GAY POWER!" into the astonished faces of the crowd. It was a speech met with boos and indignation, which has subsequently gone on to become a legendary statement of anger, defiance, and support for the disenfranchised, powerless, and ignored.

Demoralized and depressed by her reception, Sylvia went home and tried to kill herself by slitting her wrists. Marsha found her bleeding to death, got her help, and nursed her back to health, representing the very best of the queer community at the time, the way LGBTQ folks reach out to each other when they need it—even if the damage done to them was by other people in that community. Sylvia would later say of her anger, "I will not forgive the movement for anything they have done to my family." She and Marsha would both spend the rest of their lives screaming their rage, protecting their sisters, and fighting, fighting, fighting back for rights and respect—a never-ending, decades-long struggle that they both willingly took on, with flowers in their hair, color on their lips, and polish on their nails.

You Betta Werk

That quality of being loud and confrontational, fearless and bold—all in service to your own vulnerabilities—is at the heart of queer boldness, the heart of drag. It's why we all love to see the queens go at it in the Werk Room, throwing shade and stating their rights. It isn't just because most queens have a way with a comeback or know when to pull out their earrings to get down and dirty. It's because *Drag Race*, fully aware of the history of warrior women like Marsha and Sylvia, has always used drag as a metaphor for personal strength and a tool for self-actualization. Ru, who has called Marsha "the mother of us all," believes that drag queens have a special responsibility and ability to pull from deep inside themselves, the darkest, most painful parts of their psyches, and use it to make good drag. Confrontations aren't in the mix just because they make good reality television. They're in the mix because Ru believes an awful lot of drag is about confrontation, whether it's confronting your fears, the gender paradigm, your detractors, or who-ever's standing in your damn way. Despite its drag-slang name, the Werk Room truly is the room where the work gets done, whether it's tucking or baking or sewing or rehearsing; it's a space devoted to queens doing their damn thing. But *Drag Race*, aware of the long history of communal spaces for queens and queers, made sure that the Werk Room was also a space for speaking your truth, confronting your demons, shouting down your detractors, and calling out bad behavior. This is why the Werk Room scenes owe so much to queens from ancient times, like Sylvia Rivera. She never backed down and she never stopped fighting. She lived for confrontations.

Without being so presumptuous as to speak for either of them in terms of how they'd wish to self-identify today, we would understand Marsha and Sylvia to be transgender women, even though it was not a term in wide use at the time they were alive. As was the fashion, they tended to refer to themselves as transvestites or drag queens—when they weren't identifying as women outright. Like all communities struggling toward self-acceptance and societal acceptance, the early years of the organized post-Stonewall LGBTQ community cycled through a lot of terminology before settling on the terms we all know and use today. And this takes us right back to one of the biggest controversies in the history of *RuPaul's Drag Race*, the result of a quickly established Werk Room tradition that ran afoul of the modern transgender community.

For the first five seasons of *Drag Race*, challenges were launched by a video introduction from Ru, which she announced each week with, "Ooooh girl! You've got she-mail," as a reference to the old AOL sign-on. Transgender writers, commenters, and activists called the show out for using an offensive slur (she-male) against transgender women. Ru defended the use of the phrase by explaining that it was also historically a slur against drag queens and that he was just trying to reclaim it and strip it of its power to hurt. Transgender rights advocates countered that it wasn't his word to reclaim. Eventually Ru backed down and the phrase was retired for the slightly nonsensical "She done already done had herses." This was the correct thing to do, of course, but this clash came about largely because of that very shifting of terminology over time and because one side of the debate was taking the long view and the other side was arguing from the current moment. This is a big indicator of how the show tracks with social and cultural changes within the LGBTQ community over the past half century or so, the span of Ru's life. The history of *Drag Race* and the history of the LGBTQ community and the history of RuPaul himself—they're all bound up together. And we can't imagine Sylvia and Marsha wouldn't have cheered their modern transgender drag queen sisters along as they once again got in the faces of their fellow LGBTQ family members and demanded the respect due them.

Of Hankies and Zhuzhing: Queer Mentoring

But there's another side of the Werk Room and also of queer life—a gentler, more conventionally supportive side without which LGBTQ life in the pre-Stonewall era would have been unbearable and *Drag Race* would pretty much be unwatchable. As much as we all remember the legendary confrontations and rivalries that played out, some of the best scenes in the Werk Room happened when one queen saw another queen struggling with something and took the time to check in on her or offer her help. Sometimes it's a little sewing help, sometimes it's a little makeup help, and sometimes it's just to lend a struggling girl some hip padding and a corset because Michelle Visage keeps complaining about her boy body on the runway every week.

It's also a place where Ru can come in and offer his thoughts while the queens are still in process, as opposed to when they're on the runway and all the tea has been spilled already. Even though these exchanges with Ru often end a little defensively and even contentiously (Pearl asking Ru, "Is there something on my face?" after a classic stare-down would be probably the most referenced example of this), they're essential to Ru's idea of drag and how a queen should be expected to commit to it. The Werk Room is not just a place where you do the work, it's where you'll be expected to defend it—if not to Ru, then to the roomful of bitches competing with you.

There's also the physical aspect of the work—how it relates to the mechanics of drag, from tucking to contouring to corseting. Like all drag queens backstage, the queens on *Drag Race* share tips and techniques from time to time—when they're not engaging in that age-old drag technique of simply stealing from or copying each other. Drag is an old art form, and quite a bit of what you see the queens do in that Werk Room is born out of decades of men and women perfecting the form and passing on their technical expertise to the next generation.

This is queer culture writ small, a series of gestures, references, slang terms, and technical knowledge that gets passed on and mutated as it moves through generations. Queer folks have always had to exist in the world, find each other, and until comparatively recently, fly under the radar so as not to be detected. All subcultures and countercultures come up with their own lingo and stories, but queer culture is especially rich in myths, tips, and fables. It's because LGBTQ people come from every culture on earth and can appropriate freely from any of them.

Our favorite example of queer oral culture and history is Polari, the slang lingo of carnies, theater folk, and travelers. It was later picked up by British gay men as a way of signaling their belonging to a secret and highly illegal group without actually coming out and saying so, which could have resulted in jail or hospital time, depending on their luck. Polari is where we get the terms *drag*, *butch*, *zhuzh*, *queen*, and many other recognizable words (and not-so-recognizable ones: "Bona vada your lovely eek and riah, darling!").

Polari was a way for queer men of the past to find and openly support each other without necessarily endangering themselves. And while it's not in usage much today, its long reach into gay history and culture is a prime example of how LGBTQ folks navigated a world hostile to them by creating a pretty little secret, something for themselves, a cultural possession kept closely guarded and then slowly revealed to each new member of the group as they entered it. Polari was referenced on iconic gay singer Morrissey's album *Bona Drag* in the song "Piccadilly Palare." The Polari word *zhuzh* came back in popularity through the efforts of none other than *Drag Race* judge Carson Kressley, who brought it to the mainstream in the original *Queer Eye for the Straight Guy*. Everything queer is tied up in the mix of *RuPaul's Drag Race*.

And if you want a less whimsical example of this sort of thing, there's the hankie code, a secret system of signals based on the placement and color of a hankie in the back pocket of a gay man's jeans. Its purpose: to let other gay men know what kind of sex they were into and which position they would prefer to be in when doing it. These sorts of things developed in the community when it was a strictly underground one and got passed down from older or more experienced members to newer or younger ones as they entered the community.

The Politics and Personal Side
of the Makeup Mirror

The makeup mirror on *Drag Race* is part confessional, part therapy session, part storytelling circle. The scenes of the queens putting on their faces, throwing shade, kiki-ing, and telling their stories mimic the backstage camaraderie and sniping you'll find at any drag show or revue. This is a very deliberate re-creation of the long history of the drag circuit and what it's like to be in a roomful of queens preparing—and vying—for the spotlight. It also helped launch a few careers and trends as the show's popularity grew. Not only have beauty magazines and websites pushed makeup trends based on drag techniques with increasing frequency in recent years (often using *Drag Race* alums to demonstrate them), but several queens from the show have become spokesmodels for beauty brands. A few have even launched their own beauty lines, following in the footsteps of Ru himself, who made history as the first drag queen spokesmodel for a mainstream cosmetics company when he became the first Viva Glam girl for MAC Cosmetics in 1995.

Between swipes of the brush and flicks of the wrist, queens have stood before that mirror and talked about their addictions, their assaults, their eating disorders, and their issues with self-esteem, racism, mental health, money, and self-loathing. Magic occurs in front of that mirror, not just in the transformation of boys into girls or normies into goddesses, but in the truths told and the walls that crumble in the telling of them.

This idea of the makeup mirror as a place for telling truths isn't just a metaphor. Departing queens are expected to write their final good-byes in lipstick on the mirror before leaving, while surviving queens are expected to ceremoniously wipe them clean and say a few words, like some sort of cosmetics-based burial ritual. One of the things *Drag Race* is very good at is taking the tropes and shorthand of drag life and spinning rituals, catchphrases, and new traditions out of them. But as with so many of the show's traditions, you can find their roots in either pop culture history or LGBTQ history. In the case of the mirror messages, they grew out of the spot where the two histories overlap.

In the 1960 film *BUtterfield 8*, the dragfully named Gloria Wandrous, played by Elizabeth Taylor, gay icon and eventual honorary auntie to an entire generation of plague-ravaged gay men, wanders the lush, empty apartment of the married man with whom she just spent the night. Dressed in a slip and heels, she nurses a morning cocktail and riffles through the closets, as one does. After sampling some of his wife's perfume and trying on her mink coat, Gloria, who later describes herself to her mother as "the slut of all time," is horrified to discover that her lover has slipped $250 into her handbag with a note asking if it's enough. Angered and hurt, she takes out her lipstick and scrawls NO SALE on the grand gilded mirror of his living room before storming out. She takes the mink coat with her because that's how self-described slut queens roll. Cash is out, but stealing is still on the table. Is it any wonder she became a gay icon? Is it any wonder Ru would make his queens sign off from the show in the same way, paying tribute to one of the great Hollywood fruit flies of all time? But that's not the only iconic diva with a famous predilection for communicating via cosmetics.

Twelve years after Taylor's declaration via lipstick, Diana Ross, former Motown diva Supreme and icon to Ru, was starring in *Lady Sings the Blues* as legendary jazz singer Billie Holiday. In one of the film's most memorable scenes, Billie is backstage after having been attacked by the Klan, sitting before a makeup mirror, lightening her skin with powder and crumbling under the weight of heartbreak, addiction, and unrelenting hatred and racism. She reaches for her tube of lipstick, and before she knows what she's doing, she's scrawling her inner feelings wordlessly across the mirror, a streak of greasy pink rage.

Both of these lipstick warriors used their tubes of tint to express something raw and basic about themselves. The combination of mirror and lipstick makes the perfect medium for each of them to declare who they are or how they suffer. It's certainly not for us to say that the lipstick-on-the-mirror send-off that ends each episode of *Drag Race* and begins each subsequent one as the queens react to it was directly inspired by these two scenes, but it's hard not to see them as in the mix of the show's inspirations. One of the things queer art and drag are very good at is taking bits and pieces of mainstream culture and giving them a particularly queer little spin.

Pay It No Mind and Make It Werk

Marsha and Sylvia never stopped doing the work of securing their rights and protecting their sisters—in drugstore makeup and nail polish, with whatever bits of flair they could piece together but very little else, because they didn't have the resources for high, glamorous drag as we know it today. They never had money, which means they always had to express their queerness through creativity, sass, and street savvy. Marsha strung Christmas garland or flowers in her hair because that was literally all she had at hand, loving to tell people that the middle initial of her name stood for "Pay it no mind." That rough, homegrown style of street drag is not only part of Ru's own past as a Club Kid, but it's also one of his favorite types of drag.

Every time you see a queen in the *Drag Race* Werk Room struggling to make a lewk out of scraps of pickins, they're paying tribute to all those street queens who had to pay it no mind and make do with whatever life laid at their feet. Many a queen has shown up to compete on *Drag Race* with trunks full of custom couture and stage wear that would make a Vegas showgirl gag, especially in the later seasons of the show. But there has always been a DIY undercurrent to the competition. And Ru's always had a special place in her heart for the make-do queens, the ones who don't have lots of money or resources but are determined to make do with what they can get, like Chi Chi DeVayne or Nina Bo'nina Brown. There's usually at least one challenge or mini-challenge per season that demands a level playing field, one in which all the queens have to put their outfits together from whatever they can find in bins strewn throughout the Werk Room. Just like Marsha putting flowers or Christmas lights on her head, paying it no mind at all.

"No pride for some of us without liberation for all of us," Marsha would say. She and Sylvia worked tirelessly to elevate and situate the voices and experiences of people of color, drag queens, and transgender women in the LGBTQ community at a time when they were being systematically ignored or erased by a movement more concerned with respectability, which was an option being considered by the early leadership for only white and cisgender queer people.

While she was well celebrated by parts of the queer community, posing for Andy Warhol for his series of paintings of drag queens and transgender women, Ladies and Gentlemen, in

1975 and performing with the Hot Peaches drag theater company, sometimes it seems that Marsha's greatest job was simply being Marsha, which brought her joy but also contained a great deal of struggle. She struggled with homelessness and mental health issues sporadically her whole life and contracted HIV sometime in the 1980s. In July 1992, on Pride weekend, her body was found floating in the Hudson River under mysterious circumstances, which the police called suicide but her friends—including Sylvia—insisted was murder. While it might be wrong to make the violent or tragic end of her colorful, expressive life the focus of any discussion of it, it's hard not to see Marsha's death existing on the continuum of violence suffered by transgender women that continues to this day. We think Marsha would probably rather be remembered for her light and color and beauty, but we also think the darker, harder side of her would want people to remain angry about her death and the deaths of her many mothers, sisters, and daughters.

Sylvia, for her part, continued to work for her transgender siblings and other members of the queer community. Years after Marsha's death and the original group's dissolution, Sylvia relaunched STAR in 2001, renaming it the Street Transgender Action Revolutionaries. The group went on to fight and advocate for the New York City Transgender Rights Bill and for inclusion in New York's Sexual Orientation Non-Discrimination Act, which passed in 2003 but would not become fully inclusive regarding gender orientation until 2019. Sylvia died of liver cancer in 2002, a fighter for her rights and the rights of others until the very end. After her death, the Sylvia Rivera Law Project was formed in her honor. It has continued to fight for the rights of transgender people in New York to this day.

At its heart, every confrontation or declaration made in the

Werk Room is the same one Sylvia and Marsha had to make every day: I'm here. I have a story. I matter. Back off, bitch. Those queens aren't just doing the work of trying to win a cash prize and reality television immortality; they're doing the kind of work Marsha and Sylvia understood best: fighting for recognition, for respect, for just a little more time on the stage.

The Tea On:

Elizabeth Taylor, from Fruit Fly Supreme to Auntie!

When she wasn't playing fabulously badly behaved women on-screen, collecting massive diamonds, or tearing through a baseball team of husbands, Elizabeth Taylor was surrounding herself with the A-list gay men of her Hollywood generation, like Montgomery Clift, Rock Hudson, and Roddy McDowall, who all adored her. When Hudson succumbed to AIDS in 1985, one of the first high-profile celebrities to even admit to having the disease, Elizabeth was inspired to devote her time to finding a cure. To that end, she helped form what later became known as amfAR, the Foundation for AIDS Research, as well as the Elizabeth Taylor AIDS Foundation. She is directly responsible for raising hundreds of millions of dollars for AIDS research. Her highly dramatic personal life, stunning beauty, lust for the finer things (including food, drink, and diamonds), blunt personality, and bone-deep glamour made her a particular favorite of drag queens of the mid- to late twentieth century. You will often see her name cited by drag queens of that period. John Waters said Divine originally used to dress up in drag using Taylor as an inspiration before he eventually adopted his iconic punk trash drag look. Dorian Corey, in the 1990 documentary *Paris Is Burning*, about the ball scene, spoke of the old days of drag, when queens wanted to look like Elizabeth Taylor and Marilyn Monroe. In the final years of her life, Taylor was known to hold court in her wheelchair at the legendary Los Angeles gay bar the Abbey, ever the fruit fly. While her drag and queer history bona fides are unquestionable on their own merits, we think she inadvertently defined drag when talking about how she's handled the ups and downs of her own tumultuous life: "Pour yourself a drink, put on some lipstick, and pull yourself together."

Herstory Lesson:

The Half Century of Continual Stonewall Rioting

There is a reason why LGBTQ history is divided into pre-Stonewall and post-Stonewall. Prior to the riots, only the most radical of queer thinkers and activists could even dream of a world where queer people could openly live their lives. The three-night outbreak of rioting on Christopher Street in queer safe haven Greenwich Village in 1969 was barely reported in the New York papers at the time. It was such a discreet and relatively under-attended sort of public display of fighting back when civil rights and anti–Vietnam War demonstrations were gaining much more attention. Its effects were not like a lightning bolt hitting all queer people at once. In fact, over a half century after this small event, the effect of the Stonewall Riots is still rippling outward, still affecting marginalized queer communities all over the world as they tentatively step out into the streets of their cities and towns, sometimes in the face of a repressive regime or religious fanaticism, and bravely wave their rainbow flags in recognition of their place in the queer community as well as in the larger community. The Stonewall Riots are still happening—serving as a flash point not just for queer rights but also for queer culture, changing irrevocably how LGBTQ people see themselves and their place in society, which naturally affects how they express themselves both personally and artistically.

Stonewall was as much a cultural explosion as a political one, in which queer folks of every stripe of the rainbow—gay, lesbian, bisexual, transgender, genderqueer—saw how much they needed to group together and rely on each other to change the world. Stonewall solidified, for the first time, the queer community as one worth fighting for. It was pure in the moment. What happened after wasn't necessarily the shining moment it could have been, as the movement's leadership was largely overtaken by white gay men, with an organized shunning of drag queens and transgender women. The thinking behind this distancing was that in order to secure gay rights, the more "freakish" aspects of the community needed to be excised from it. In the fifty years since Stonewall, the LGBTQ community has slowly been making its way back to being the inclusive, tightly bound community it was the night a bunch of gay men, transgender women, and drag queens looked at each other after a butch lesbian told them to do something—and they all bonded together to throw rocks and set fires.

The Tea On:

Werk Room Celebrity Visitor Showdown! Who Was the Most Sickening?

In this corner, Nancy Pelosi, holding up her rainbow bracelet and telling the tearful queens, "You're an inspiration because you really know your power and you're taking pride."

In the other corner, Lady Gaga, making all the queens gag and telling them, "Just remember when you have a bad day that I was nobody and now I'm somebody."

In yet another corner, Miley Cyrus, doing a pretty terrible job at being a drag king.

You make the call! (Although the Gaga one sounds a weensy bit self-absorbed in retrospect—*No tea, no shade!*)

Herstory Lesson:

Stormé DeLarverie, That "One Girl"

In the annals of Stonewall legend, the name Stormé DeLarverie looms large. She's a near-mythical figure in LGBTQ history, often mentioned as the butch lesbian who got thrown into a paddy wagon at Stonewall, kicking and screaming and cursing her rage at the stunned crowd of queer folks who'd never seen anyone fight back. She was, however, often coy about her involvement in the riots. Like many queer people who frequented or lived in the West Village at the time, she was known to have been at Stonewall for at least some of the action during the three nights of protests and disruption, but she often demurred on the question of whether she was the spark that set things alight. "I'm a human being that survived," she would say of herself, adding, "I helped other people survive." It was almost as if she understood that the legend of Stonewall was more important than its somewhat hazy documentation. Besides, even if she wasn't that one legendary figure at Stonewall, the fact of her status as a survivor as well as her life spent helping others in her community is enough to keep her legend secure around her.

She spent her later life working as a bouncer in lesbian bars, but for many years, she was an extremely talented and well-regarded drag king, spending almost fifteen years as the "one girl" in the Jewel Box Revue's *25 Men and 1 Girl* drag show. She was celebrated for her smooth baritone, pencil mustache, and fine men's suits. For several decades, she patrolled the streets of the West Village in New York, always on the lookout for any "ugliness," always in service to her stated mission of protecting her "girls," the loose collection of lesbians, drag performers, and other queer folks who made up her home and by extension, her family. After decades living with, working with, and protecting an expansive family of queer people, Stormé spent the final years of her long life being taken care of in one of the nation's first facilities for aging LGBTQ folks. She spent her life taking care of an extended family, and at the end her extended family embraced her, took her in, and returned that care. She died in 2014 at the age of ninety-three, not just a survivor but a legend.

Chapter 2

Shady Dames
in the Library

You're beautiful and you're young. You deserve to have the best
in life. But you did not deserve this. I don't say she's not
beautiful, but she wasn't looking beautiful tonight. She doesn't
equal me! Look at her makeup! It's terrible!

Crystal LaBeija, The Queen

I magine you're in a social setting and you've made the
mistake of saying the wrong thing at the wrong time.
Imagine you've managed to step on someone's toes in
front of a whole group of people. Imagine you took something
that didn't belong to you and the person you took it from, or the
person whose toes you've stepped on, or the person on the receiving end of your social faux pas is a queen. Oooh, you just got
a chill, didn't you? Now imagine that queen sizing you up, locat-
ing every single one of your psychological buttons, and then
pushing them all, one after another, methodically ticking off all
your insecurities, embarrassments, and fears in front of a group
of your peers. Imagine you have been left speechless, open-
mouthed, and chastened by this onslaught, which has only
served one purpose: to establish that you are the lesser person

in this scenario and your social better has just asserted their royal right to state so. Honey, you might want to sit down for a while because you just got read for filth.

The Library Is Open

The Library mini-challenge on *RuPaul's Drag Race* has always been among the raunchiest, most hilarious, and most cringe-worthy parts of the show—and because of that, it's always been one of the challenges most likely to give the viewer insight into the talent level of any season's crop of queens. The Library is about all the things Ru values most in her queens: being quick on your feet, quick with a comeback, and thick-skinned. It's about staking out your place in the pecking order and putting your lessers in their place beneath you. It's about stinging someone with your words but not necessarily being hurtful with them. A good read can land like a vicious slap or a hilariously loving send-up, depending on the skill of the reader and their intentions. But even a lightly delivered, lovingly applied read is about letting the recipient of the read know where they stand with the queen doing the read. On *Drag Race*, it's a way to settle scores, put a high-riding queen in her place, secure more camera time, audition for future gigs, or simply have a little fun dragging on each other. In the way of all reality competition traditions, skill at reading can be both strategic and frivolous to a *Drag Race* queen. But the history of reading in queer culture is long and colorful, and the Library challenge on *Drag Race* is a reality television–filtered version of an aspect of queer culture that arose out of its marginalization and response to potential violence.

"At least I am a showgirl, bitch! Go back to
Party City, where you belong!"

Phi Phi O'Hara to Sharon Needles, season 4

But what is a read, anyway? Oh, don't sit there looking at this
book with that face on your head. You're a *Drag Race* fan. Of
course you know the *literal* definition. But shade and reading
are oral traditions born out of oppressed subcultures, which
means a strictly literal definition is going to be extremely limit-
ing in describing it. These things evolve and change over time,
and one might even argue that the definitions of both have
changed as a direct result of *Drag Race*'s popularity. Even as
you pore through the words of the drag elders on this matter,
you're going to find some slight variations. As Ru said when he
introduced the Library challenge for the first time in the sev-
enth episode of season 2, "As drag queens, we shrug off a lot of
insults. So when we get our chance to throw an insult, we turn
it into a high art form. We call it reading or throwing shade, and
it's part of our culture." In the manner of so many of Ru's utter-
ances, not a word of that was false or unnecessary. Like so many
parts of *Drag Race*, it serves as a concise summation of queer
culture and history. But even then, Ru's explanation doesn't
quite cover how deep the roots of shade and reading go.

"It's a lovely gown. A shame they
didn't have it in your size."

Princess Angel, Vegas in Space

The legendary Dorian Corey in *Paris Is Burning* (the sacred
text of shade) described reading in terms of finding someone's
flaws and exaggerating them. "That's the idea—knock them out

if you can . . . hit them below the belt." She called reading "the real art form of insult," noting that a queen reading another queen requires a certain amount of finesse and creativity. She also helpfully provided possibly the best definition of shade, which she characterized as a more evolved form of reading. "Shade is . . . I don't tell you you're ugly, but I don't have to tell you because you *know* you're ugly." And believe us, Dorian was one lady who knows from shady.

> "You know, there are two things I don't like about you,
> Felicia . . . your face. So how 'bout shutting both of them?"
>
> *Mitzi,* The Adventures of Priscilla, Queen of the Desert

Sometimes a read is simple and direct, like Mystique Summers's "I am from Chicago, bitch!" or Bianca Del Rio's "If I was gonna come for you, I'd come to your room at night and cut your fucking wigs up." In those cases, it's a basic threat offered with a bit of flair or wit, because the best reads are eminently quotable. Other times, the shade takes over, leaving a queen wondering just what the hell was said to her, like Willam's "Your tone seems very pointed right now" to Phi Phi O'Hara's tirade against her, or like Katya's one-word response of "Party" to Alaska's pleading to let her stay. In the manner of really good shade, that last one requires so much groundwork to lay and background to fill in that it almost doesn't seem worth it to explain it. Suffice it to say, Alaska called Katya "Adore Delano" one too many times (because on *Drag Race*, one of the most concise reads is the one that compares a queen to another—usually messier—queen from a previous season), and when Alaska was at her lowest point, Katya's coolly delivered two-syllable response of Adore's catchphrase landed like the most epic of bitch slaps. To quote Latrice Royale, who became a ridiculously popular meme on this one line, "The *shade* of it all."

The Art of Shade and the Performance of Reading

"I don't have a sugar daddy. I never had a sugar daddy. If I wanted a sugar daddy, yes, I could probably go out and get one because I am what? *Sickening!*"

Shangela to Mimi Imfurst, **Untucked!** *season 4.*

Being able to throw shade or read someone has always been a survival technique for drag queens and queer folks. And if you want to reign as a top queen or a celebrated queen, you simply don't get to that point without learning how to wield your tongue like a razor.

A thick skin and a quick mouth are part of the working drag queen's job description. Reading is a form of social control and the upholding of mores inside a group. In other words, you read someone when they have stepped out of line in some way, violated the agreed-upon social contract. You read someone because they have stepped into your space or made themselves unwelcome to you in some way. You read someone because they are a threat, pure and simple. And if you read someone without coming from those starting points, if you read someone simply because you're bored or they're weak or you think they're beneath you, you won't get the support or finger snaps from the people hearing the read, which is essential to any read. A queen throwing shade is just a shady queen, easily dismissed or put in her place. But when a queen reads someone—especially when it's another queen—there's a social contract being observed by everyone involved, from the reader to the readee to the read's audience. And there is *always* an audience for a read; otherwise there's no point to it. Sure, you can take a queen aside and read her beads, but once you strip the performative aspect out of a read, you're just having a conversation or an argument. Without a jury of your peers to witness the read, it has very little social power.

> "Girl, if I was gonna judge anyone, I would judge you on that body where those shoulders should match them hips, but they don't, so . . ."
>
> *Jade Jolie to Alyssa Edwards,* **Untucked!** *season 5*

An intra-community (queen-on-queen) read tends to focus on matters of looks, realness, and talent—or the lack of all three. On *Drag Race*, the most common topics of Library reading are a queen's teeth, a queen's feet, a queen's body shape, a queen's whiskers, and a queen's wigs. While other body parts may get called out now and then, there's often a reaction that a line's been crossed. Very few of the big girls on the show ever found the "You're fat" reads all that funny, for instance, but some of the biggest laugh-getters in the Library challenge came when a queen made fun of another queen's janky teeth or untended feet.

> "Why don't you just light your tampon and blow your box apart? Because it's the only bang you're going to get, sweetheart."
>
> *Bernadette,* **The Adventures of Priscilla, Queen of the Desert**

The flip side of an intra-community read is the survival read—the kind of read required by a queen when she's dealing with a tricky trick or a harassing cop or just a bunch of boys looking to intimidate someone. As Dorian Corey noted when she schooled the world on such matters in *Paris Is Burning*, it's different when a read occurs "between the gay world and the straight world." In those instances when the two worlds clash, it becomes, in her words, "a vicious slur fight." In that kind of read, a queen doesn't need to be witty, she just needs to find a person's buttons and push them hard and fast. This is a read not meant to garner finger snaps or laughter or *Oooh girls*. This is a read meant to throw a predator off his game, a read meant to give a queen an opening to either run or get into fighting position while the other guy sputters and reels from your tongue-lashing. When you see the queens on *Drag Race* put on their reading glasses and go to town on their competitors, you're seeing the end result of a century of drag evolution. Yes, reading is fundamental to drag queens and transgender women and always has been; it's one of several tools in their arsenal to help them survive, just like brass knuckles, a brick in a handbag, or pepper spray. Drag queens have personalities that span the entire spectrum of humanity, but truly successful ones naturally develop the ability to slap someone down when they violate their space or their rights.

> "About five minutes ago, I looked across at Ms. O'Hara and
> I realized that she was ugly. And I'm at peace with that."
>
> *Latrice Royale, season 4*

The long history of learning to read for filth was born out of the idea that a cutting wit and a sense of self is all a queen has to protect herself in the world. A drag queen of yore would've had to deal with not only the prospect of being bashed but also the prospect of being harassed by the police. Learning to cut a man down by verbally pushing all his buttons often meant the difference between life and death, a trip to the emergency room, or a trip in a paddy wagon. In a harsh world, the ability to read someone's beads was a necessary survival tactic—and still is for many queens and queers. Bottom line, for most working drag queens, for the entire length of time there have been working drag queens as well as transgender women existing and living as women, life has been harder than it would be otherwise. And if a queen doesn't learn how to fight back against her oppressors, whether those oppressors are straight cops or narrow-minded or bigoted gays, then a queen is going to find it hard to survive. But shade and reading can be indicators or harbingers of so much more. Shade can lead to art. Reading can lead to revolution.

When we say things like that, we should be clear that the types of queens we're talking about in the previous paragraph were predominately queens of color, who faced such enormous backlash for every single aspect of their being that simply stepping out of the house expressing their true self was literally placing their life in danger. Like so much of modern drag if not LGBTQ culture generally, shade and reading were born as formal concepts in the ballroom scene immortalized in *Paris Is Burning*, a direct result of the marginalization and disenfranchisement of the people—almost entirely black and Latinx—who made up that community. It's no surprise, then, that one of the most legendary reads ever documented also happens to have been delivered by the one queen most responsible for the modern ballroom scene.

Crystal LaBeija, Mouth Like a Whip, Mind Like a Revolutionary

"She won't make money off of my name, darling. She can make money off of Harlow and all the rest of the fools that will flock to her, but not Crystal, darling. Anybody but her. That's why all the true beauties didn't come."

Crystal LaBeija, The Queen

In 1967, at the Miss All-American Camp Beauty Pageant held in New York, the reigning Miss Manhattan, a big-haired, kohl-eyed glamour queen named Crystal LaBeija, walked offstage mid-ceremony upon learning her status as a third runner-up. She wanted no part of what was about to go down, although as it turned out, she had plenty of thoughts she was willing to express on the matter. Highly unusual for the time, cameras were there to record her reaction. In fact, there's a pretty decent argument to be made that those very cameras amplified her reaction, much in the manner of a reality TV show a half century later. But this was no television show. The very idea of featuring drag queens on television in the 1960s—let alone black drag queens like Miss Crystal—was completely unheard of. This was something almost as shocking: a documentary about drag queens. The brainchild of a drag pageant impresario named Jack Doroshow, who emceed the pageant and narrated the film in his drag persona Mother Flawless Sabrina, *The Queen* was released in 1968 and eventually played at the Cannes Film Festival. Its initial fame was rather short-lived, although it became a cult classic and eventually, thanks first to video stores and later to streaming services, became something of an ancient text of drag, a glimpse into the murky, shaky, pre-Stonewall past, when drag was literally illegal.

Competing in drag pageants and balls of the 1960s, when queens of color like herself were expected to whiten their appearance, Crystal LaBeija persevered with a fierce fabulosity and every reigning drag queen's best weapon: a sharp tongue. In *The Queen*, she established herself as the patron saint of shade, reciting the urtext of reading as she . . . shall we say . . . offered her thoughts (*"I will sue the bitch!"*) on the quality and ethics of the pageant in which she had just placed as third runner-up. Rachel Harlow, a pretty, realness-serving white queen from Philadelphia (who achieved greater fame a few years later when she dated Princess Grace's brother after she came out as a transgender woman and became something of a social doyenne of the Philadelphia nightclub scene of the 1970s), was crowned the winner of the pageant, much to Miss Crystal's consternation. What follows is probably the only truly interesting part of the documentary outside of the sobering curiosity of drag queens congregating furtively in hotel rooms to practice their illegal art in pre-Stonewall New York. Miss Crystal, clearly happy to have someone filming her, reads poor Harlow's beads (*"Get a picture with me and Harlow and we'll see which is more beautiful, darling."*) and leaves her speechless before turning her ire on Mother Flawless Sabrina, accusing her of favoritism and exploitation. When Sabrina tries to counter that Crystal's invective shows her true color, Miss Thing doesn't waste herself a nanosecond, shooting back with her voice rising on each syllable, "I have a right to show my color, darling! *I am beautiful* AND I KNOW I'M BEAUTIFUL."

"I am beautiful and I know I'm beautiful." That's pretty much the drag credo right there. It should always be followed by a trumpet blare. That's what makes Crystal's read so fabulous to behold. It's pure in its rage and also in its expression and turns of phrases. Every syllable reaffirms her supremacy, the tragedy of her lessers, and the injustice that these things are not being recognized to her satisfaction. This is a *queen*, darling.

What's notable about Crystal LaBeija's read is her skillful use of shade, the ability to leave a recipient wondering whether they've been insulted or complimented. In some ways shade can be worse for the recipient because there's no good way to react to it without leaving yourself open to accusations of being defensive. A read is direct, and while it's best not to respond to a savage read, it's understandable why someone might choose to do so, if they feel their honor has been sullied. But shade is subtle and wily. It is deliciously ambiguous and deviously witty at times. And Crystal, as a queen of color watching yet another white queen get favored over her, made a particularly good avatar for shade in that moment.

In 1977, Crystal was asked by her friend and fellow drag queen Lottie to help her launch a drag ball. Crystal, having spent her entire drag career fighting for recognition in venues that didn't value queens of color, including the balls, agreed and took the idea one revolutionary step further by founding the legendary House of LaBeija, one of the first drag houses, with a titular mother in Crystal herself. Lottie and Crystal launched their first drag ball, at a Harlem bar called Up the Downstairs Case, with a flyer that was simple but seismic in its own way: "Crystal & Lottie LaBeija presents the first annual House of LaBeija Ball at Up the Downstairs Case."

A manifesto it was not. And yet it signaled what would become a stunning change in queer history and culture and, more important, a life-changing development for generations of queer people of color. Drag houses sprung up immediately after, all legendary from the start and legendary to this day. The House of Xtravaganza. The House of St. Laurent. The House of Dupree. The House of Ninja. Queer and transgender people of color took back a portion of LGBTQ culture, re-centered their own perspectives, aesthetics, and artistic voices, and gave untold numbers of people an outlet and form of expression that developed from within their communities.

In this way, Crystal responded to the racism she encountered in the drag pageant community with not just an epic read but with a revolutionary action that had far-reaching consequences for queer culture, echoing down the decades to today. It's perhaps a bit too easy to draw a straight line from her one media appearance in *The Queen* to her one major contribution to queer culture. Life rarely works out that neatly or cinematically. But when you take the long view, it's not hard to see how her epic read dressing down an undeserving white winner and her legendary introduction of drag mother houses to the ball community are connected, all part of the same larger picture of her life. Like so many important LGBTQ figures of the past, she lived her life and made her contributions in the underground, away from the historians and journalists who could have—and should have—immortalized her. And like so many trailblazers, she changed the world not because she felt like it but because she had to in order to survive in the way that she wanted. Respect. She demanded it, she knew it was owed her, and if the world wasn't going to give it to her on their terms, she'd damn well change the terms to suit her better. This is why a read or skillful application of shade can be about so much more than simply getting one over on someone or putting them down. Reading comes from deep inside a queen's need to be understood, respected, and, in many cases, worshipped for her beauty and grace.

Frank Ocean paid tribute to Crystal by sampling part of her read in the track "Ambience 001" in his 2016 video album *Endless*, helping underline her importance to queer cultural history and African American cultural history. On *Drag Race All Stars* season 3, Aja rather expertly channeled her for the Snatch Game challenge. Aja later said they felt their legendary read of Valentina in the season 9 reunion special ("You're perfect, you're beautiful, you look like Linda Evangelista, you're a model." "She could walk out there in a fucking diaper and they're like, 'Valentina! Your smile is beautiful!'") was a direct descendent of Crystal's form of shade and the kind of long-term rage that inspires it—that specific mix of anger and exhaustion at constantly being othered or less-than'd that can often fuel great art or performances. Alaska's song "Your Makeup Is Terrible" is based on Crystal's legendary read. She has more than earned her status as a legendary queen because both her words and her actions continue to resonate through the generations.

Voguing, the Art of Nonverbal Shade

Forget what Madonna told you in her 1990 hit "Vogue." It's a fun little dance song, but it has little to do with the art and history of this particular form of dance. For one thing, her "it makes no difference if you're black or white" lyric could not possibly be more off base. Voguing came from the drag balls, arising out of a dance form perfected specifically by black and Latinx queer people in order to not only express themselves but to fight for dominance or to establish their proper place in the world. Voguing is throwing shade without using words.

Willi Ninja is largely considered either the godfather or the grandfather of voguing. Regardless of which title you apply to him, the point is the same: He looms large in the pantheon of voguing, doing more to popularize and explain the art form than pretty much anyone else. In *Paris Is Burning*, he explains voguing's form as body-based shade, describing it as "a dance when two people don't like each other." Some legends maintain that it originated with queer inmates of color at the Rikers Island facility, who developed it as a way of fighting while not actually touching each other. Whether that particular aspect is true or not, there's no question that it's a specifically queer form of art and even more specifically a form created and developed by people of color.

Originally utilizing moves taken from fashion magazine editorials and named after *Vogue* magazine, the dance form also took inspiration from mime, Egyptian hieroglyphics, gymnastics, and, over time, other forms of modern dance. Today, it is recognized and celebrated worldwide as a particularly vibrant form of modern dance; but more important, voguing and the drag balls have evolved so that the art of voguing is also a highly competitive form of sports dance, allowing queer people of color the opportunity to express themselves and to channel that expression into a show of strength and skill. It still serves as a proxy for fighting or throwing shade, but it's also a gorgeous, brilliant, life-affirming form of self-expression that, like shade, asserts the rightness of a person's dominance and the tragedy of anyone who can't even come close to their perfection.

Just don't ever call it a "death drop." That's a classic voguing move, and no one in the ball community calls it that. It's a dip, thank you very much.

When Reading Isn't Enough: The Compton's Cafeteria Riot

It was 1966, a year before Crystal LaBeija launched her legendary read, and on the other side of the country, an entirely different group of queens also reached their breaking points. It was the sixties, after all, a time when a whole lot of disenfranchised folks in America were reaching their breaking points. This time, however, the response wasn't verbal. It was violent.

Much has been said of the 1969 Stonewall Riots and their place in LGBTQ history, but in August 1966, a group of pissed-off queens and trans women, realizing that a sharp tongue or a way with an insult wasn't going to cut it, did what so many oppressed folks do when they've had enough of their oppression: They fought back. Hard. And that same Darwinian viciousness that makes strong queens so formidable in their tongue-lashing is no less potent when it's translated into actual violence.

The Tenderloin neighborhood in San Francisco in the mid-sixties was a haven for the queens and queers who populated it, but it was also a minefield of danger, from angry johns to harassing cops and even to transgender-targeting serial killers. Gene Compton's Cafeteria, an all-night diner on the corner of Taylor and Turk in the heart of the Tenderloin, was a place where queens could congregate late at night, check in with each other, trade stories and warnings, and generally do the work of being a supportive community in a world that didn't want them to exist at all.

Some of the queens and trans women who gathered at Compton's were performers of one sort or another, but a good deal of them were sex workers because no one would hire them for conventional work. Marginalization is about denying options to groups of people based on how closely they adhere to the ideal. In mid-twentieth-century America, a black or Latinx queen or trans woman, seen by most as a man with a serious psychological issue, if not a criminal tendency, was so marginalized and fetishized that sex work was literally the only option available to many of them. "Nobody cared whether we lived or died. Our own families abandoned us and we had nowhere to go," is how transgender activist, drag performer, and Compton's rioter Felicia "Flames" Elizondo described this community in a speech given at the fiftieth anniversary observation of the riots. The entire history of drag, transgender, and nonbinary expression is one that demands a hardening and toughening on the part of its players, as well as a fierce need to congregate and communicate with those like them.

In that summer of 1966, temperatures were high and the Tenderloin was teeming with more tension than normal. The queens of the Tenderloin were starting to see the power in their congregating, but the management of Compton's routinely called the cops in to get them to leave. When a cop grabbed a queen sitting in Compton's with her friends one night in August, it turns out she was the wrong queen with whom to try that shit. Whoever she was—and history didn't record her name, unfortunately—she threw a cup of coffee in the cop's face. This act of rebellion sparked an instantaneous response from the surrounding queers and queens who saw it (remember, these things require an audience, not just in a read session, but because queer people in general and queens especially are more protected and more powerful when they band together). Tables got overturned; sugar shakers got thrown, shattering the plate-glass windows of Compton's; a newsstand was set on fire; and the queens of the Tenderloin roared their rage into the night. This act of ignition caused a ripple effect in the lives of so many involved, many of whom used this moment to formally band to-gether, to form outreach committees to the queens working the streets, and to serve as liaisons to the police department, who learned the folly of pushing a queen too far, past the point when even a good read will get them to back off. In other words, when reading failed these queens, fighting back had to take its place—and in making that leap toward revolution, they began the pre-viously unimagined work of forming a community.

Compton's Cafeteria is long gone, but a simple plaque marks the site for the important place in LGBTQ history it is: "Here marks the site of Gene Compton's Cafeteria, where a riot took place one August night when transgender women and gay men stood up for their rights and fought against police brutality, pov-erty, oppression, and discrimination in the Tenderloin. We, the transgender, gay, lesbian, and bisexual community, are dedicat-ing this plaque to these heroes of our civil rights movement."

The importance of drag queens and transgender women, especially those of color, in the earliest violent clashes with authority and the struggles of oppression is directly connected to the art of shade and the skill of reading. Black and Latinx queens, trans women, and nonbinary people were literally on the front lines of queerness, living their lives in full view of the world. This made them the first, most likely targets for police harassment and hate crimes, which in turn made them the first to get fed up. As Junior Labeija put it so well in *Paris Is Burn-ing*, "With y'all vicious motherfuckers, it do take nerve."

Herstory lesson:

The Original Reality Queens

The Queen, the seminal 1968 documentary on drag that introduced Crystal LaBeija to the world, follows the story of Jack Doroshow, a twenty-four-year-old drag pageant promoter and part-time drag queen named Mother Flawless Sabrina (a maternal persona he took in an attempt to appear unthreatening to the beauty queens in his shows), as he plans and mounts the 1967 Miss All-America Camp Beauty Pageant held at the town hall in New York, with none other than Andy Warhol sitting on the judging panel. Sabrina was a bit of an operator and fast-talker; a read between the lines seems to indicate that Crystal LaBeija was totally on the nose when she accused Sabrina of favoritism. The film was shown at Cannes in 1968 and received no small amount of attention, given its rough nature and taboo-for-the-time subject matter. It helped that one of the film's stars, the pretty and glamorous Harlow, attended Cannes in full drag to promote the film. While it tends to depict an extremely narrow slice of drag life in the late 1960s (lots of ragtime and showgirl numbers and a focus on white middle-class gay men), it nonetheless offers a sobering look at how furtive and conformist drag was, back in the days when drag could get you sent to jail. The scenes of the various queens in their hotel rooms talking about their boyfriends and families, their desire to serve in the military or get married, and the vehement denials that any of them "want to be a woman" are a surprisingly candid and on-point look at gay life at that time. Keep your eyes peeled for an appearance by *Paris Is Burning*'s Pepper LaBeija (before she took that name), practically unrecognizable in full drag and even less so in her straight-and-narrow boy clothes.

Herstory Lesson:

Dorian Corey, Shady Queen Surviving in a Shady-Ass World

Some of the most illuminating and gently entertaining segments in *Paris Is Burning* occur when Dorian Corey just chats to the camera as she slowly, patiently, and painstakingly applies her face. Miss Dorian was a snake dancer with the legendary Pearl Box Revue in the 1960s and is one of four queens featured on the 1972 Pearl Box LP, *Call Me MISSter*. For years, she was known for her drag performances at the Times Square drag bar Sally's. But her biggest, most colorful tale was not revealed until after her death in 1993, when a friend of hers was going through her old costumes, thinking to sell them, and instead found a mummified body with a bullet in its head, in a garment bag stored deep in the recesses of Dorian's overstuffed apartment. An ensuing investigation determined that Dorian may have known and dated the man, although there was purported to have been a note included with the body that he tried to break into her apartment and she was forced to defend herself.

We may never know what truly happened, but it's a reminder that a queen sometimes has to get rough with the world, and the world needs to understand just how dangerous a queen can be when cornered. It's not for us to say whether Dorian was the hero or the villain in this tale, just a queen trying to survive in a hard-ass world. "Everybody wants to make an impression, some mark upon the world," she mused in *Paris Is Burning*. "Then you think, you've made a mark on the world if you just get through it, and a few people remember your name. If you shoot an arrow and it goes real high, hooray for you."

Herstory Lesson:

When Cross-Dressers Collide: RuPaul vs. Milton Berle

"You know, RuPaul, forty years ago, when I was on TV, I used to wear gowns myself."

"Is that right? You used to wear gowns and—that's funny, now you wear diapers."

RuPaul's legendary showdown with Milton Berle on camera at the MTV Video Music Awards in 1993 is a shining example of a queen using her mouth to beat back an aggressor.

A comedy legend from the vaudeville tradition and pioneer of early television, Milton Berle was known for the many times he wore "ugly drag" (how straight male comedians use drag for comic purposes) during comedy sketches on his shows. As part of a jokey bit at the awards podium, Berle mentioned that he used to wear gowns just like the one Ru had on. What the audience didn't know was that Berle and Ru had an altercation backstage in which he grabbed Ru and made some inappropriate comments. Ru, fairly new to fame and only a few years removed from the club queen and street performer he once was, clapped back hard with the unplanned line about diapers. In recent years Ru has said that he regrets that this confrontation happened onstage, while also noting that he should have taken care of Berle backstage. In other words, it wasn't the confrontation or the standing up for himself that he regrets; it's that he allowed it to happen onstage, when he was trying to be a professional. Still, we think he shouldn't be so hard on himself. Sometimes, a little bit of lip is all a queen has to protect herself.

The Tea On:

Drag Race's Most Legendary Library Reads

"Jiggly Caliente, you're such a fat slut, after sex, you smoke ham."
Sharon Needles, season 4

"Legendary you think you are. Legendary?
Looks like leg and dairy."
Jujubee, season 2

"Joslyn Fox. She's so gay even her ass has a lisp."
Bianca Del Rio, season 6

"Adore Delano. I'm. Going. To. Say. This. Slowly. So.
You. Can. Understand. You're dumb."
Darienne Lake, season 6

"Bob the Drag Queen. You may be from New York, honey,
but those feet are from Mississippi."
Chi Chi DeVayne, season 8

"Roxxxy Andrews. I think of you all the time.
Especially in the morning, at the bus stop."
Katya, All Stars season 2

"Trinity the Tuck. You on *All Stars* is just like
what's in your face: filler."
Manila Luzon, All Stars *season 4*

"Miss Tyra, was your barbecue canceled? Your grill is fucked."
Jujubee, season 2

Herstory Lesson:

Paris Is Burning Helped Build the Library

"Touch this skin, darling. Touch this skin, honey.
Touch all of this skin. . . .
You just can't take it. You're just an
overgrown orangutan."

Venus Xtravaganza

As Ru notes with every introduction of the Library challenge
("In the great tradition of *Paris Is Burning* . . ."), *Drag Race*
takes a great deal of inspiration from the legendary 1990 documentary when it comes to matters of shade.

Venus Xtravaganza in particular figures heavily in the legends of reading on *Drag Race*. A soft-spoken princess of the
drag balls, Venus gave an impromptu tutoring session on the
art of reading ("You wanna talk about reading? Let's talk about
reading.") in *Paris Is Burning*, a session that birthed several
deathless drag phrases. Tyra Sanchez, the first contestant on
Drag Race to play the Library challenge, referenced Venus
within the first minute, calling Jujubee an "undergrown orangutan." Willam quoted the "Touch this skin . . . Touch all of this

skin" line in the Werk Room. Ru has used Venus's phrasing about going through "a psychological change in your life" on several occasions; Carson punned "Touch this fin, touch all of this fin" during the Bette Midler mermaids runway challenge. That Venus was murdered only adds to the poignancy of her scenes in the film, especially when you consider the close relationship between the ability to read and life in a harsh and violent world.

Chapter 3

Serving Snatch to
Middle America

*S*ome queens consider it the one challenge worth entering the competition for and some queens grit their teeth and hope they can just make their way through it. Some queens giggle and clap with glee at the prospect of it and others fall apart at the daunting task in front of them. It's the Snatch Game challenge, and it's always been one of the hardest parts of the *Drag Race* competition. Snatch Game determines "who is a contender and who is just roadkill," as Ru said. Aquaria called it "an iconic challenge." Put more succinctly by Trixie Mattel: "The Snatch Game is fucking hard."

The Snatch Game has its roots in both pop culture history (as a parody of the 1970s game show *Match Game*) and in drag history, and it's very much in line with RuPaul's vision and version of drag: witty, pop culture–based, and celebrity worshipping in a joking, bitchy way. As Ru said while judging the Snatch Game efforts in season 4, "That's what drag is about. You have to have a knowledge of pop culture." It's also a challenge that asks the queens to be on their toes, with jokes at the ready, a fully conceptualized and recognizable character look, and the ability to play off all the pandemonium around them. The two most important aspects of Snatch Game involve Ru as the host of the sketch and later as the judge of the competition. You have to make him laugh, which is an order/piece of advice usually repeated a dozen times throughout a Snatch Game episode. And just as important, but much more subtle: You have to hit the balls he pitches to you. (This will probably be the only sports analogy you'll find anywhere in this book, so savor it for a moment, would you?)

Our point is that the Snatch Game is as much an interaction between Ru and each queen as it is a performance put on for Ru as a judge. This makes it one of the hardest challenges in all of *Drag Race*. While you're trying to get your established jokes and bits out, you also have to play off Ru, come up with funny answers to the questions, and try to avoid what Latrice famously called the *"Romper Room* fuckery" that happens when a queen starts going off the rails and takes the surrounding queens with her. You have to play off every single thing around you, make your voice heard, and if mayhem breaks out, rise above it. "Snatch Game challenges your improv skills, your wit, and your impersonation skills. Without these three things, a drag queen might as well not call herself a drag queen," as Jinkx Monsoon put it succinctly in season 5. And these skills—the kinds of things a queen learns working the bars, nightclubs, and cabarets, making her way through the drag circuit, dealing with rowdy crowds and other queens trying to steal her spotlight—are some of the most essential skills for any queen to become a major star, in Ru's considered opinion.

Which brings us to the other reason the Snatch Game is important—and the reason why so many queens shudder at it: Impersonating female celebrities is a very old form of drag with a long tradition behind it and some truly legendary players to live up to. Some of the biggest stars in the history of drag worked their way up the drag revue and drag cabaret circuits doing exactly what the Snatch Game asks the *Drag Race* queens to do: Show us your best celebrity impersonation and make us believe it.

So when the queens take part in the *Drag Race* tradition of the Snatch Game, they're also paying tribute to a form of drag that made huge inroads into mainstream acceptance of queer performers and performing styles in twentieth-century America. It's a lot to live up to, and Ru knows it.

Selling the Illusion

"In the grand tradition of drag," Ru said when he introduced the first Snatch Game challenge in the second season, alluding to the fact that drag entertainment has long had a celebrity female impersonator component from which countless slightly off-brand Judys, Barbras, Bettes, Chers, and Madonnas have made their entire careers. Going back as far as the 1920s, various nightclubs, cabarets, supper clubs, and casinos featured revues of drag performers mimicking famous women for a living. Going even further back, to the mid- to late nineteenth century, comedic "wench" or "crone" drag was as essential a component of vaudeville as blackface—and roughly as complimentary to its subjects. In the early years of the twentieth century, Julian Eltinge bridged these two styles and became one of the highest-paid entertainers in the world, famous for his somewhat revolutionary form of drag, which eschewed the bawdy comedic aspects associated with it for true glamour and beauty. Eltinge was a pioneer of the modern drag idea of the female impersonator, a man who could effectively pull off the illusion of being a woman, instead of simply making a joke of the very idea. That was the approach that spurred on a new form of entertainment for the new century. Because once you establish that men can cast an illusion of womanhood and that people would be fascinated enough by the idea to pay to see it, it's only a matter of time before female impersonators with a gift for mimicry and the right facial structure start casting the illusion of being *specific* women. Famous women. And just as all this started springing up as a legitimate form of entertainment in the first half of the twentieth century, Hollywood exploded as a cultural force and perpetual celebrity-making machine, serving up generation upon generation of glamorous, larger-than-life women for female impersonators to build a career around emulating.

The Jewel Box Revue: Queer Entertainment for the Straight and Narrow

Frank Marino, one of the most successful female impersonators of all time, whose three-decade career on the Vegas Strip is legendary (and whose *Divas Las Vegas* show has employed *Drag Race* alums Coco Montrese, Chad Michaels, Shannel, and Derrick Barry), once explained the success of his style of drag in an interview: "I'm not selling people a lifestyle." Marino, who's famous for his Joan Rivers impersonation, is happily and proudly out and gay, so this isn't quite as judgmental as it might sound at first. The history of celebrity female impersonation is one of largely queer men and transgender women seeking out mainstream acceptance from predominantly straight audiences, often by obscuring, downplaying, or outright denying their queerness.

The Jewel Box Revue was a glittering, high-quality drag revue that launched at the Jewel Box club in Miami in the 1930s and later became a traveling show, spending decades bringing the hard work and undeniable talent of an enormous stable of queer folks offering the very best in drag entertainment to cities and towns all over America, until it eventually closed down in the late 1960s, when drag had come to be seen as an overtly queer form of entertainment.

The masterminds behind the Jewel Box Revue were a pair of two-fisted lovers named Danny Brown and Doc Benner, who liked to bill the show—and themselves—as a perfectly normal and even masculine enterprise put on for family entertainment by family men. No, really. As Brown liked to brag in press materials, "We took the degeneracy out of female impersonation. . . . The Jewel Box Revue is just a clean, family-type show." With a marquee line of "25 Men and 1 Girl," the show's programs and press materials liked to tout how many of the performers in the show were married men and fathers (not many, it turns out). And yet, backstage was a tight, communal, totally queer safe space of chorus boys, costume designers, musicians, and drag queens, a space that many of its participants spoke fondly of half a century later. Some modern scholars of queer history have singled out the community of the Jewel Box Revue specifically as one of the earliest spaces created for queer folks, even though the times forced them to deny it and the culture caused them to seek out mainstream acceptance in order to survive.

Celebrity female impressions weren't the sole draw of the

Jewel Box Revue, which was mainly about large musical production numbers and shticky vaudevillian comedy. But plenty of its most famous queens over the years were known for their mimicry skills and homages to famous women, the most celebrated of whom would probably be Lynne Carter, a white man who wowed midcentury audiences with his eerie skill at mimicking the vocal styles of African American entertainers Pearl Bailey and Josephine Baker. Offering illusory and entertaining impressions of famous women allowed an almost entirely queer enterprise like the Jewel Box Revue to gain mainstream acceptance. What better way to get Mom and Dad out for a night of queer entertainment than by packaging it as a winking take on the mainstream Hollywood stars they love? The Jewel Box Revue plucked glamour from its rarefied perch and served it to the masses, in town after town, theater after theater, for more than a quarter century, launching the careers of hundreds of drag entertainers.

Taking this back to *Drag Race*, the Snatch Game is a particularly subtle bit of brilliance on the show's part because it takes one of the most mainstream forms of drag—and not coincidentally, the form most obsessed with being seen as respectable if not downright wholesome—and married it to that great bastion of wide mainstream appeal, the daytime game show. *Match Game* was a staple of 1970s daytime television and a showcase for a lot of hammy B-listers (at best) and comedians to try to outdo each other in outrageous commentary and bawdy-for-the-seventies double entendres. Combining these two tucked-away corners of the culture, in a manner only a pop culture–obsessed queen could truly understand, was one of the show's earliest strokes of genius.

Respect and Respectability

Because twentieth-century female-impersonation revues like the Jewel Box were packaged and played to straight audiences, female impersonators and illusionists were often obsessed with respectability on a level queens from other communities never could be. Crystal LaBeija and Marsha P. Johnson demanded basic respect and (in Crystal's case, at least) to be recognized as beautiful and worthy of celebration, but mainstream-facing drag entertainers, with their focus on artistry and glamour and their attempts at passing themselves off as non-queer entertainment, wanted something different. They wanted legitimacy and acceptance. The history of female impersonators, gender illusionists, and celebrity female impressionists is a history of performers who most definitely did not see themselves as "mere" drag queens and were focused less on the respect of their peers (like Crystal LaBeija) and the basic dignity owed them (like Marsha P. Johnson) and more on gaining the respect of that vast consumer demographic known as Middle America. Or for the purposes of this conversation, straight folks. We'll get into this idea more in subsequent chapters, but just note for now that the drag performing community has a history of being hierarchical, with many drag artists and entertainers spending their entire careers denying the term *drag queen* for their work. This distinction tended to play out along lines of class and artistic value. The nicer (and straighter) the venue, the less likely the person doing drag on the stage prefers to call themselves a drag queen.

We'd like to make it clear that, from our perspective at least, there's no judgment against these men for how they navigated a world that was even more dangerous for the gender-nonconforming than it is now. A white gay man from a pre-Stonewall era expressing his need or desire to perform in drag is going to see more of himself in the white middle-class audiences of supper clubs and cabarets than he is in the drag balls of Harlem or the streetwalkers of the Tenderloin. But you can't deny the hold a closeted existence can have over your self-worth, and even the upscale, white, celebrated queens of the early days of female-impersonation entertainment have to be respected for the boldness of their lives at a time and place when it was extremely dangerous for them.

Here you have the curious situation of queer performers plying the drag trade to heterosexual middle-class audiences as a form of respectable entertainment. The backstages and caravans of these shows were as queer and bitchy as any episode of *Untucked!* or argument at a Werk Room makeup mirror, but the marketing and promotion stressed the more or less wholesome masculinity and assumed cisgender status and heterosexuality of the players. To be fair, this respectability was a thin veneer, and audiences of the day were in no way naive or dumb about the kind of men most likely to be found working in a female-impersonation revue. But that's the funny thing about social veneers; they're really just agreed-upon delusions by everyone involved. This dynamic was one of the reasons why so many drag performers in this kind of revue used "Mr." in front of their stage name, whether it was male or female.

To take a broader view, this focus on respect and respectability is drag's essence—a demand for acceptance, appropriate deference, and the use of preferred terms; an insistence upon the illusion; the right to determine what's real; and the ability to make everyone else see it through your eyes. When Alexis Mateo makes you believe she's a butch pregnant Alicia Keys or when Raja makes you believe she's a slightly insane Tyra Banks or when Bob the Drag Queen makes you believe he's a black Carol Channing, they're winning the game because they're getting to the heart of what it's all about.

Faking the Truth vs. Finding the Truth

Part of the reason so many queens find the Snatch Game challenge so difficult is because it asks them not just to perform in the grand drag tradition of celebrity female impersonation but also to pull from various disciplines (for lack of a better word) of the art form. The queens have to manage mimicry of some sort as well as inject comedy that somehow feels truthful to the person being portrayed. Asia O'Hara got a lot of criticism for her utterly humorless Beyoncé not just because she wasn't funny, but because no one could understand why she was portraying her so angrily. It just didn't feel right for Beyoncé. When Alaska changed Mae West's signature line "Come up and see me sometime" into a blunt demand for anal sex (thereby setting off one of Ru's hardest-laughing jags in the history of the Snatch Game), he was getting to the truth of Mae West's persona by saying something she'd never actually said. Not in public, anyway.

But a pure comedy approach isn't always the best route, and sometimes a queen has a much better chance of winning the Snatch Game when their impersonation is both visually and aurally correct. In other words, they have to look and sound like the person they're mimicking. To be fair, it's no guarantee of success. So specific is the Snatch Game's required balance of comedy and mimicry that professional Janet Jackson impersonator Coco Montrese and professional Britney impersonator Derrick Barry barely managed a mention for their efforts—not because they didn't look like Janet and Britney, but because they didn't offer any sort of observation or hidden truth about them.

The only time a queen ever truly wins Ru over with a bad impersonation is if they somehow turn the very awfulness of it into a part of the joke. When Alyssa Edwards could do little more than offer up *Mommie Dearest* quotes as Joan Crawford, she ran with it, going full-bore wild-eyed and clownish to the point where the joke stopped being about Joan Crawford and became about how ridiculous Alyssa's version of her was.

But that kind of approach led to way more failures than successes in Snatch Game, largely because of that tension between portraying the truth of a woman, and finding a certain underlying truth about her and using that to build a portrait. The history of celebrity female-impersonation drag is long, with so many players and influential performers that it would be impossible to give a comprehensive account of it here; but with the Snatch Game as a frame, we can look at two artists whose drag performing styles represented the very best and most celebrated forms of the celebrity impersonation drag the challenge is based on. Charles Pierce was a performer who knew how to get to the comedic truth of an impersonation without necessarily nailing the mimicry, and Jim Bailey became internationally famous for the eerie precision and meticulous re-creation of his celebrity impressions. Both of them are unquestionably legends.

Charles Pierce's Hilariously Sloppy Illusion

"You've heard of *Women's Wear Daily*?
This is what men wear nightly."

Charles Pierce

Born in 1926, Charles Pierce began his lifelong vocation of drag like so many who took up the form did: by dressing up as his favorite actress on Halloween as a young boy. In his case, it was Mae West—and it would be the last time he'd put on the famous sex symbol's face and voice without collecting a fee or a bra stuffed with tips. He spoke many years later of rummaging through his grandmother's things in the attic of his Watertown, New York, childhood home, trying them on and making believe that he was out in the world doing glamorous things, saying witty things, and making people laugh. He eventually got his start as a radio announcer, trained as an actor, and did summer stock. At one point he was even a department store Santa. Eventually he landed in the world of cabaret, saw that he could get paid a living wage doing it (as opposed to his acting career), and in 1954, put together an act composed of a little singing, a little patter, more than a few jokes, and impressions of the stars of Hollywood—but no drag. Not yet. He would perform in a tuxedo or in a pair of black pants and a black turtleneck, a blank canvas that allowed him to use props like hats and feather boas—but not dresses, wigs, or makeup. Not at first, anyway. A single performer on a cabaret or nightclub stage in the 1950s didn't have the leeway an entire revue of professional female impersonators provided, and Pierce knew that the laws about men wearing women's clothing were different from town to town (something many revue owners, like the Jewel Box's Brown and Benner, got past by bribing the local police), so his drag career was, at first, completely sans drag. This was probably a huge help to him in the long run because it allowed him to build an act based on his own wit, charming personality (with a heavy dose of classic Bitchy Queen), and tremendous love for the grand ladies of the golden age of Hollywood. When he eventually did start doing his act in full drag—something he later noted happened gradually without a definitive decision being made—it remained for the rest of his career a performance devoted entirely to making the audience laugh and cheer, with the accuracy of his impressions coming in way down on the list of considerations.

It wasn't that they were bad impersonations—far from it. His Bette Davis is legendary. He only semi-faithfully gets her voice down and wildly exaggerates her mannerisms, but Pierce was fine-featured and slight of build, with enormous blue eyes. In other words, he was built for female impersonation and in the case of Bette Davis had the benefit of actually resembling her. More important, he had a gifted comedian's knack for truly observing the heart of a person and putting out a version that felt true—and hilarious. "I'll never forget my films," his Davis mused lightly as she arched an eyebrow and artfully flicked her cigarette, "and I'll never let *you* forget my films." All his other ladies—Mae West, Joan Crawford, Joan Collins, Katharine Hepburn, Tallulah Bankhead, Marlene Dietrich (whose signature song "Illusions" Pierce sang to close his show)—were easily recognizable, based on this same ability to evoke them using a few theatrical tricks, a movie fan's ardent knowledge, and a comic's acid-tinged ability to skewer. The jokes were old-fashioned and sometimes pretty groan-worthy from a present-day perch ("Sex is like bridge," said his Mae West. "If you don't have a good partner, you better have a good hand."), but he clearly held his adoring and appreciative audiences in his palm and never let go until the final bow. And perhaps his early years being forced to go drag-free had something to do with it, but the man eventually compiled a stunning array of glamourous gowns to help him achieve his effects. At the end of his four-decade career, he estimated that he'd worn more than ten thousand dresses onstage. "Drag is dirty work," he said, "but somebody's got to do it."

Having said that, like so many female impersonators, he didn't prefer to be called a drag queen at all. If you go through the interviews and documentation of these performers, practically every one of them, from Julian Eltinge to Lynne Carter and all the way up to Frank Marino today, had a slightly different name for what they do. Illusionist. Impressionist. Gender illusionist. Female impersonator. Drag artist. Pierce himself preferred a term a reviewer used to describe him: "male actress." He could hardly be said to have been all that coy about his gayness and he spent a huge chunk of his career playing gay venues to gay audiences, so he didn't have the hang-ups or need to separate his professional identity from his queer one, like other female impersonators have done. But Pierce also enjoyed a considerable amount of mainstream success. His *Charles Pierce Show Featuring the Legendary Ladies of the Silver Screen* comedy special, taped in 1982 at the Dorothy Chandler Pavilion ("Who knew Dorothy Pavilion's middle name was Chandler?" he quipped), was a staple of late-night eighties basic cable, running on the Playboy Channel for most of the decade, making his Bette Davis a familiar sight to countless sleepless hotel room occupants. He worked as a character actor, both in and out of drag, making guest appearances on a bunch of popular mainstream TV shows, from *Wonder Woman* to *Laverne & Shirley*, *Starsky & Hutch*, and *Designing Women*. Near the end of his career, he played the drag queen Bertha Venation in the movie adaptation of Harvey Fierstein's *Torch Song Trilogy*. And his cabaret act routinely saw luminaries and legends such as Lucille Ball, Bea Arthur, Carol Channing, and Stephen Sondheim sitting in the audience. This queen did all right for himself, is what we're saying, going from tiny gay bars to the toast of café society in Hollywood and New York.

At his funeral in 1999, longtime friend (and frequent character in his act) Carol Channing said, "He did Carol Channing better than I did." Bette Davis was reported to have not found his act flattering, and several famous women have tried to sue their impersonators (like Joan Rivers, who initially went after Frank Marino for stealing her act but eventually relented and gave her blessing), but in the end, with someone like Charles Pierce, who spent four decades serving up Gloria Swanson and Joan Crawford and a couple dozen other big-screen divas, it's hard not to see the sheer love and fannish joy underlying the performances. Carol understood this, which is why she appeared on the *Drag Race* season 8 finale to commend Bob the Drag Queen on his hilarious (but like Pierce's, not technically perfect) impersonation of her in the Snatch Game.

Charles Busch, the great drag performer and playwright, put it better than we ever could, in an interview for the 1997 documentary *Dragtime*: "Charles Pierce is a great artist who fought many of the battles that I reap the benefits from."

The Fierce and Eerie Precision of Jim Bailey

Jim Bailey would never have called himself a drag queen and didn't even like to call himself a female impersonator or impressionist. Instead, he preferred "character actor" or "illusionist" for what he did. And what he did was largely considered the very best Judy Garland in the game for decades—with a Streisand that was no less legendary.

Reviews of his shows all note the eeriness of his impersonations, especially his Judy, whose legacy he kept alive for four decades after she died. Unlike Charles Pierce, whose form of impersonation was broad and comedy based, Bailey's female stage personae were meticulous and dignified re-creations of the women he was performing, using the precision of his operatic-trained voice to mimic them exactly. Looking back on his career, he professed wonder at how it ever started. As a young man in the mid-1960s, he was known to sing classic songs—including many of Judy Garland's—at parties. He had begun doing a small cabaret act impersonating comedian Phyllis Diller, whose outrageous personal style and unmistakable voice made her a favorite among the celebrity female impersonator set. But one day at a party, for reasons he couldn't articulate even forty years later, Jim Bailey opened his mouth to sing "Over the Rainbow" and instead of his own well-trained voice, Judy Garland's came out, surprising even him. The crowd was dazzled, and Jim's cabaret career started taking off once he brought his Judy into the fold.

The real Judy Garland came to see him perform her act while he was headlining at a club in Los Angeles around 1967; she was so enraptured and enchanted by it that she did the very

Judy thing of leaping up onstage at the end and throwing her arms around him in a hug before singing a duet of "Bye Bye Blackbird" with him as an encore. She took him under her wing and trained him on all her onstage moves: physical, vocal, and emotional. She once played the entire album of her legendary Carnegie Hall performance for him at top volume and walked him through the entire thing, shouting every bow, wink, and gesture at him over her own overpowering vocals. What a scene that must have been. Judy died tragically in 1969, a victim of her own demons and an entertainment industry that had abused and exploited her since her childhood. Her grandiosity, vulnerability, and stunningly dramatic talent had already secured her a place of honor in the female impersonator pantheon, with many having already made a career out of her and countless more to come in the decades ahead. But there was only one Jim Bailey, and only he could seemingly resurrect Judy from the grave and invite her to take over his body.

In 1970 he got his first big break, performing on the hugely popular *Ed Sullivan Show*, singing "The Man That Got Away," from Garland's 1954 version of *A Star Is Born*, dressed in full—and of course flawless—Judy drag. This was only a year after Garland herself died, and many home viewers assumed it was a rerun of an old episode or a tribute clip, the illusion was so perfect.

If Charles Pierce could get to the essence of his women with a wink and a gesture, Jim Bailey took the exact opposite route. He studied and studied and studied—their movements and gestures, the way they breathed and blinked, the exact way they applied their makeup, using precisely the same shades and finishes. The costumes were meticulous re-creations of their signature looks. Glamour wasn't the most important item on his list in compiling his drag, partly because he favored women who had signature and iconic looks of relatively low glamour. But when you read or watch interviews with him over the years, despite the intense and very queer love he had for his divas, he was far more intent on capturing their image rather than indulging in their glamour. Charles Busch spoke of catching a Jim Bailey performance as Judy and being astonished to see that he padded himself like the middle-aged woman with the non-model figure she was at the time he was portraying her. Busch saw this as a testament to Bailey's obsession with meticulous accuracy over surface glamour or light ridicule. "I become them," Bailey said of his impressions, speaking many times of the feeling of turning his body over to the women he portrayed. Despite having a repertoire of famous women he was known for mimicking—not just Garland and Streisand but also Peggy Lee and Diller—Bailey almost always stuck to one impression per performance because it took hours for him to get into character and costume, so precise and involved were the details. Charles Pierce, by comparison, dashed offstage mid-show to change costumes several times—all while still performing his act, singing and joking into an offstage mic.

Like Pierce, Bailey achieved an admirable level of mainstream success and exposure, in live performance and television. He played Carnegie Hall nine times and the Palladium in London seventeen times, as well as headlining more Vegas revues than we can bother counting. On TV, he introduced his drag to America by making appearances on *The Lucy Show* (because Lucille Ball apparently loved herself some drag queens), *The Carol Burnett Show*, multiple appearances on *The Tonight Show* and *The Ed Sullivan Show*, and a whole bunch of other variety shows of the period, as well as portraying a transgender woman on an episode of *Night Court.* And it should be noted that at the same time Jim Bailey and Charles Pierce were serving their particular brand of nonbinary queerness to America's living rooms, a succession of films and television shows portrayed drag queens and transgender women as serial killers and psychopaths. Bailey and Pierce weren't trying to do anything but entertain people; but in retrospect, their work and success helped to temper the public's idea of queerness at a time when most people were deeply uncomfortable with and suspicious of it. In fact, Jim Bailey was so good at serving drag to mainstream audiences when they weren't exactly all that receptive to queerness that he played the halftime show at Super Bowl XII in 1978 *in full Barbra Streisand drag.* You don't get more mainstream and heterosexual a venue than that. And yes, his version of "Don't Rain on My Parade" brought the crowd to cheers.

He continued to perform as Judy and Barbra and Peggy for more than forty years, almost the entire life-span of Garland herself. His final performance, at seventy-five years of age, was for the S.T.A.G.E. benefit in 2013, in which he sang three of Judy's classics in—what else?—flawless Judy drag. He died in 2015, a legend among his kind and the keeper of Judy's flame.

The Tea On:

Legendary Snatches

Over the course of the Snatch Game's history, many contestants have made the bold choice of portraying one of the legendary inspirations of female impersonators of ye olden days of drag, which gives you some idea of how aware of their drag history some of the queens are.

Carol Channing: Pandora Boxx and Bob the Drag Queen

Marlene Dietrich: Sasha Velour

Barbra Streisand: Manila Luzon

Eartha Kitt: Chi Chi DeVayne and Valentina

Cher: Chad Michaels

Marilyn Monroe: Ivy Winters

Joan Crawford: Mariah Paris Balenciaga and Alyssa Edwards

Bette Davis: Chad Michaels

Mae West: Alaska

Liza Minelli: Alexis Michelle

These were generally considered risky choices because so many legendary queens had made their careers doing these same impressions. That makes for an interesting commentary on how *Drag Race* works in relation to all the queer cultural history it references. The competition is full of challenges deliberately devised to pay homage to aspects of drag or LGBTQ culture and history, but it tends to reward those queens who move the form forward or at least don't rely on aping the past. If you're going to do Bette Davis on Snatch Game, you can bet that Ru will be comparing your work directly to Charles Pierce's, and you can bet he's going to want to see you do something new with it. In other words, know your legends, but don't rip them off.

The Tea On:

Boy Drag in the Snatch Game

Part of *Drag Race*'s evolution as it became more popular and more critically beloved (meaning it had a much larger audience with a much broader demographic) was the way it slowly and sometimes begrudgingly embraced those things it used to denounce. Much of the criticism in the earliest episodes of the show centered on any queen who did not come out in full feminine drag. Queens have been called out for wearing pants or not wearing corsets or shapers, but as the show's audience started skewing younger and more broadly queer (as opposed to the gay male audience of its origins), such restrictive ideas about gender presentation have largely been loosened up. There was a time when it was considered not just questionable or risky for a queen to portray a man on the Snatch Game, but downright wrong. It's a choice that still occasionally raises some eyebrows, but there were enough winning or lauded boy-drag performances over time that eventually the show embraced the idea and now no one tends to get all that fussed if a queen wants to do some form of male drag. It should be noted that many of the male drag entries were men who were flamboyant, like Ben-DeLaCreme's Paul Lynde, and known to wear makeup, like Thorgy Thor's Michael Jackson and Kennedy Davenport's Little Richard. Since gender illusion revues like the Jewel Box showcased famous drag kings such as Stormé DeLarverie, it feels not only forward-thinking but also respectful of queer history for the show to embrace drag's many forms of illusion, presentation, and impersonation.

Herstory Lesson:
Julian Eltinge's Fragile Masculinity

At one time a huge star in vaudeville and the movies, Julian Eltinge is generally considered to be a central figure in drag history, having inspired entire generations of the female impersonators who followed him. When you look through the contemporary drag documentation of the 1950s up through the 1980s, countless older drag queens cite him as an influence or inspiration. Both Lynne Carter and Charles Pierce mentioned him as an inspiration in interviews. The *Female Impersonator's Handbook*, published in 1967, said of Eltinge, "Of the impersonators who have achieved 'Greatness,' he alone excels as the top, only to be imitated by hundreds of others." He had a somewhat conflicted attitude toward his choice of career, often winding up in the papers for getting into fistfights with men who disparaged his masculinity. He successfully brought his drag to the silver screen and starred in several hit movies, making a fortune for himself in the process. He noted as he got older that drag was less of an option for him because, as he insightfully (and bitterly) put it, people had no interest in looking at women over forty.

He couldn't make the transition into non-drag character actor work, and eventually, because of changing laws about public decency, his career consisted of standing onstage singing his old songs and pointing to the costumes he used to be allowed to wear, displayed on dress forms. As we'll illustrate further in subsequent chapters, the past hundred years saw a constant waxing and waning of the public's acceptance of drag as a form of entertainment. Public decency laws throughout the twentieth century prohibited cross-dressing in public, sometimes under severe penalties. When the dominant culture went through periods when they found drag entertainment cheeky, naughty fun, such as in the vaudeville era and the Roaring Twenties, these laws were lightly and sporadically applied. When social mores shifted, as they do constantly, many drag entertainers found themselves without a viable outlet for their careers and skills. For Julian Eltinge, society had turned his performed exuberance into performed shame.

If you ever get a chance to pass by the Empire theater on Times Square, just a few steps down from the famous wax museum, buy a ticket to a movie, step into the grand lobby, and look up. It used to be the Eltinge Theatre, and there on the ceiling is the final lasting monument to Julian Eltinge's career: a mural of the Three Muses of mythology. It's one of the purest representations of the feminine ideal in Western culture, and all of them are portraits of Julian Eltinge in drag, providing his best illusion.

Herstory Lesson:

Lynne Carter's Taxicabs Full of Dior

Lynne Carter came home from serving in World War II and, with the newfound freedom granted postwar queers congregating in urban centers, he found himself working in cabarets and strip clubs, perfecting an eventual drag-based act of songs and jokes. A contemporary of Charles Pierce and a longtime headliner with the Jewel Box Revue, Carter became famous for many different celebrity impersonations, the more notable of which may have been his versions of Pearl Bailey and legendary bisexual singers Josephine Baker and Billie Holiday—all black women whom the white Carter performed without the use of blackface or even any attempt to look like them. He often performed these women while in a platinum blond wig, a look none of them were known for. Blackface drag wasn't exactly unheard of in the history of the art, which makes it fairly admirable of Carter to have avoided any attempts at race-based mimicry, letting only his vocal talent do the work of making people believe. This lack of racial mimicry may be one of the reasons why Bailey, Baker, and Holiday supported him. Josephine Baker caught his act and gave him what he described as several taxicabs full of Dior and Balenciaga gowns. She also tutored him in French and taught him her act. Bailey saw him do one of her numbers in a strip club and immediately took him under her wing, coaching his singing and providing him with her own musicians and arrangements.

She even went so far as to provide a quote for one of his show programs at a time when supporting female impersonators publicly wasn't something most stars would consider. "When I hear Lynne sing," she wrote, "it is like listening to a playback of my own voice."

Joey Arias is a drag entertainer who first became famous in the 1990s as a star of New York cabaret society, wowing audiences by dressing like 1950s fetish queen Bettie Page but sounding almost exactly like Billie Holiday when he opened his mouth to sing. Joey is a legend in his own right and doesn't need to be compared to anyone, but we always felt like his whiteface glamour over a black female vocal style was lightly descended from Lynne Carter's work half a century before. Lynne Carter died from AIDS complications in 1985.

Herstory Lesson:

Pudgy Roberts's *Female Impersonator's Handbook*

Pudgy Roberts was a female impersonator who not only wrote a handbook for the profession in 1967, the following year he published the first professional female impersonator industry magazine, called *Female Mimics*, and he had a consulting business for professional female impersonators on matters of hair, makeup, and costumes. This queen was *serious* about her drag.

With tips from Roberts on everything from what type of wig to wear to his favorite method of creating a vulva out of electrical tape ("This gives the illusion of lips."), spirit gum, and fake hair ("Needless to say, this is another illusion that's quite effective."), the *Female Impersonator's Handbook* is admirable not only for the boldness of its author but also for its very clear and often-declared insistence that female impersonation is an art form that requires enormous technical skill and practice. "It is within the power of every impersonator to create for himself an illusion of beauty," he wrote.

If you need help or guidance on ensuring that your feminine presentation is flawless, Pudgy's got you covered:

Here are some helpful hints to give that ladylike appearance.

    Lift your neck out of your shoulders.

    Place your chin parallel to the floor.

    Relax your shoulders; strain them neither backwards or
        forwards.

    Elevate your chest as on a deep breath.

    Pull your waist out of your hips.

Pudgy, you lost us on that last one, dear.

Herstory Lesson:

The Marilyn Impersonator Who Wasn't

Aleshia Brevard left her life on the farm and her life as a boy
behind forever in the late 1950s, headed out into the world to
figure out how to live as a woman, and eventually found herself
at the world-famous drag cabaret Finocchio's in San Francisco,
where they took one look at the six-foot, yet daintily feminine
curvy blonde and hired her on the spot as a Marilyn impersonator. Brevard noted later that she not only did nothing in particular to evoke Marilyn, she in fact had absolutely no skills in
female impersonation whatsoever. In the manner of queer folk
passing on their lore and skills, the girls of the Finocchio's revue
took her under their wing and taught her everything they knew
until she had the crowds roaring to their feet in approval—
including Marilyn herself, who reportedly attended one of
Aleshia's performances. Like many transgender women in entertainment, she didn't feel particularly at home in the world of
drag for the long term, and after going to the extreme length

of self-castrating in order to force a doctor to undertake her surgical transition, she left drag, completed her transition, and lived her life as a woman, taking jobs as a stripper, a Playboy Bunny, and a low-level actress and day player in films and television. She married three times, and according to her, only two of her husbands knew she was a trans woman while they were together. For many years, she didn't see herself as part of any queer community or lineage; she simply saw herself as a woman who passed through the drag world because it was the only option she had to get to her goal of living life as a woman.

There are many transgender actresses and performers in addition to Aleshia Brevard who spent time working as drag queens before deliberately focusing their career attentions away from that world, including present-day actress-model Laverne Cox and 1960s soul singer Jackie Shane. Laverne said of her time as a drag queen that it was interesting and fun for her, and a way to work on her performing skills, but ultimately it wasn't her world. Aleshia Brevard eventually came to the same conclusion, writing two autobiographies before she died, telling her story proudly and calling herself a transgender woman. After a long career as an acting teacher after having attained her master's degree in theater arts, she died in 2017. All that from the young person who showed up fresh from the farm at Finocchio's and found herself headlining as Marilyn to sold-out crowds.

Chapter 4

Watch Out for Those
Sketchy Queens, Gurl

America's next drag superstar needs to respect the craft of acting,
so when the spotlight hits you, you can deliver your line with conviction.
ahem
"FREEZE, YOU HONKY BITCH!"
Thank you.

Ru, introducing the 9021-HO challenge

On February 24, 2019, just a couple of weeks after *Drag Race*'s tenth anniversary, three-time show alum and fan favorite Shangela leaned out of her limo, gathered up the enormous satin embroidered skirt of her custom Diego Montoya gown, and put a well-shod toe onto the red carpet of the ninety-first Academy Awards before stepping out to face the cameras, a huge smile on her face. It was the most high-profile acting-award event of the calendar year and a *Drag Race* sister was there to represent for her role in the multiple-award-nominated Lady Gaga film *A Star Is Born*. Halleloo. Fellow *Drag Race* sister and *A Star Is Born* costar Willam, a seasoned actor with an impressive IMDb listing in her own right, was right there with her, providing red carpet commentary and generally making a draggy nuisance of herself in that Willam sort of way.

A few weeks before, Monét X Change's Pepsi commercial with Cardi B debuted during the Grammy Awards, and Valentina made her network television debut playing the iconic drag queen/transgender woman/nonbinary performer (depending on whose interpretation you prefer) Angel in a live production of *Rent* on the Fox network. In the months before that, Peppermint was collecting huge press and critical acclaim on Broadway in *Head Over Heels* and Ginger Minj was making waves costarring in the Jennifer Aniston film *Dumplin'* as a Dolly Parton–impersonating drag queen. Drag acting was having a moment—and it was no coincidence that so many of the most notable acting performances were coming from *Drag Race* queens. Because whether they want to admit it or not, *Drag Race* did its best to make sure its top girls left with the basics of acting technique down. It may not be *RuPaul's Best Friends Race*, but the show has always served as a career training program filtered through its host's own experiences and understanding of the arena or genre of entertainment highlighted in each challenge. It's a show structured around the career of its titular host, hence the focus on modeling, hosting, comedy, singing, and occasionally acting. That's Ru's professional arc in a nutshell.

The *Drag Race* queens are put through their paces (and the wringer) on at least one acting challenge per season, the results of which are often as easy and pleasant to sit through as the first table read of a high school production of *Hamlet*. The acting challenges tend to be some of the hardest in the show's run and have reduced many a lesser queen to a puddle of tears and embarrassment. Some queens found these challenges frustrating and unconnected to their form of drag, but acting, theater, sketch comedy, and films were all conquered by drag performers decades ago.

We hope we've made it clear by now that *Drag Race* sits on a continuum of queer cultural history, so it shouldn't be a surprise that we see connections to a long line of queer theatrical traditions and figures when we look at the acting and sketch comedy challenges. But in order to trace a through line connecting these challenges on the show with the history of drag, queer, and non-gender-conforming artists in theater and film, we have to first define what the acting challenges are about and then pull at the threads of queer cultural history a little to show why the challenges are constructed and critiqued the way they are. Pack a lunch and a thermos, because we've got a long walk ahead of us.

Mama Ru's Vocational School for Working Queens

"These are two loud bitches, so you've gotta overpower them."

Michelle Visage to Trinity during the "Mary, Mother of Gay!" sketch

Ru values boldness and bravery in her drag and has long promoted the idea of drag as a tool for self-actualization as well as self-expression. It's a particularly good way to coach a nonactor into giving some sort of performance that isn't a disaster—by telling them to be bold, to put aside their fear, and to find something inside themselves or in the script that they can work with and develop into something. It's why the show tends to single out the queens who took the nothing roles or the difficult roles—which are deliberately written into every script—and made something out of them. Whether it's Raven playing a chicken in a cooking grease commercial or Darienne Lake playing a head in a box in a horror film sketch or Manila playing a space monkey in a sci-fi spoof, the acting challenges expect those queens handed impossible roles to figure out a way to make them funny or entertaining.

It's also why Ru and the judges tend to single out those queens for praise when they play well against their type or the expectations people have of them. That's always been the main goal of these challenges—not to get Oscar-level performances out of anyone, but to get fun and brave and well-realized ones out of them. No one ever criticized a queen for not giving us Meryl Streep or Dame Judi Dench in the acting challenges. The critiques are almost always the same. "I wanted more." "You weren't bold enough." "You didn't take it far enough." "You let other people overshadow you."

The acting challenges on *Drag Race* are always focused on the bare-bones technical skills that every single actor needs to learn early in their careers: memorization, blocking, emphasis, not stepping on lines, and knowing where the camera is, where the audience is, and how to remain in character. And because this is a drag competition, the ability to take and give a stage slap seems to come up with some frequency. As Tori Spelling advised in season 7's "9021-HO" episode, giving the best indication of the level of technical skill they're expecting from the queens: "Hey, a lot of actresses have made a big career on a hair flip and one-note bitch delivery." She's not wrong, America.

The essence of acting (to be someone you are not) and the idea of drag (to perform a stylized version of gender you may or may not be) are impossible to disentangle from each other. The judges of *Drag Race* have always been open about their thoughts on this connection. During the Scream Queens challenge in season 6, Vivacious, who comes from the Club Kid tradition, mentioned that she had no theatrical training, to which Michelle shot back, "Uh, look at yourself. What you do for a living is theater!" There's an assumption built into the show that drag, no matter what form it takes, is unquestionably a theatrical form by definition, and that all drag queens are putting on some version of a theatrical performance. Michelle, again, said to Jaidynn Diore Fierce during the ShakesQueer challenge, when she complained that she had no experience in theater, "Girl, you are a drag queen. You are experienced at acting." She's got decades, if not centuries, of precedent to back up that claim.

Drag Your Skirts Across the Stage

Drag and the theater are linked from the very earliest days of both forms of art, with a theatrical tradition of men playing female parts that stretches back centuries and spans cultures and continents. Theater legend—repeated by Ru during the "ShakesQueer" episode—holds that the term *drag* was an acronym from Shakespeare's stage direction for the actors to "dress resembling a girl," although there's no evidence for this. *Drag* as a term is more commonly thought to have originated in Polari slang, as a joking reference to actors dragging the full skirts required of classical theater female parts across the stage, in productions or eras in which female actors were prohibited. During Shakespeare's time, all the female roles in his plays were played by male actors because of social restrictions against women appearing onstage. This tradition continued on and off in classical Western theater, giving it just enough time and ubiquity as a theatrical practice to possibly inspire a central word of queer slang. This explanation has a little more appeal to us, first because it implies a straight actor's perspective, which lends its origins some credence. After all, no queen would have to drag her skirts across a stage, because she'd be thrilled at the chance to wear them and would be well versed in the skill of working them with finesse. Remember, Polari was a slang language of seventeenth-century origins that spanned subcultures, used by both performers and queer men, arising naturally out of the places where their existences overlapped: the theater. We like to think that straight actors complained about having to drag their skirts, queer actors thought this was hilarious, and eventually the term *drag* started being applied to a particularly queer form of the practice.

It's hard to delineate the exact second drag acting performances go from a straight-presenting man in a dress (like Robin Williams as Mrs. Doubtfire, Dustin Hoffman in *Tootsie*, or Tyler Perry as Madea) to something truly representative of queer artistry and culture. What makes Divine's Edna Turnblad in *Hairspray* a legendary "queer" performance aside from the sexual orientation of the player? Were the three straight lead actors in *To Wong Foo* or *Priscilla, Queen of the Desert* truly representing queer drag on film? Can one really make the argument that Tim Curry's Frank-N-Furter in *The Rocky Horror Picture Show* isn't a seminal queer performance, even if the actor never identified as such? It depends who you ask, of course, but we think queer theatrical drag has certain qualities that help identify it other than how the artists identify themselves.

First, there's the subversive and anarchic qualities of the queer theatrical tradition. Madea, Mrs. Doubtfire, Hoffman's Dorothy Michaels, and other such straight forms of drag acting tend to be far more focused on mainstream sensibilities such as parenting, family, and heterosexual romance. The queens of *To Wong Foo* seemed more concerned with solving the problems of the straight community around them than advancing any queer agenda. Even the queens in *Priscilla*, probably some of the most unabashedly queer performances by a trio of straight-identified actors, focused on heterosexual romance (with a transgender woman and a straight-identified man, to be fair) and parenting.

To get a sense of truly queer drag acting, you have to look in the same place you always have to look when you talk about the roots and the history of drag: the underground. Specifically, the underground theater and experimental film scenes of the mid- to late twentieth century. Compared to the drag cabaret acts or female-impersonation revues of the same period, which looked to the mainstream for acceptance, the queer theater and queer underground cinema scenes flipped the bird to the mainstream and dared it to accept them. The point was to be shocking and bold, not to find solace in hearth and home—and *certainly* not to ask for respectability. When queerness was outlawed, its natural tendency toward upending the social order was more of a burning need than a cheeky response to the culture. Queer folks weren't going to survive if the culture didn't change around them, so queer artists of the period basically got down to the task of making that happen through their art. Just as shade was a response to oppression and reading was a response to potential violence, queer art, from Warhol to John Waters, grew out of a survival response to restrictive conventionality and oppressive normalcy. Queer art exists to question the normal, make fun of it, filter it through the point of view of those people society has not allowed to be considered normal or acceptable. This is the tradition from which most of the sketch and acting challenges arise on *Drag Race*, all of which are satirical, parodic, and occasionally scatological in tone.

This is also a big reason why the *Drag Race* acting challenges span a range of genres: telenovela, commercial, Shakespearean spoof, science fiction (both retro and modern), horror, sitcom, soap opera (both daytime and nighttime). The queens have been put through their paces in spoofs of *Beverly Hills, 90210*, *West World*, and *Empire*. They've acted in "shequels" to classic films such as *Thelma & Louise* and *Showgirls*, and spoofs of *The Queen* (the Helen Mirren version, not the Crystal LaBeija one), *The Help*, *Black Swan*, *Erin Brockovich*, and *Sex and the City*. The sketches have consistently targeted conservative politics, Christianity, parenting, teenage social norms, heterosexual romance, and other forms of mainstream culture. While it's traditional for most TV sketch comedy shows to spoof other parts of pop culture, *Drag Race*'s campy approach and deliberately over-the-top style of acting, as well as its devotion to skewering parts of the culture with broadly queer appeal or with whom a queer and queer-friendly audience may have a few issues, set it apart from, say, a *Saturday Night Live* sketch.

You can see the DNA of *Drag Race*'s sketch challenges in the work of postwar queer performance (and occasional drag) artist Jack Smith, who shocked and dazzled mostly New York underground audiences throughout the conformist 1950s with

multimedia performances that incorporated drag and experimental films and sought to provide commentary and level criticism at modern middle-class aesthetics and mores. You can see
it in the underground cinema of Andy Warhol in the late 1960s
and early '70s, with its star-making turns by legendary drag
queens Holly Woodlawn and Candy Darling. You can see it in
Richard O'Brien's *Rocky Horror Picture Show*, a big, queer,
draggy ode to Hollywood musicals, physique magazines, and
sci-fi B movies of the 1950s. You can see it in the work of theatrical drag giants like Charles Ludlam from the 1960s to the
'80s or Charles Busch in the present day. There simply is no
question that the iconic trash cinema of John Waters, partner-
ing with the legendary Divine, hangs over *Drag Race*'s acting
challenges like a creative umbrella. All these artists and movements overlapped and inspired each other for half a century,
establishing a particularly queer form of art designed to make
high points using low culture. When queerness, drag, and acting overlap, the results tend to be a broadly delivered slap in the
face to the mainstream, a skewering of the lowest common de-
nominator aspects of culture, and a veritable encyclopedia of
queer references or obsessions. How is that not a perfectly rea-
sonable description of most *Drag Race* acting challenges?

Yes, there has always been drag in theater, and a very
mainstream-friendly form of drag has been popular in the
theater and films for years—not just *To Wong Foo* and *Priscilla*, but *La Cage aux Folles*, *Kinky Boots*, *Torch Song Trilogy*,
Hairspray, *Hedwig and the Angry Inch*, and *M. Butterfly*, which
have all taken mainstream audiences by storm, secured or
furthered the careers of many queer artists, and won award
after award. But it took some very talented queer folks working
away from the big spotlights and loudest applause to turn the

intersection of drag and theatrical tradition into something truly representative of queer identity and culture. In short, it's about being cheeky, shocking, satirical, and completely obsessed with culture both high and low. It's about deliberately focusing the most mainstream parts of mainstream culture through a queer prism designed to break it down into its components. It's about one very basic quality that Ru constantly asks of her queens: Be brave enough to be ridiculous.

Charles Ludlam's Very Queer Ridiculousness

> "You have to make the character work with
> what you have in your wheelhouse."
>
> *Ru to Asia O'Hara, after her disappointing
> Sarah Palin spoof in "Breastworld"*

Charles Ludlam pioneered a form of experimental theater starting in the 1960s that made major use of drag and gained him mainstream respectability and critical acclaim to the point that his 1989 death from AIDS complications was the first to be announced on the front page of the *New York Times*. Ludlam settled in Greenwich Village in the mid-1960s after graduating from Hofstra University, where he studied drama and, in the manner of more than a few theater majors, came to the realization that he was gay. For a time after graduation, he was involved with the Playhouse of the Ridiculous, an anarchic experimental theater group that sought to overturn the conventions of the theater by stressing broad acting styles, pastiche, the parody of high and low culture, and the goal of being shocking to the audience. It took inspiration in part from celebrated midcentury

underground queer performance artist Jack Smith, who was occasionally affiliated with the movement, as was Andy Warhol. A
broad spectrum of queer theatrical and cinematic artists were
drawn to the ridiculous theatrical tradition or took inspiration
from its tenets and works, from *Rocky Horror* creator Richard
O'Brien to underground filmmaker John Waters to celebrated
playwright and drag artist Charles Busch, who saw Ludlam as a
direct inspiration for his own theatrical career.

Ludlam split with the Playhouse of the Ridiculous to start
his own Ridiculous Theatrical Company in the early 1970s, in
part because he felt the Playhouse troupe was too reluctant to
dive deeper into queer themes and motifs, especially his own
fascination with drag as a theatrical tool. "I wanted to create an
outrage," he said of the choice. The Ridiculous Theatrical Company achieved intense critical acclaim as Ludlam used it to
mount a succession of his own plays. These plays, with titles
like *Conquest of the Universe or When Queens Collide*, *Eu-
nuchs of the Forbidden City*, and *Turds in Hell*, were pastiches
of works by Christopher Marlowe or Alexandre Dumas with re-
mixes of *Camille*, B movies, Victorian penny dreadfuls, and
comic book references in order to explore concepts of queerness, gender, and sudden death at the height of the AIDS crisis.
He used drag, camp, anarchy, and parody with a wickedly queer
sensibility underlining them at all times. "We take the abandoned refuse, the used images, the shoes from abandoned shoe
factories, the clichés, and we search for their true meaning," he
explained to the *Village Voice* in a 1973 interview. The most famous and longest-running of his plays is *The Mystery of Irma
Vep*, which eventually became the most produced play in America as well as the longest-running play in Brazil. Like so much of
his work, the play incorporates drag and cross-dressing into the

performances and utilizes pastiche and parody of cultural motifs both high and low. Ludlam was an award-winning playwright, director, and performer in his time and at first glance, you might not see how his work has anything to do with *RuPaul's Drag Race*. But he saw drag as a way of paying homage to or drawing inspiration from parts of the culture, by remixing it in order to make a comment about it.

Ludlam probably shouldn't be thought of as a drag queen, since it encompassed only part of his theatrical work, but he was a creator, writer, and artist who took tremendous inspiration from the art and world of drag and the exploration of gender in theater. Ludlam was known as a playwright first, a talented actor and performer second, and a drag performer a close third. His drag wasn't precise or impersonating in effect. It was a slash of paint on a canvas, the details of which he filled in with his performance. Ludlam was dark and dangerous, his drag sloppy and less concerned with mimicking femininity as evoking it through performance and pastiche. "Wanting to look like a woman was not the point," he later wrote. "Wanting to create the illusion of Dumas' heroine was."

Drag Race makes the queens act and perform in conventional if not downright clichéd genres and forms and expects them to find something new, different, queer, and funny within them, very much in the tradition of Ludlam and his Ridiculous Theatrical Company. Ludlam likened naturalistic acting to people wanting him to act civilized "in a room," evoking just how oppressive he found the traditional approaches to theater at the time. We can't help reading that sentiment and thinking of all the outrageously broad acting the queens on *Drag Race* were encouraged and directed to do during the acting challenges.

His interest in drag as a parodic form, incorporating aspects of camp and pop culture references, had a long-lasting impact on both mainstream and underground queer theatrical traditions. He was an intensely talented openly gay man (at a time when that was shocking) who understood how to use drag both dramatically and comedically on the stage, under theatrical principles that have not only been advanced and carried forward by a succession of legendary theatrical drag performers but that also inform every single sketch or acting challenge on *Drag Race*. He was part of a satirical queer theatrical tradition that almost instantly expanded way past the boundaries of the New York underground scene.

The Balls-Out (Literally) Anarchy Drag of the Cockettes

"All you have to do is, like, make big, weird googly eyes and do funny things with your mouth."

Carson's acting advice to Alyssa after her What Ever Happened to Baby Jane? spoof

It's not only one of the most famous images of the anti–Vietnam War movement, it's largely considered one of the most iconic images of the 1960s, if not the entire history of photojournalism. A blond, floppy-haired young man in a sweater, surrounded by military police pointing their rifles at him as he boldly yet delicately places a carnation down the barrel of each gun. It was October 1967, the movement was marching on the Pentagon (to levitate it, because that's just how political theater rolled in 1967), and the young man serving up that iconic image was an actor on his way to San Francisco named George Harris.

He would shed his clean-cut image, his name, and any pretenses toward normalcy when he got there—as so many folks tended to do when they arrived in San Francisco at the height of the 1960s counterculture.

Gay, flamboyant, handsome, and raised in a family of actors who prized such things, Harris bloomed in San Francisco, falling in with a group of hippie anarchists, flower children, and drag queens; festooning himself with flowers, glitter, and makeup; and renaming himself Hibiscus, as one did in those days. He eventually became the founder and leader of a hippie acid-freak drag queen theatrical commune called the Cockettes, because let's face it, if you're gay and cute, love drugs and drag, and grew up in the theater, San Francisco in the late sixties was simply going to be a magical playground for you. Naturally charismatic, with the soul of an artist and a love of marrying anarchy with creativity, Hibiscus was the perfect leader to encourage his merry band of drag-wearing brothers and sisters to fly their freak flags, drop acid, and let it fuel the exploration of their wild sides on the stage. The kind of drag the Cockettes practiced—wild, without rules or borders, with little thought given to gender presentation or glamour in the traditional sense—was nothing like the drag of Lynne Carter's torch singers or Crystal LaBeija's balls and pageants. The Cockettes picked their drag from trash and charity shops, made bras out of pineapples, draped themselves with feathers and flowers, glitter and face paint. Part commedia dell'arte, part Ringling Brothers, and part *Godspell* on acid, the drag practiced by the Cockettes was about as far as possible from the serious glamour of the drag pageants and the rehearsed professionalism of the major female impersonation revues that existed at the same time. There was no tucking, shaving, or contouring here; indeed, there was rarely any underwear at all, and many of the Cockettes' early performances ended with them in a nearly naked kick line—balls-out drag while tripping balls.

Hibiscus, a drag messiah conjured up by central casting, with the long blond beard and hair of a blue-eyed Jesus straight out of a Hollywood Bible flick, encouraged his troupe to be wild in their explorations of creativity, to overthrow the natural order, to challenge the mainstream, and mostly just to have a whole lot of fun. They were, said John Waters, who found them to be kindred spirits with his own band of Baltimore freaks and geeks, "the only drag queens I ever knew that read Lenin."

Virtually no one in the group had technical skills, training, or even talent, yet they became the hottest ticket in town, largely for the unrestrained glory of their self-expression, the freedom and joyousness of their drag. Mounting shows put on for midnight movie audiences at the Pagoda Palace, and drawing on references to classic Old Hollywood films, with titles like *Gone with the Showboat to Oklahoma*, *Journey to the Center of Uranus*, and *Tinsel Tarts in a Hot Coma*, the Cockettes' shows were bawdy, hilarious, cheeky anarchy, mixing high and low culture, nostalgia, and satire all at once.

In June 1971, the group released a short film, *Tricia's Wedding*, a shockingly vicious satire of the recent White House wedding of President Richard Nixon's daughter Tricia. The film features drag versions of first ladies Mamie Eisenhower (fall-down drunk), Jackie Kennedy Onassis (a total snob), and Lady Bird Johnson (a Minnie Pearl–like, down-home country gal). Future disco superstar Sylvester, who was a member of the group at this point—the only one besides Hibiscus with any true performing talent—makes a notable appearance as Coretta Scott King singing a gospel solo before the whole wedding gets dosed with acid and an orgy ensues. This was only three years after Martin Luther King Jr.'s assassination. Dignified, tasteful art house cinema this was not. It was gross, stupid, shocking, offensive, hilarious, and awful. It was perfect anarchy drag.

The group became the toast of New York very briefly in 1971, flying out for a series of highly anticipated performances, appearing at all the right parties and chic night spots and often coming up against the more sophisticated, fashionable, and precise New York–style underground drag of Warhol queens Candy Darling and Holly Woodlawn, who were under-impressed with their wild West Coast ways. The Cockettes were so committed to their anarchic lifestyle that they partied away their time and did virtually no rehearsing while in New York. By all accounts, their opening night was a disaster, with no less than Angela Lansbury and Andy Warhol (drag queens in tow) walking out. Chastened by the experience, they headed home to the ever-welcoming arms of their beloved San Francisco, where they continued to ply their trade and upend traditions for a little while longer. Eventually, they invited Divine, fresh off her early underground film success with John Waters, to perform with them—which she did, hopping on a plane with no money to her name and finding a family of freaks waiting for her at the other end with literal open arms and cheers. There she found a home for a time, singing "A Crab on Uranus Means You're Loved" to ecstatic crowds while dressed in a lobster costume before moving on to bigger and better things.

Hibiscus broke away from the group, largely because many of the players were tired of performing for little or no money, a principle he was unwilling to bend or change. He headed back to the same New York experimental theater scene Charles Ludlam was currently queering up with his own anarchic work and started his own theater company, Angels of Light, which occasionally hosted performances by none other than Marsha P. Johnson when she was part of the act Hot Peaches. Hibiscus would continue to perform in experimental theater, as part of a punk band called Hibiscus and the Screaming Violets, and eventually started making inroads to a mainstream career in television as George Harris (underneath all the hippie drag was a leading man's face), but then he died of complications from AIDS in the early 1980s.

The Cockettes burned brightly and briefly, before fading out in the early 1970s, with several of its members dying from drug overdoses and later from complications from AIDS. They were hugely influential on the vibrant and important San Francisco drag and experimental theater scenes for decades to come. As for the group's effect on *Drag Race*, while Ru would never have appreciated Hibiscus's love of anarchy and disdain for rehearsals or planning ("You owe it to your talent to do your homework," Ru advised Adore Delano after she tried to wing her way through the Scream Queens challenge), the Cockettes' love of pastiche and parody, their intense focus on completely letting go and giving yourself over to the performance, and their ability to spin magical drag out of trash pickings and vintage clothing all play out constantly in the *Drag Race* challenges.

The power of Hibiscus's vision and charisma can't be understated, especially when you consider the ways in which his career and work intersected with some of the most important drag and transgender figures of the twentieth century. You don't cross paths with Sylvester, Divine, Candy Darling, and Marsha P. Johnson unless you're doing something really interesting. You don't transition from the heights of San Francisco hippie queerness to a New York punk band and on to a legitimate acting career unless you have considerable talent, vision, and ambition. It's almost hard to imagine where Hibiscus would have gone had he been allowed more time on this planet to explore the possibilities only he seemed capable of seeing.

Divine, the Original Drag Superstar

"At the end of the day, you just have to be
memorable in the presentation."

Carson, during the Shequels challenge judging session

There is no discussing the sketch challenges on *Drag Race* without talking about Divine. In fact, there's no discussion of drag acting and high camp without centering on the work of Divine, who was the first drag queen to truly become a household name. Before RuPaul became the first person everyone thought of when they heard the term *drag queen*, the only other drag queen to reach that same level of recognition was the former Harris Glenn Milstead of Baltimore, who eventually shed his fears and his past to give voice to his anger and shock the shit out of a nation. "People like to laugh at sex, people love to laugh at dirty things, and people love to be shocked," she once said. "So that's my job: to get out there and shock them."

As John Waters said, even long before Glenn discovered drag, "He could *never* pass as normal." In his teen years, during the early 1960s, after a decade of bullying about his weight and impossible-to-camouflage queerness, he started exploring the competitive drag pageant scene, dressed as his favorite movie star, Elizabeth Taylor. But he found that world and the queens who ruled it far too serious for his liking. They may not have crossed paths, but the respect-demanding seriousness of Crystal LaBeija storming off a pageant stage would have been the kind of thing Glenn would have likely rolled his eyes at. Embracing his large size in his drag, he leaned into it and used it to shock, get laughs, or turn people on by devising a much sloppier, trashier form of glamour than the Hollywood kind most queens traded in. Quickly leaving the pageant queens behind, the not-yet-Divine embraced the freaks of 1960s Baltimore and channeled his anger at years of being bullied into this terrifyingly glamorous and trashy character. Divine found his maestro in trash cinema pioneer John Waters, who in turn found his muse in Divine. It was Waters who actually gave Glenn his drag name and pushed him to take the presentation to further and further extremes.

People tend to remember Divine for her work with John Waters—not just *Pink Flamingos*, but their incredibly rough, first relatively successful collaboration *Mondo Trasho*, which featured a scene of Divine getting raped by a giant lobster; *Female Trouble*, which introduced the world to the immortal Dawn Davenport and her undying love of cha-cha heels; and their final collaboration, *Hairspray*, which wound up being the most popular of them all. But Divine also spent years in the underground and experimental theater, not only performing with the Cockettes in San Francisco, but making several highly talked-about and heavily buzzed turns in off-Broadway plays, which helped secure her position as a queen of the New York nightlife scene of the 1970s and become a mainstay at Studio 54. Like Ru, she also explored a fairly successful career as a singer, releasing a string of disco, new wave, and early electronica hits and touring the world performing them.

Divine's signature look was hugely influential, moving drag away from its Hollywood-obsessed roots and focus on traditional beauty and toward an underground, punk-inspired aesthetic and a much more aggressive form of glamour. It was simply unheard of for a conventional pageant queen, ball queen, or female impersonator to shave off half her hair so she could draw her eyebrows all the way to the crown of her head; but Divine did it, and now forty years later, *Drag Race* queens like Eureka O'Hara, Alaska, Sharon Needles, Acid Betty, Trixie Mattel, and Kim Chi can trace their extreme makeup effects to Divine's groundbreaking face work. And virtually every "big girl" queen of the past forty years owes some minor debt to Divine for making plus-size drag not just acceptable but exalted. Trixie said Divine's films "made me feel like it was okay to be as unbeautiful as I wanted to be." Divine's drag wasn't interested in being pretty, and it certainly wasn't interested in being real. It was only interested in being shocking.

Divine was terrifying and sexy and campy. She used drag as a form of cultural terrorism, turning herself into such a spectacle that she used to force people to look at her. John Waters noted that Divine's form of drag shattered the way people thought of it before then: "He took it to a level of anarchy." While Hibiscus may have been advocating anarchy to his band of glitter-hippie drag queens, he never got any of them to eat fresh dog shit on camera. When she was pursuing a more mainstream acting career later in life, Divine got tired of the focus on the history-making scene in Waters's *Pink Flamingos*, where she did, in fact, eat a turd fresh from the back end of a dog. Thirty years after his death it's still one of the most discussed things about his career. It was even the subject of a song in the Divine Intervention challenge on *Drag Race* (with extra-special guest judge John Waters). But in the end, Divine's brief dabble in canine scat became one of two immortal contributions she made to the culture, two contributions so far apart in meaning and style that they can't help but sit as the perfect summation of her career. Her Edna Turnblad in *Hairspray* was not only her most popular and critically acclaimed role, it established a tradition through every major iteration and evolution of *Hairspray* (from film to Broadway to musical film to live television production) that demanded the role always be played by a man in drag, in tribute to the history-making queen who first made the role come alive. From eating dog shit in underground trash films to establishing one of the most beloved maternal figures in musical theater history—now that's range.

Divine used drag to channel her anger and indulge her freakiness, yet practically anyone who knew her talked about what a warm and genuine person she was. It was as if drag allowed Glenn to work through his demons, which is very much in line with Ru's idea of drag as a way of connecting to your true self and facing your darker parts in order to produce a fearless performance.

Ru has called Divine "the first drag superstar," but not surprisingly, John Waters summed her up best: "Divine stood for all outsiders."

Tim Curry, Queen of the Midnight Scene

> "I just wanted you to go further with it. You weren't letting go completely."
>
> *Michelle Visage to Sasha Velour during the 9021-HO challenge*

If Divine terrified and fascinated the mainstream 1970s with his size, demeanor, and rage-based drag, then Tim Curry terrified them, because his drag made them want to fuck him. Crossing the draggy aggression of glam rock with the sensual archness of Mick Jagger, Curry tapped into his nasty feminine side and created the immortal sweet transvestite from Transylvania, Frank-N-Furter, in the greatest cult film of all time, *The Rocky Horror Picture Show*. Curry has never stated or articulated his sexuality publicly, so while we can't claim him as a queer man, we can still claim him as a queer icon, because his performance was like a big pansexual nonbinary sex bomb going off smack in the middle of the most sexually open decade in centuries, the 1970s. Curry's Frank-N-Furter was simply hot and up for anything, regardless of who was involved or which way they swung. Coming at a time when people like David Bowie had already cracked open the door on nontraditional, nonbinary presentation styles, Curry's thick lips, heavy eye makeup, and sinewy body turned on everyone and made the young queer and trans folks in *Rocky Horror*'s countless midnight audiences feel like they weren't such freaks after all—or even better, like they were freaks and wasn't that a glorious thing to be?

The cult success of *The Rocky Horror Picture Show* spawned a subcommunity around it, full of its own traditions, slang, and mode of dress, all based on or playing off the film itself, similar to the midnight movie traditions that spawned the Cockettes. None of this is notable in the general sense because all subcultures, from underground comics fans to S&M clubs, have all the trappings of their own cultures. But starting in the mid-1970s, because the film's cult following practically demanded cosplay from its most ardent fans, it allowed and encouraged countless young men to step out in public on a Saturday night wearing fishnets, heels, a face beat to the gods, and a corseted bustier—for over four decades. For the entire span of a generation, *The Rocky Horror Picture Show* encouraged men—queer, questioning, or not—to get in touch with their feminine sides and then show them off to the world. For some of these men, it was a doorway opening up new ideas about their gender identity or sexual orientation; but for the majority, it was about existing in a space that allowed them to do something they'd never normally think to do in their own life. In some ways, getting cishet men to try drag and feel a little freaky about it was a more significant achievement on the film's part than the countless men it walked up to the closet door and opened it on the realization of their own queerness.

If Divine used drag in part to express her rage and to let loose her id, then Tim Curry used it to express his desire and desirability. Curry's drag was the first time mainstream folks openly admitted they found drag *hot*. Of course there have always been plenty of folks who found the non-gender-conforming sexually attractive, but it was a big damn deal for people to go around admitting it in the (more or less) mainstream in 1975. People tend to think of drag as something composed of glamour and focused on beauty or a style of performance designed to get laughs, but it can just as easily be a vehicle for anger or a tool to explore desire, which is why it makes such great inroads to acting and why Michelle Visage considers every drag queen an actress.

Tim Curry straddled all the lines of drag—boldness and camp; male, female, and nonbinary; gay, bi, and pansexual—in an underground film that satirized old Hollywood horror films and musicals in order to explore themes of desire, fear, and personal freedom of expression. What does that have to do with *Drag Race*?

What part of that *doesn't* have something to do with *Drag Race*?

Serving Intergalactic Fish: The Stunning *Vegas in Space* and the Legacy of Doris Fish

"Maybe it didn't need the Meryl Streep treatment?"

Sasha Velour to the judges

"HAHAHAHAHAHAHA!"

The judges, in response

Just as George Lucas was ending his first trilogy of game-changing outer space films with *Return of the Jedi* in the early 1980s, San Francisco drag queen Doris Fish was beginning work on her singular entry into the genre, which was in some ways no less game changing for the drag aesthetic than *Star Wars* was for special effects blockbusters. Doris, also known as Philip Mills, a Sydney transplant in San Francisco's queer scene, was part of an underground drag theater group called Sluts A-Go-Go, along with fellow drag sisters Miss X and Tippi. Mills had a burning desire to film a drag-filled homage to drive-in sci-fi B movies of the 1950s—again demonstrating the intense focus on parody and pastiche of low culture that unites nearly all underground drag theater and inspires *Drag Race*'s acting challenges.

Mills wrote, cast, art-directed, and costumed an underground trash cinema sci-fi extravaganza he quite aptly titled *Vegas in Space* and enlisted Sluts A-Go-Go's resident "straight man," Phillip Ford, to direct the film for him. Part Warhol, part John Waters, with a 1980s-style psychedelia, and in the San Francisco drag tradition of anarchic creativity embodied by the Cockettes, *Vegas in Space* is more experience than narrative, more visual than verbal. These are the kinds of things you say about a bad film when you're trying to make it sound like more than it is, but we can assure you, that's not the case here. Sure, the quality of the acting varies from moment to moment, scene to scene, queen to queen, but there's no denying the passion and the incredible amount of work put into the film. Okay, yes, technically it's a bit of a mess, but visually, there are moments of real cinematic art that leave the viewer sitting there in silent, sometimes bemused wonder—an effect achieved almost entirely by placing stunning drag queens in front of colorful (but cheap) backdrops and lighting them like they were made of tubes of neon. Virtually all the visual language of the film is owed to Doris Fish, who designed the costumes, makeup, hair, sets, and miniatures. The city of Vegas on the planet of Clitoris, which looks like a bunch of glittering perfume bottles under a pink sky and whimsical cardboard mountains, is "an oasis of glamour in a universe of mediocrity," as the mysterious Princess Angel (played by Sluts A-Go-Go member Tippi) calls it—a description of the set that sounds more like a mission statement about the film itself. Planet Clitoris is populated by bitchy ("Don't they have mirrors on earth?") but stunning drag queens who pose and mug in a rainbow of candy-colored wigs and shockingly colorful faces hovering over the most broad-shouldered new wave '80s fashion you've ever seen. In the present day, it exists as both a time capsule and a shockingly prescient prediction of where the art of drag was going in the new millennium.

Mills financed the film over its seven-year stop-and-start production partially through non-drag sex work, joking, "No one ever told me you couldn't make a feature film on a prostitute's salary." This is the same drive, the same cocktail of charisma, uniqueness, nerve, and talent that allowed Sylvia Rivera and Marsha P. Johnson to turn tricks to provide housing for their community, or for a street queen in the Tenderloin to throw a hot cup of coffee in a cop's harassing face at Compton's Cafeteria, or for Marilyn impersonator Aleshia Brevard to force the truth of her existence on her body whether it killed her or not. It takes some serious CUNT to survive as a queer outlaw in a straight world, to love as a queer outlaw, to express as a queer outlaw, to make art as a queer outlaw. The history of LGBTQ culture is full of stories of queer folks who will sell their bodies, endanger their bodies, force the truth on their bodies, because the first line of attack to fight against oppression is through the use of those very bodies. *Vegas in Space*, after a long journey, finally saw its release in October 1991, eight years after Doris Fish launched the idea. She would not be there at the premiere, however. She died four months before of AIDS complications.

There are times when the dialogue or aesthetic of the film looks like something straight out of a *Drag Race* sketch comedy or acting challenge. For many of the players, the acting would not have met with Michelle's or Ru's or Ross Mathews's approval. Despite the sometimes hard-to-ignore technical deficiencies, the grandeur, humor, and even power of the film shines through unexpectedly at times, offering images as indelible and dramatic as any German impressionist, French new wave, or American film noir classic, lines as bitchy and hilarious as any read from a street queen at three a.m.

Popular San Francisco drag queen and longtime midnight movie hostess Peaches Christ, who has called *Vegas in Space* a seminal part of San Francisco drag history, has been a huge booster of the film over the years and in 2016 hosted a twenty-fifth anniversary screening and Q&A with director Phillip Ford and the surviving members of the cast. Sasha Velour has also been a passionate fan of the film for years (you can see the influence of it on her own drag) and introduced a screening of the film at New York's Museum of Modern Art in 2019. Like Charles Pierce's *Legendary Ladies of the Silver Screen* on HBO a decade before, the film got a boost by becoming a long-running perennial on the USA network throughout the 1990s on its *Up All Night* program, making it possibly as influential to millennial queens as *Rocky Horror* and Divine were to baby boomers and RuPaul was to Gen Xers.

RuPaul Charles: From Supermodel to Butch Thespian

"I don't want to hear any more goddamn excuses! Fucking make it happen!"

Ru to Kennedy Davenport during the ShakesQueer challenge, season 7

Because virtually every challenge on the show is based on Ru's version of a successful drag career, they also draw on a cinematic tradition in drag of which Ru remains one of the top performers. From her motion picture debut in Spike Lee's *Crooklyn* as a woman dancing in a bodega to her early movie roles in *The Brady Bunch Movie* and its sequel and *To Wong Foo, Thanks for Everything! Julie Newmar*, Ru was making her cinematic splash in largely the same manner her immediate forebear Divine did—in total drag, often playing female characters. But for a lot of reasons, mostly the changing times and her desire for a more mainstream route to success than her predecessor, Ru had the benefit of working for hot directors or on popular mainstream films from the beginning of her career. There's no doubt that Ru wants to see her girls move on to mainstream success if that's where their interests lie, but there's no denying that *Drag Race*'s acting challenges are far closer to her underground low-budget classic *Starrbooty* than any of her more mainstream work. Full of incredibly bad production values and highly questionable performances (recognizing a theme here?), it's also hilarious, loaded with more drag queens than you can shake a stick at, and very much in the tradition of trash cinema drag, from *Female Trouble* to *Vegas in Space*.

Ru's version and vision of drag requires his girls to reach into themselves to find core emotions and memories to fuel their work, much in the way a method actor might. This is of a piece with many of the hoops Ru forces the queens to jump through and the situations the show puts them into in order to secure a reaction. It's a melding of performance and self-actualization, much in the same way Divine used drag and performance to work his way through a lot of rage and come to a place of self-love. Many *Drag Race* contestants struggled under the acting challenges, but ten years on, it's amazing how many of the show's alums have gone on to compile some fairly impressive IMDb listings.

This is very much in line with how Ru talks about drag, both in interviews and especially on the show. She wants her queens to use their drag to get in touch with their inner selves, to cast aside fears and doubts, and to express something real about themselves.

When you get right down to it, *The Mystery of Irma Vep* and *Starrbooty* are cut from the same sparkly cloth. Who's to say Bianca Del Rio's low-budget *Hurricane Bianca* films or Ru's

Starrbooty won't be playing in an exhibition at the Museum of Modern Art someday? You can bet the Cockettes never thought their trash-picked drag would wind up in museums.

Herstory Lesson:
Queens of the Legitimate Theater

In addition to the many talented and anarchic queens mentioned in this chapter, there are several extremely talented and prominent figures in American theater whose work produced some of the most important drag characters ever to grace a stage. Harvey Fierstein first rose to fame in 1982 by writing and portraying Arnold Beckoff, a drag queen in search of love and acceptance in *Torch Song Trilogy*. He would go on the next year to write the book for the legendary *La Cage aux Folles*, which included the enduring anthem of all drag queens for all time, "I Am What I Am," written by the show's lyricist, Jerry Herman. He then went on to win a Tony playing Divine's immortal Edna Turnblad in the Broadway musical production of *Hairspray* in 2002 and wrote the book for *Kinky Boots* in 2012, about a drag queen saving a factory from ruin. The man's got some drag bona fides, is what we're trying to say here.

Charles Busch is the author and star of such plays as *The Divine Sister*, *The Lady in Question*, *Red Scare on Sunset*, and *Vampire Lesbians of Sodom*, and a groundbreaking drag artist who helped define modern drag-based theater. Busch came to his drag through drama and theater rather than through, say, Halloween, parties, or cabaret, the way so many other drag artists did. Early on in his stage career, writing small pieces for himself and friends, he realized not only that he had an affinity for the female roles, but that he had all the trappings of being a leading lady, and he subsequently built a career around his own skills and preferences. Charles Ludlam's love of pastiche and pop culture infuses Busch's work. Busch has said that Ludlam's legendary portrayal of Marguerite in the Ridiculous Theatrical Company's 1973 production of *Camille* had a greater influence on his own work than any other performance.

In the manner of a pop culture– and Hollywood-obsessed queen, he has a great love of the grand ladies of Old Hollywood, but rather than becoming an impressionist, he used these women as inspiration to launch new characters and entire stories. Busch spun tales and monologues, observations and patter with a cabaret sound. His women are dignified but completely his own creations.

Chapter 5

Sing Out, Queen!

A great drag queen is like a rock star. She pushes it to the limit.

Ru introducing the Rocker Chicks challenge in season 2

As with the acting and Snatch Game challenges, which occur like clockwork every season of *Drag Race*, the competing queens can always expect that they're going to be asked to open their mouths and sing at least once during the competition—if they're good or lucky enough to stay in it that long. Despite this inevitability, the singing challenges still tend to send at least one queen per season spiraling into a minor meltdown or freak-out over it. If we had to guess, it's the one challenge that will raise the anxiety levels of practically every queen going into it. You give a funny, quick-talking, focus-pulling queen a sketch comedy script or an improv challenge and at least half of them will dive right in, talent level be damned. But even the accomplished singers in *Drag Race* herstory—and there have been many—tend to approach the singing challenges with some caution.

Season 2's Rocker Chicks challenge was the first time the queens had to sing live, a revelation that shocked them and caused more than a few to question whether even attempting it was worth it. It simply wasn't something most of them were expecting, although Ru's own career automatically puts the lie to any "Drag queens don't sing" sentiments. Coached by guest judge Terri Nunn of the band Berlin, the queens were instructed to focus on ephemerals like connection, emotion, and relating to the song. "You don't have to sing perfectly. You just have to feel it and make us feel it," she told Raven. This would set the tone and the criteria for how all the ensuing singing challenges were judged.

If the acting challenges on *Drag Race* are all about encouraging the queens to be bold enough to be ridiculous, the singing challenges ask them to be brave enough to bare their true selves and take their drag personae to emotional and presentational extremes, to connect with the audience by finding a truth in the song and getting it across effectively. That's a lot to ask of someone who isn't used to that kind of thing. Many drag queens took up the art as a way of shielding themselves from the world, not as a method for baring their souls—but as many queens have discovered over the years, that's exactly what Mama Ru wants them to do. As in the sketch challenges, queens are expected to be bold and free with their singing, not technically perfect. They have to take musical direction well and learn choreography on the fly. "Whatever you excel at, fucking apply it to everything," Ru told Monét X Change in season 10's Cher: The Unauthorized Rusical challenge, when the opera-trained Monét expressed doubt that he could pull off a Cher vocal.

This is why *Drag Race* works so well as a reality show, because you can see the queens learning and growing on camera. One of the reasons the show is such an Emmy-winning success is that it takes very basic reality television tropes—facing your fears, confronting your foes, showing personal growth—and maps them perfectly onto the realities and implications of drag. It makes reality TV actually mean something. Accomplished, high-level queens with trophies or Vegas gigs or a fully booked calendar will always tell you that it took time, rehearsal, and many failures to get them to the point where their drag was lauded and celebrated. Every drag queen's story eventually comes back to two themes: growth and transformation (which is why they tend to make such perfect avatars for the broad spectrum of queer life). Nearly all the challenges in *Drag Race* play on the growth theme, but the singing ones tend to really emphasize it.

Even more than the acting challenges, the singing challenges expose the nervousness and insecurities of the queens, making it more or less the point of the challenge. It's a flaming reality television hoop designed to work their nerves and produce drama. But live singing and recorded tracks are without a doubt a major component of mainstream drag performing. You don't have to leave *Drag Race* an opera diva, but Ru wants you to face your fears, learn a few technical tricks, and give it your all.

There are plenty of drag queens—possibly even the majority of them—who have never sung a note in front of an audience. "I'm a drag queen," complained Trinity K. Bonet during the Shade: The Rusical challenge in season 6. "I lip-sync. I don't sing live." This was a common complaint in earlier seasons of the show, but in light of so many queens going on to release singles and music videos (Trinity went on to drop several herself), you don't tend to hear this complaint as often in later seasons. Now almost every queen who appears on the show has a track ready to drop the day after her elimination episode airs.

Like Mama Ru, her girls have all learned that music is a tremendous promotional tool for a working drag queen, and anyone who gets the opportunity to make it part of her drag package would be foolish not to take it. Besides, the vast majority of tracks released by *Drag Race* alums tend to be highly produced, auto-tuned, electronic dance mixes, which don't necessarily require a lot of technical training or vocal prowess. If you can hit the beat and sell it, you're good to go. Once again, *Drag Race* shows itself to be both a tribute to RuPaul's career and a vocational school for her drag queens.

Having said that, there were plenty of queens who came into *Drag Race* with either advanced training or a high level of unskilled talent. In the case of queens like Adore Delano, Courtney Act, and Jinkx Monsoon, it was a moment to step up to the mic and show what they already had.

Nasty Boys

Despite Terri Nunn's cheerful, uplifting inaugural coaching session in season 2's Rocker Chicks challenge, the singing challenges on *Drag Race* went on to develop and return to a stock character loaded with meaning: the hard-ass choreographer/coach/producer/composer character. Whether it's Todrick Hall snapping at Asia that he will not allow her to represent black women with such terrible rhythm or Lucian Piane sparring with Bob the Drag Queen about the correct musical references to pull from, the song-and-dance challenges expose the queens to a nastier-than-normal (for *Drag Race*) form of coaching. Practically everyone brought in to whip the queens into shape for their musical numbers or recordings tends to lay their criticisms and grimaces on a little thick—this being a reality TV show, after all. But this strikes us as a very clear representation of the kinds of people and attitudes they will encounter in the music industry, which is infamously harsh. That's part of the whole vocational school aspect of the show, which expects its queens to toughen up because drag is hard, the entertainment industry is hard, and the music industry may just be the hardest of all, especially when you consider the difficulties and hardships faced by non-gender-conforming queer artists.

Unlike the acting challenges, which pull from a drag tradition in underground theater and trash cinema, the singing challenges trade strictly in mainstream musical forms and genres: Pop, rock, dance, disco, new wave, punk, and musical theater styles have all been drilled into the queens over *Drag Race*'s first decade. This tracks with Ru's own career as a pop star, which was mainstream from the jump, starting with her star-making turn dancing in the B-52s "Love Shack" video in 1989, to dropping a culture bomb on the world with his breakout hit "Supermodel (You Better Work)" in 1993. Like everything else on the show, the song-and-dance challenges also subtly pay tribute to a history of brave gender-bending performers working their way through mainstream musical forms. You can look at tons of queer singers, from Little Richard to Elton John to Freddie Mercury, Indigo Girls to Melissa Etheridge, Frank Ocean to Troye Sivan, to note how queer folks have been part of popular music for decades. And while we certainly have no intention of ignoring those trailblazers, *Drag Race* and its singing challenges specifically focus on the freedom and bravery of the legendary singers who would not fit the gender mold.

Interestingly enough, the history of popular music in the past century is full of examples of non-gender-conforming artists who were embraced wholeheartedly by musicians and the public. From Little Richard to Prince, David Bowie to Boy George, Annie Lennox to Phranc, the audiences for popular music going back nearly a century had the easiest time accepting the otherwise unacceptable so long as there was a good beat involved and you could dance to it. It helped a lot if you were a non-gender-conforming artist who was otherwise heterosexual and cisgender. In other words, Annie Lennox's androgynous buzz cuts were easier to accept than k.d. lang's or Phranc's because Lennox is a cisgender straight woman (who sported a lot of gender-affirming makeup and glamour), and the latter two couldn't help but underline or showcase their queer identities (and eschew most feminine-coded presentation). Bowie's glitter makeup was celebrated and considered sexy and otherworldly, but even at the height of his 1980s Culture Club fame, Boy George's version of soulful queer made-up glam was viewed as exotic, if not a little off-putting, largely because his voice was high and soft and his affect was more feminine in appearance.

We should note that from the minute the Beatles grew their hair to the point where it barely grazed the top of their collars in the early 1960s, the press and the older parts of the public said they looked like girls. Even Elvis's 1950s gyrations were considered alarmingly queer and inappropriately "Negro" in tone, largely because any man who made overt displays of his own sexuality was not considered either masculine or civilized. The mid-twentieth century was an unbelievably conformist time in terms of gender presentation. Even so, there appears to have been an unspoken understanding that displays or presentation styles that weren't strictly gender conforming as it was defined at the time were accepted in pop singers so long as they weren't *actually* or *openly* queer in any way.

And while Bowie flirted with bisexuality (which he later denounced and claimed was overstated), the vast majority of men who flipped the norms on gender presentation in music were straight. Thanks to the popularity of glam rock in the 1970s, any dude could slap on glitter makeup and a wig and never once have his cishet status questioned. This trend toward androgyny or nonbinary presentation waxed and waned over the history of popular music during the past century, sometimes making the careers of queer performers, only to break them when the tide of acceptance went out again. Any glam rocker could scrub off their makeup and return to cishet presentation without repercussions when the trends shifted, but queer artists who didn't conform to gender norms often found themselves floundering in their careers when they stayed too visibly queer for too long.

If there's a point to the song-and-dance challenges on *Drag Race* aside from the obvious entertainment and competitive value, it's to demonstrate that yes, drag queens do sing, that some of them are quite good at it, and that virtually all of them are going to face a hard time trying to make their way in the music industry. Ru and Michelle both know this from experience, but the history of queer, drag, trans, and non-gender-conforming musical artists backs it up nicely. Those trailblazers had it *rough*, so you better toughen up, buttercup.

Let's look at some of those trailblazers and how they rode the tide of the times so they could get up and do the two things they most wanted to do in the world: stand up as their truest selves and open their mouths to sing that truth to cheering audiences.

Gladys Bentley's Butch Blues

"I don't want no man that I got to give my money to."

Gladys Bentley singing "Worried Blues," 1928

The past is often bolder and queerer than you think.

Go back nearly a century and you'll find Gladys Bentley, the blues-singing, piano-playing, black lesbian performing sensation of the Harlem Renaissance of the 1920s and 1930s, wowing the audiences at Harlem's legendary gay speakeasies and nightclubs such as Harry Hansberry's Clam House and the Ubangi Club by performing in a top hat and tails while singing raunchy blues songs and openly flirting with the women in the audience.

Born in Philadelphia in 1907, she ran off to Harlem by her late teens, tired of clashing with her family over her masculine presentation and tendency to get crushes on women. At the height of her butch, piano-banging fame, she was often billed as a "male impersonator" but in reality, she was simply a butch queer black woman, whose preference for male attire extended into her day-to-day life (as much as she could get away with) and who didn't try to do a thing to camouflage that fact. Given her presentation, it may even be correct to view her as transmasculine. Legendary Harlem Renaissance poet Langston Hughes wrote of her performances in his autobiography, describing her as "a large, dark masculine lady" and "a perfect piece of African sculpture, animated by her own rhythm." Her performances were characterized as large, bombastic, thundering, and as raunchy as it gets. They called her the Brown Bomber of Sophisticated Songs. Her charisma, uniqueness, nerve, and talent secured her a spot as one of the highest-paid black entertainers for a time in the 1920s. The folks who came to Harlem nightclubs weren't naive about what Gladys's presentation and onstage behavior may have revealed about her personal life, but this was at the height of that queer cultural moment of the late 1920s and early '30s, the Pansy Craze, a period when audiences accepted and even sought out queer musical performers, happy to indulge in their talent and charisma, so long as they didn't have to hear about the rest of it. Keep it onstage (where it's fabulous) or keep it to yourself (where it's sinful). The 1920s and '30s were a time when the prohibition of alcohol gave rise to an entire underground nightlife scene in places like Harlem and Greenwich Village, where many of the rules of the outside world were suspended and a woman like Gladys could receive huge accolades and wealth based on the power of her overtly queer persona.

But the Pansy Craze, like so many of the brief flirtations LGBTQ folks made with mainstream acceptance, ended quickly and without much warning. When the Great Depression kicked in, a weary, stressed America turned to wholesome Hollywood entertainment to forget their woes and embraced a formalized sense of public morality as outlined in the newly adopted Hays Code for motion pictures. The police crackdowns on the gender-bending drag revues and Pansy-hosted shows in the early 1940s sent a message that was loud and clear to queer performers like Gladys: Conform or get out. She left Harlem and eventually wound up playing in a lesbian nightclub called Mona's ("Where Girls Will Be Boys!") in San Francisco for a time in the early 1940s, but eventually she had to give up her male drag if she wanted to continue to work.

As the Depression gave way to World War II, which eventually gave way to the highly conservative decade of the 1950s,

Gladys wound up publishing an essay in the August 1952 issue of *Ebony* with the unfortunate title "I Am a Woman Again." Complete with pictures of Gladys in dresses and makeup, doing the dishes in her kitchen, and turning down the bed for her new husband (!) before he comes home, the essay tells a tale of someone saved from a life of sin and perversion by the love of a good man and hormone treatments. It would be so easy from our present-day perch to speak derisively of this turn of events, or to cast them as a tragic example of someone whose fire and passion was beaten out of them by a society that had no room for nonconformity. But the life and choices of a black lesbian in the mid-twentieth century, at the height of McCarthyism and with the threat of imprisonment or worse hanging over her, these things are not to be questioned by us. Gladys had to live and work in that world as a symbol of everything conformity hated most: a large black woman who didn't bend to gender roles.

Gladys was, like many queer folks of her generation (and several other generations), at the mercy of the rapid shift in social mores that often happens when queer folks make some cultural progress, only to have conventionality and tradition slap them back. We can't imagine what forces came into play to result in the choices she made. It's not for us to say what would have been the correct or more fulfilling course for her life to take. For all we know, she was happy living in gender conformity later on—but the fire and passion and boldness of her youthful queer presentation and bawdily sexy performance style could not be denied. She was an incandescent talent who burned bright, inspiring poets and playing to ecstatic crowds as boldly and truthfully as she possibly could.

Gladys Bentley died suddenly of pneumonia in 1960 after completing the training to become a minister in her church.

Ru and the judges and coaches on *Drag Race*, knowing all that came before, all the brave and rebellious men and women who got up to sing in front of audiences in full defiance of the social mores and laws of the day, simply don't want to hear that someone's too scared or nervous to sing.

The Defiant Soul of Jackie Shane

"You know what my slogan is? Baby, do what you want, just know what you're doing. As long as you don't force your will and your way on anyone else, live your life, because ain't nobody sanctified and holy."

Jackie Shane, during a live performance of "Money (That's What I Want)" around 1963

Jackie Shane was born in 1940, appropriately enough in the place many people consider the heart of American music, Nashville, Tennessee. From the age of five, she knew and asserted that she was female, even if the world refused to agree with her. "I would dress in a dress, hat, purse, and high heels and go up and down the block—and enjoy it," she said in a 2017 interview. "What I'm simply saying is, I could be no one else."

She shocked her elders with her ability to walk in high heels several sizes too large for her by emulating no less a figure than Mae West, whose signature style of bump-and-roll walking helped the young someday-entertainer to perfect her own style. From a remarkably early age, she had a singularly uncompromising and impressively rock-solid understanding of herself, her identity, and how she was going to navigate the world. As a child, she was happy to display her impressive singing talent in the church, but only so long as everyone understood she had no interest in sticking around and listening to the preacher, who she understood would have no understanding or kindness for her clearly queer self. By the age of thirteen, she had the support of her mother to live her truth—a highly unusual sentiment for the time and place, but a testament both to Jackie's unshakable sense of herself and to her mother's love for her.

By the late 1950s Jackie was working as a singer and drummer. She eventually joined a traveling carnival and wound up in Canada, a country she fell in love with quickly as the weight of America's Jim Crow laws evaporated from her. Soon, she was fronting a band called Frank Motley and His Motley Crew, which quickly started gaining a reputation among Montreal nightclubs for being one of the hottest acts in town, thanks to its charismatic, soulful, and unquantifiable lead singer.

Jackie was occasionally billed as a female impersonator, a misnomer she put up with even though it misgendered her. While transgender identity wasn't unheard of at the time, in the wake of the international fame accorded to Christine Jorgensen after she pioneered the first transition, most of the world of the 1950s and '60s still saw someone like Jackie as an effeminate queer man, imposing a drag persona on her that didn't actually exist. When her recording of "Any Other Way" became a regional hit (something that was quite frequent in the days when thousands of independently owned small radio stations existed), a local station in Toronto invited her in to appear on one of their programs, only to promptly cancel when she showed up and they didn't know what to make of her. Her mode of dress when playing clubs tended to be oversize men's-style suits in bold colors, occasionally with glamorous touches like sequined tops. She wore makeup and styled her hair in a pompadour, for which she often got compared to Little Richard or mistaken for a lesbian. Other times, she wore her hair long and dressed in the styles of most women of the time: dresses and heels, hosiery and handbags. But by necessity, she often had to straddle a sort of genderqueer line in her presentation, leaving folks confused as to her gender and orientation. Our point is not to in any way deny her womanhood but to note that Jackie, presenting as a woman the whole time, had to navigate a world that absolutely didn't see her as one—and yet it never shook her confidence, presentation, or poise. The radio station invited her back, by the way. The song had become too popular and she'd been too firm in her self-regard for them to deny her.

To watch a performance of her singing "Walking the Dog" on Canadian television in 1965 (her only TV appearance, despite multiple requests, which she usually turned down) in makeup and a sequined top, to an audience who saw her as a man, is a study in bravery, poise, and confidence that demanded people accept her. Jackie was an inscrutable figure to midcentury audiences. People didn't have the language to describe her back then, and she was so singular in her presentation that it seems she mostly skated past judgment by being talented and so wholly original.

Her charisma, uniqueness, and nerve are in some ways more legendary and impressive than her talent. When representatives from *The Ed Sullivan Show* came calling, they told her she would have to perform dressed as a man on the show. Jackie not only told them to take a hike, she also apparently threw in a few choice words about their boss looking like Frankenstein's monster, effectively slamming that door behind her for good. She took no shit whatsoever. She absolutely lived her life and performed her music on her own terms.

She stepped away from performing in 1971, partly to take care of her mother and partly because she was worn out from giving so much of herself to the stage and the audience. Simply existing and presenting her true self to a public who didn't even try to understand who she was must have been exhausting. For many years after she left the spotlight, her legend only grew, along with wild suppositions and theories about what might have happened to her. Many thought she'd been killed. Music journalists finally tracked her down and in 2017, her compilation album, *Any Other Way*, was released, which garnered Jackie's work its only industry recognition: a Best Historical Album Grammy nomination. Jackie died in 2019, but she lived long enough to learn that her work, her bravery, and her fiercely immovable sense of herself had turned her into a legend. As she said in one of her final interviews, "I don't bow down. I do not get down on my knees. The lowest I go is the top of my head. This is Jackie!"

The Shimmering and Mighty Realness of Sylvester

"Sometimes, folks make us feel strange, but we're not strange. And those folks—they'll just have to *catch up*."

Sylvester, onstage in 1978

Just as Jackie Shane was ready to retire from the scene in the early 1970s, soon-to-be-legendary disco queen Sylvester was beginning to make his mark on it.

Born Sylvester James in Los Angeles in 1947, he had a rocky relationship with his religious Pentecostal mother and stepfather, partially over his unapologetic queerness. He was known in the church community both for his stunning voice while singing gospel and for being flamboyantly queer in an undeniable way, which generally didn't mix well with most church communities back then—and of course still doesn't. In a somewhat horrifying turn of events that Sylvester was usually fairly sanguine about in the retelling, he was molested by a man of the church when he was thirteen, and the community, because of his overt queerness, blamed and shunned him. Remember, he'd wind up singing gospel dressed as Coretta Scott King for the Cockettes' underground film, *Tricia's Wedding*. Given his background with the church, it's perhaps not that hard to see why he'd do such a shocking scene so early in his performing career.

After clashing with his mother and stepfather over both his rape and his queerness, Sylvester moved out in his mid-teens to live with his grandmother, who used to be a blues singer herself and didn't mind socializing with gay men. She introduced him to a local clique of gay black men who called themselves the Disquotays, a singing group that dressed flamboyantly and were known for throwing legendary house parties. Sylvester learned to walk the walk of queerness and gender expression with these men, one of whom recommended he move up to San Francisco and join a wild band of drag performers known as the Cockettes. Sylvester enjoyed his time with the group, but while freedom of expression was definitely his bag, anarchy most certainly wasn't. When the group's disastrous New York debut went down, Sylvester often apologized prior to the remaining shows for the sparkly train wreck about to follow.

The Cockettes were not going to be his pathway to artistic expression and he knew it. When they disbanded, he started making a name for himself doing live shows in the clubs and theaters of San Francisco, often surrounding himself onstage with barely dressed chorus boys or go-go boys. He was advised to be a little less overtly gay in his stage shows and find a couple of female backup singers who could keep up with him. He dragged his feet on the idea—possibly because he tended to get antsy anytime anyone suggested he act less gay—until he came upon a pair of plus-size backup singers who called themselves Two Tons O' Fun, Martha Wash and Izora Rhodes. The trio clicked and the ladies would go on to sing backup on the legendary songs "You Make Me Feel (Mighty Real)" and "Do You Wanna Funk?" Two Tons O' Fun would later rename themselves the Weather Girls and produce their own legendary gay club anthem in 1982, "It's Raining Men."

It's probably more accurate to call Sylvester's talent immeasurable. He was blessed with a falsetto that could soar above a crowd like a howling disco wind, and his performing style and presentation were unquestionable and unapologetically queer— all turbans and sequins, robes and dresses, wigs and makeup. The boldness of his presentation, like that of Jackie Shane's a decade earlier, was simply astonishing in the context of the times. Famous female impersonators like Jim Bailey simply never discussed their private lives or sexual lives; at the time, most people considered performers like him or flamboyant pianist Liberace to be clearly queer, even if such things were never openly stated. Sylvester's queerness, while similarly unstated, was completely undeniable, especially when you put it up against the relative coyness of his contemporaries like Freddie Mercury and Elton John.

Somewhat derisively called the Queen of Disco (much in the same way legendary gay crooner Johnny Mathis was routinely referred to as the African Queen by underground comics of the 1960s), Sylvester helped embody the popular dance music form of the late 1970s. Disco was a musical form that bubbled up out of black and Latinx dance clubs where queer people congregated, a combination of African American and Latinx musical motifs and queer aesthetics.

Like so many men who performed utilizing drag tropes, he did not like being called a drag queen. When asked what he was, he would reply, "I'm Sylvester." It was answer enough.

Sylvester died of AIDS complications in 1988 and, per his wishes, was buried in a red kimono and full makeup. He bequeathed all future royalties from his music to HIV/AIDS organizations. His unshakable sense of self was no less potent than Gladys Bentley's or Jackie Shane's, but he rose to fame in an ever so slightly more accepting post-Stonewall world, during another of those periods in which queer folks were celebrated in certain spaces. The plague took him too soon, but his life was free, open, and without shame until the day he died. Boldly performing in makeup, sequins, and turbans, with stacks of bracelets and oversize rings, Sylvester had talent and popularity that broke down barriers and allowed artists like Boy George and RuPaul to stomp through.

In March 2019, Sylvester's recording of "You Make Me Feel (Mighty Real)" was entered into the National Recording Registry of the Library of Congress as a historically significant and culturally important work that "reflected his childhood background in both African American gospel music and his work as a drag performer in San Francisco." Sylvester probably never imagined his work would receive that level of recognition, but we suspect he'd correct the Library of Congress's description. Sylvester wasn't a "drag performer." Sylvester was Sylvester.

From Punk Wrecker Drag to New Romantic Drag: Jayne County and Boy George

"It was commercial suicide, but I didn't care.
I did it because I loved it."

Jayne County on her career

The musical artists we've highlighted so far either flirted with, pursued, or achieved success in the mainstream, but we have to take a second here to pay tribute to one queen who not only refused to flirt, pursue, or achieve anything that could be considered mainstream, she actively fought against the idea throughout her career. Jayne County didn't want to be your next pop star. She wanted to be, in her words, "a wrecker."

The punk pioneer and performing artist who would eventually become Jayne County abruptly left her hometown of Atlanta in 1968 after a couple of "rednecks," as she called them, started firing on her and a friend as they were walking down the street. That was enough for her. She turned to her friend as they dodged bullets, said, "I'm getting the hell out of here," and promptly left for New York with twenty-five dollars in her purse, to become the person she was meant to be, surrounded by the types of people who don't tend to shoot at people like her. She wanted to break into the burgeoning underground art scene happening there at the time, populated and embodied by people like Charles Ludlam and Andy Warhol. She became a frequent patron of the Stonewall Inn and participated in all three nights of the riots that ignited the community in 1969. Eventually she met Warhol queens Jackie Curtis and Candy Darling, and the three of them wound up sharing an apartment together. Curtis asked Jayne to be in her play *Femme Fatale*, playing off-Broadway, where she made her debut with the immortal opening line "Oh my God! You scared the shit out of me!" and produced a plastic prop turd from under her skirt.

She made enough of a splash that she spent some time bouncing around the underground theater world, including work at the Playhouse of the Ridiculous, which spawned the career of Charles Ludlam. During this time, through her friendships with Jackie and Candy, she was bouncing around the Warhol orbit as well, constantly surrounded by artists, performers, and boundary pushers of all stripes. She seemed to be one of those people always on the scene, always knowing the beautiful people, and always ready to move on to the next scene. In 1972, she left the theater behind and formed her first band, the glam rock group Queen Elizabeth, which was named not, as it turned out, after the monarch of England but after an infamous Atlanta drag queen who got fired from her department store modeling job when management clocked her. This open, in-your-face queerness in a lead singer at a time when queer men like Elton John and Freddie Mercury were tearing up the charts while remaining coy about their identities is as brave, defiant, and deeply admirable as Jackie Shane and Sylvester refusing to deny their truths and expecting the world to catch up to them instead of the other way around.

Similar to her theater stints, Jayne bounced around the music scene, knowing all the best people, playing in various bands, and making a name for herself in legendary rock clubs like Max's Kansas City and CBGB—an underground drag queen with an edge, living her truth and rocking the shit out of it. In 1977 she wound up—as if she had a nose for such things—in the heart of the burgeoning punk scene in London, where she formed her band Wayne County and the Electric Chairs. Releasing tracks like "Fuck Off," "Man Enough to Be a Woman," and "Toilet Love," they became underground legends and influenced countless punk and post-punk bands up until the present day. "I took it really to a point where no one else was taking it," she said.

Punk had a limited initial run in the mainstream and Jayne County never became a household name, but much like Gladys Bentley and Jackie Shane paving the way for the much more mainstream success of Sylvester, punk and new wave drag and transgender performers like Jayne County and Divine (who was touring the world around the same time performing her dance club hits) laid the groundwork for someone like Boy George to come along just a few years later, offering a much more vulnerable, working-class, multicultural drag for the pop scene of the 1980s.

The former George O'Dowd escaped life with his "sad Irish family" and served up a very eighties British form of working-class melting-pot drag that not only didn't prevent him from superstardom, it actually helped him gain it. George occasionally jokingly referred to himself as a drag queen, but he didn't truly consider himself one, largely because his aesthetic came out of the early eighties New Romantic music movement in his native Great Britain, which produced a string of popular and even legendary musical performers from that period. Like his musical contemporaries Duran Duran, A Flock of Seagulls, and Klaus Nomi, George wore a ton of feminine-style makeup. And yet, stripped of the iconic undertones, Boy George's classic eighties look could walk a *Drag Race* catwalk and no one, not even Michelle Visage, would question it was drag (although she'd probably want him to wear a waist cincher). He has an iconic image as locked into the public mind-set as RuPaul's, Divine's, and Tim Curry's, and he rose to international fame at a time when the United States and England were in the throes of Reagan- and Thatcher-based conservativism and the gay male community was ravaged by AIDS, forcing many back into the closet.

Inspired by Leigh Bowery and thrust into international stardom as a non-gender-conforming gay man in the early 1980s as the lead singer of Culture Club, when the acceptance of the 1970s had started to give way to the fear and hysteria surrounding gays in the era of AIDS, Boy George not only wore his queerness on his sleeve (and face and head), he wore his heart there, singing songs of broken hearts and unstated queer love, using the pain of his own romantic past to fuel success with songs like "Do You Really Want to Hurt Me," "Karma Chameleon," and "Time (Clock of the Heart)." Like Sylvester's and Jackie Shane's, his queerness and gender nonconformity were inseparable from his singing and performance. George sang of the pain of his own breakups and romantic obsessions, universal themes that came through with a queer undertone to them—in ribbons and bows, lipstick and eyeliner.

The Unprecedented Success of Divine and RuPaul

Note that everyone we've mentioned in this chapter so far was not technically a drag queen. If you want to talk about the history of self-identified drag queens with popular music careers, there really are only two names, and we've already mentioned them. But a discussion about the history of gender nonconformity in pop music without mentioning RuPaul and Divine is a rather lopsided discussion. In truth, they're probably the most successful drag queen singers of all time—if you're going by a strict definition of drag or simply acknowledging those performers who identified as such. Divine was known far more for her film work, but she spent a good portion of the 1980s recording minor chart hits like "You Think You're a Man" and "I'm So Beautiful" and touring the world promoting them, performing in nightclubs and on music shows like *Top of the Pops* in England. She was the first performer to achieve success in popular music while unquestionably identifying as a drag queen.

RuPaul picked up the mantle Divine laid down and achieved even greater success. "Supermodel (You Better Work)" is a bona fide classic and in recent years, Ru has become a master at promoting his constantly dropping dance tracks through *Drag Race*, whether by featuring the songs for lip syncs or actually making the queens sing them. And because of that somewhat easily ridiculed sense of promotion (check out Trixie Mattel's Ru impression during Snatch Game, where she constantly plugs her next single), more of the *Drag Race* alums have gone on to record songs and make music videos than act onstage or do stand-up or walk runways. Taking their cues from Ru and Divine, many of the queens recorded dance and electronic music that didn't necessarily require the most advanced or trained singing talent. No tea, no shade, ladies! The point being that even though many queens complained their way through a singing or a dance challenge, a whole lot of them wound up using the skills they either picked up or refined and showcased while on *Drag Race*. Mama Ru's Vocational School for Girls strikes again. And the next time you hear a queen on *Drag Race* complain that drag queens don't sing, you can roll your eyes with great abandon. Practically every drag queen mentioned in this book stood up and sang in front of audiences at some point in her career. Singing and drag are irrevocably linked.

Herstory Lesson:

The Pansy Craze

Masculine women, feminine men!
Which is the rooster? Which is the hen?

Lyrics from the 1926 song "Masculine Women! Feminine Men!"

In the 1931 Busby Berkeley musical *Palmy Days*, an officious man raps on the glass counter of a bakery and snippily informs the shopgirl that he needs a cake in twenty-four hours. "What kind of cake would you prefer?" she asks him. "Chocolate. *All* chocolate," he replies firmly, then as he grows wistful and looks off into the distance, "I just *love* chocolate." "Would you like a little rose on top?" asks the shopgirl, played by a pre-fame, fifteen-year-old Betty Grable, who would go on to become a movie star and a legendary pinup girl for World War II military men. The man, coded as gay with his walking stick, brooch, white gloves, pencil mustache, and white fedora, bites his lip, raises his eyebrows, and responds, "No, make it a *pansy*." He walks out of the scene—and the film, as he never appears in it again. The exchange might seem pointless or odd to us, but the young, trend-following members of the film's audience knew exactly what was being discussed. Here was a gay man talking about his love of black men, referring to the Pansy Craze that had swept the world's nightclubs, born from the jazz clubs of the Harlem Renaissance. Fey, gay-coded walk-on characters were popular in films at the time, because Hollywood hadn't yet codified its own set of rules about what could be portrayed on film.

The passage of Prohibition in 1920 gave rise to the Jazz Age and organized crime, but it also resulted in a new form of unstated social contract, one that granted people the freedom and daring to throw away conventions and indulge in a new world of social and cultural possibilities. Women ditched their corsets, raised their skirts, bobbed their hair, and started smoking in public as the stultifying mores of the Victorian era defiantly evaporated in response to the imposition of Prohibition on an American public that didn't really want it. Urban nightlife reigned supreme as a golden age of live entertainment ensued. When people turn to the cities for the very best in live entertainment and party throwing, they tend to gravitate toward the black, Latinx, and queer night spots because they celebrate an abandon that conventional white-focused nightlife didn't always provide.

Queer people became trendy figures in nightlife and cabaret shows, including a vogue toward drag shows and the elevation of the pansy emcee figure—a mincing, effeminate caricature of the camp gay male identity dressed not in drag but in a top hat and tails, with some fey touches like lipstick or even a pansy in the buttonhole to signal his status. Think of Joel Grey's character in the 1972 film *Cabaret* as a faithful re-creation, since the Pansy Craze extended to the nightclubs of Paris, London, and Berlin.

Top pansy Gene Malin started out as a drag performer, often feminizing his first name to Jean; but when the Pansy Craze kicked in, he switched over to performing as a camp gay man in a top hat and tails and became one of the highest-paid entertainers in the New York nightclub scene as well as the face of the pansy figure to the public. He attempted to break into Hollywood films but was reportedly rejected after a screen executive saw a screen test and declared that the clearly gay Malin would never be allowed back on the studio lot again.

The sly reference in *Palmy Days* was at the tail end of the Pansy Craze, which would effectively be killed off within a year or two of its release. By 1932, the newly set up motion picture industry self-censoring body, the Hays Office, issued its infamous code to the major studios; among the first casualties were any mentions or allusions to homosexuality, which were stripped from mainstream American films for another thirty years (along with nudity, the suggestion of premarital sex, and any depictions of crime or adultery that went unpunished by a movie's end). By the early 1930s, the police had begun cracking down hard on gay speakeasies and nightclubs, making several high-profile busts that wound up shining a harsh and judgmental spotlight on them. Gene Malin died in a freak car accident in 1933, the same year Prohibition was repealed. To most, his tragic end felt like the death knell of the pansy. The Great Depression took hold, the intense desire to party with abandon dried up, and people turned their backs once again on the queer folks and people of color who had entertained them for over a decade. Many of the most popular pansies of the Berlin scene were rounded up and subsequently killed in the concentration camps of Nazi Germany.

Herstory Lesson:

The Rise and Untimely Death of Disco

The disco music craze of the 1970s bubbled up out of queer, black, and Latinx dance clubs starting in the late '60s, became briefly trendy due in part to *Saturday Night Fever*'s 1977 release, centered the aesthetics and cultural references of the communities that originated it, and suffered a cultural backlash so potent that people are still debating its significance and underlying causes four decades later.

Disco's roots were in soul and salsa music; the genre became popular in the underground nightlife scene when the DJs at gay nightclubs started playing it. Similar to the rise of the Pansy Craze, disco music became popular when white straight folks in the seventies, a time when the culture just wanted to party away their cares and woes in the wake of the Vietnam War disaster, the Watergate presidential scandal, and out-of-control inflation, snatched up the burgeoning underground musical form and pushed it into the mainstream.

It is a sadly inevitable truth that disco's moment of greatest popularity was also its whitest moment. Stripped of any allusions to gay, black, or Latinx nightlife, *Saturday Night Fever*, the 1977 film about white Brooklynites finding love and meaning on the dance floor, went off like a culture bomb, bringing disco out of its queer, colorful underground and into the limelight—literally. Despite that mainstream success, legendary discos such as New York's Studio 54 blossomed briefly on the cultural landscape, long enough to become legendary and to firmly underline the distinctly queer undertones of disco. Studio 54 was co-owned by Steve Rubell, who was gay and who made sure the club was packed with drag queens, transgender people, and gay men alongside its behind-the-velvet-rope celebrity clientele, representing a watershed moment in the culture when queer people were not only invited to the party but the whole reason there was a party to go to in the first place. Not unlike the Pansy Craze of the Harlem Renaissance at its height—and also at its decline.

In July 1979, at Chicago's Comiskey Park, a local DJ, disgruntled by his station's switch to all-disco programming and his subsequent firing, staged a Disco Demolition Night between innings of a White Sox game. If you arrived with a disco record to add to the bonfire, you got in for ninety-eight cents. Fifty thousand people showed up, records in hand, to cheer as those records got blown up by dynamite. Not content to watch it burn, the disco-phobes rushed the field; riot police had to be called in to break up the frenzied crowd, who were throwing more and more records onto the fire.

Not liking disco doesn't make someone a homophobe or a racist, but blowing up a pile of records representing queer, black, and Latinx music in the middle of a stadium to the roaring cheers of sports fans was one of the most blatantly cishet acts of cultural terrorism against queer people and people of color. Disco really did die out shortly after. The joke was on the disco-phobes, because the disco craze was closely followed by the new wave and New Romantic musical movements in pop, as well as house music and rap, each of which prized androgyny, gender-bending, or the experiences of people of color over the kind of macho white rock those fools at Comiskey were hoping for.

The Tea On:

Drag Race's Greatest Queen-Written Lyrics

"Yekaterina. Petrovna. Zamolodchikova. But your dad just calls
me KATYAAAAAAA."
Katya's verse for the song "Read U Wrote U," All Stars season 2

"D to the E to the T to the O to the—hold it! X."
Detox's verse for "Read U Wrote U," All Stars season 2

"Turning looks, stunting pretty.
I'm the bitch from New York City."
Aquaria in "American" musical number, season 10

"FACE FACE FACE, I give FACE, beauty FACE.
You can't take it, it's okay, watch my body go INSANE."
BeBe Zahara Benet's "Cover Girl" lyrics, season 1

Chapter 6

For Every Tuck,
There Must Come a Bulge

O hhh, Pit Creeeewwwww!"

With those three magic words, Ru invites her queens and the viewers at home to turn expectantly to the Werk Room door, ready to break into appreciative applause and cheers as soon as it opens. Because fit, semi-naked men are going to walk through it? Well, yes. Because many if not most of the folks who find themselves in that Werk Room tend to really enjoy the presence of fit, semi-naked men in their day-to-day lives now and then? Undoubtedly. Because drag entertainment and male bodily displays have a long tradition that stretches back a century, encompasses a wide range of drag styles and venues, and reveals some truths about how queer folks entered queer life, both in the past and today? Okay, maybe that's not why they're all clapping, but you can rest assured, when a healthy handful of oiled-up muscle men in skimpy briefs walk through that door, they're serving up a specific, iconic, and long-lasting image of queer male desire as well as continuing a long-standing relationship in the queer community, the same one you see play out on every Pride parade float full of drag queens and go-go boys.

Often used to model popular brands of underwear and

swimwear marketed to gay men, the Pit Crew is one of the more subversive aspects of *Drag Race*, putting unapologetic gay male sexual archetypes in front of the so-called mainstream. They are called on to serve drinks, model, escort the queens, dance, and occasionally act, but mostly they're expected to just stand there and be hot. Bulging and greased up, the Pit Crew members offer up their bodies for view or even as props and are not expected to speak or do anything other than what they're told. They are every go-go boy and chorus boy in gay entertainment history. They're every physique model and porn star. They're every body queen or Muscle Mary in a rainbow Speedo dancing on a Pride float. They are, in fact, a satire of the long-standing image of the perfect gay male fantasy figure: ripped, shiny, undressed, and nonverbal.

What made the introduction of the Pit Crew so perfect was that it served as a bit of a wink during a time in history (2009) when gay people were busy seeking marriage, military service, and family adoption rights while promoting a mainstream form of domesticity and public service as the premier image of queer life. The Pit Crew was meant to be politically incorrect from the get-go. In fact, a full season before they would even be called the Pit Crew, in the premiere episode of the second season of *Drag Race*, Ru had the competing queens pose for pictures straddling a cannon in a Civil War scenario while the proto–Pit Crew, Keon Hunt and Kenyon Glover—two shirtless, oiled-up black bodybuilders, each in (half of) a Union soldier's uniform—flexed behind them. By design, and even before they were named, the Pit Crew was always meant to be subversive, naughty, and even a little offensive if the situation called for it.

The little briefs and bathing suits of the Pit Crew are a direct line from the posing suits and thongs of old physique magazines as well as the eye-popping erotica of Tom of Finland, the iconic image of Joe Dallesandro posing in his briefs for Andy Warhol's 1970 film *Trash*, Robert Mapplethorpe's photographs fetishizing the male form, and Mark Wahlberg's famous ad for Calvin Klein underwear. Over and over again, the mass-mediated image of gay male desire, for over a century, has been a muscular man with visible abs in as small a brief as possible. There have been cowboys and construction workers and cops and firemen and soldiers for queer men to play with—a veritable toy box of sexual action figures—but the purest, most consistent media avatar of gay male desire is a well-built guy in a Speedo, a jockstrap, or a pair of briefs.

Drag Race deliberately frames the Pit Crew members' butts and bulges in virtually every shot, not just because it's cheeky (pun unintended) or because they're hot; not just because they sit on a long continuum of objectified muscle men in posing suits, Speedos, and briefs; but because the show lives to throw gender confusion and queer sexuality into its mix. For every tuck there must come a bulge. The push-pull of this imagery (and metaphor) permeates the history of drag. From the most glittering revues in sparkling urban nightclubs to the bathhouse and backroom Betties, from the bars of queer enclaves Fire Island and Provincetown to the cabarets of New York, drag queens have always had a tendency to find themselves in the vicinity of very pretty young men wearing as little as possible. A fit young man in briefs is as iconic an image of gay male desire as a pinup girl in a bikini is for straight male desire—and largely for the same reasons, because both images display the body without displaying the parts of the body the obscenity laws generally had problems with back in the day. Just as the girl with the perfect bikini bod is still considered a mainstream beauty ideal today, the ripped dude in the Speedo (or briefs, or jockstrap, or posing thong) continues to be held up as a queer male figure of desire. Is there a history behind all this? Darling, of *course* there is.

Come with us on a journey of body oil and posing straps.

A Short History of the Gay Male Beauty Ideal

Once the cosmic gases cooled, our planet formed, and life bubbled up in the primordial goo, single-celled gays immediately set about establishing some ground rules about who qualified as hot. We joke, but we can't say we're all that far off.

The modern LGBTQ community—and the very idea of queerness as an identity instead of an act—started forming in the late nineteenth century, riding the massive wave of change that came with the industrial revolution and the migration of America off the farms and into the cities, where formerly solitary queer folks couldn't help but start bumping into like-minded people, pairing off, congregating, and slowly forming groups and subcultures. Over time, these communities started articulating and codifying their shared aesthetics and aspirations. This was at a time when queer drag was also being codified, along with other aspects of queer culture, like lesbian salons, bars, and dance halls, as well as gay bars and bathhouses. Around this same time, in the period from the 1880s to the first couple of decades of the twentieth century, two mainstream phenomena were unfolding, the combined effect of which would dictate the image of the perfect gay male figure of desire for the next century, inspiring artists, writers, photographers, and pornographers, celebrated in museums the world over, mentioned in passing by legendary literary characters, and joyously indulged in the wedding reception dance crazes of your parents and grandparents. Those two essential ingredients to the cultural stew that eventually produced the Pit Crew? The introduction of the bodybuilding craze and the rise of the modern American advertising industry, with its ability to dictate the terms of the culture in ways big and small.

Of course you can't put a pin on a timeline and declare that *this* arbitrary notation represents the beginning of culture or history. Many factors contributed to the long-standing gay male desire for muscular, square-jawed men with six-pack abs, going back to neoclassical sculpture and the age-old hegemony of European aesthetic ideals in Western culture, not to mention the tendency of oppressed people to fantasize about benevolent authoritative figures, or for men considered by society to be lacking in masculinity to exalt and elevate the more extreme physical forms of it. But the rise of bodybuilding culture with the introduction of figures like the legendary "father of modern bodybuilding," Eugen Sandow, starting in the 1890s helped inspire the physical culture craze that began in the early twentieth century (and increased in fervor with every decade), along with its attendant rise of spaces where athletic-minded men could congregate to pursue their interests. In other words, gymnasiums, spas, and bathhouses sprung up at the turn of the century like never before—all of them not only providing a space for athletic straight men to congregate but also providing a cover story for queer men looking to . . . *congregate*. This dynamic and social arrangement continues to this very day, especially in urban areas with well-known, well-attended gyms. Virtually every metropolitan area has a handful of gyms that are known for being popular with gay men.

For all of Eugen Sandow's effects on the culture, for all the marketing that branded him as the physical ideal, society and culture of the early twentieth century in the United States didn't prize muscularity or shredded abs as physical goals, partly because both attributes implied manual labor and malnutrition to a country only a generation or two removed from agrarian subsistence living conditions. Sure, there were plenty of women who paid for private "modeling" sessions by Sandow, and there's no denying that he and other strongman figures inspired generations of men to pursue bodybuilding; but Sandow and his type were seen at the time more like living Greek statues than someone most straight men wanted to be and straight women wanted to be with—beautiful but freakish to the majority of the public. But not all the public, of course. It would be nearly another hundred years before mainstream culture (i.e., advertising) elevated the Sandow look of extreme muscularity and low body fat as an aspirational and sexual one, but queer male culture latched on to it almost immediately.

Part of Sandow's mystique and fame came down to his willingness to pose naked as early as the 1890s and in a manner designed to show off his muscles. Other strongman performers of the period (and there were many, since it was a common form of sideshow, circus, and vaudevillian entertainment) performed feats of strength, but thanks to his affiliation with master American showman and theatrical impresario Florenz Ziegfeld, who knew a thing or two about what audiences really wanted to see, Sandow performed feats of *display*—a series of poses and flexes, many of which are still performed in bodybuilding competition routines, devised to show off his extreme muscularity, both to audiences (in singlets and posing briefs) and to photographers (in a fig leaf or nothing at all). Sandow had the good looks of a film star and the kind of perfectly symmetrical and proportionate muscularity that set him apart from other strongmen of the period, which had a lot to do with his stardom and lasting impression. Thanks to the rise of cheap printing presses and the exponentially increasing popularity of the new technology of photography, queer men of the late nineteenth and early twentieth centuries were able to compile a spank bank collection of their most fervent sexual desires with an ease no other generation had enjoyed. Most of them surely had at least a few Sandow postcards and physique magazine pictorials in their stacks.

While Eugen Sandow was flexing and posing and showing queer men what their desires could be, the world of illustration was helping to show them where their desires could lead.

Setting the Stage with J. C. Leyendecker's Flawless Men

In F. Scott Fitzgerald's legendary 1925 novel of the Jazz Age, *The Great Gatsby*, Daisy Buchanan attempts to describe the lead character to himself. "You always look so cool," she says to Jay Gatsby. "You resemble the advertisement of the man . . . you know, the advertisement of the man." Given the times and Gatsby's metaphorical (if illusory) status as an awe-inspiring figure of maleness, there could be only one man to whom she was referring, the man who had after two decades become synonymous with the American ideal of physical male excellence: the iconic Arrow Collar Man, who'd appeared in illustrations for the men's shirt manufacturer Cluett, Peabody & Company since 1905. The Arrow Collar Man was an advertising figure designed by one of the most popular American illustrators of all time, Joseph Christian Leyendecker, and inspired most often by Charles Beach, Leyendecker's beautiful model and lifelong partner.

J. C. Leyendecker isn't normally considered a seminal figure in queer culture. For one thing, despite his lifelong living situation with Charles Beach in a massive Westchester County mansion not unlike Jay Gatsby's, where they were known to throw legendary parties in the early part of the century, Leyendecker never publicly came out. There are no records to confirm the nature of his life because, as legend has it, he instructed Charles Beach to destroy all his personal papers upon his death. This closeted and private form of queerness is not unusual for a man born in the nineteenth century and dead by the early 1950s, of course. But to be perfectly fair about it, no one today can say with absolute conviction where the man's desires were to be found.

On the other hand, it's nearly impossible for any queer man to look at Leyendecker's life's work and not see a man devoted to depicting a certain idealized form of male beauty, an artist willing to make male figures into shockingly sexualized beings, their nearly naked, perpetually shiny, perfectly symmetrical muscular bodies often appearing in advertisements and on the cover of the most mainstream magazine you could have found at the time, *The Saturday Evening Post*. Square-jawed beyond belief, with hooded eyes and a bored expression—especially if there was a woman in the scene—Leyendecker's men, while offered as the ne plus ultra of American masculinity, often had a decidedly effete and aristocratic feel to them, like dukes of European royalty. Dukes with extremely broad shoulders, nary a body hair in sight, and skin so shiny it looks like it would squeak with every movement and gesture, to be sure. His men posed demurely for Ivory soap ads (as medieval monks, no less), or shed their dressing gowns for Cooper union suits, revealing beautifully toned bodies (Charles Beach's) in nearly transparent and skintight turn-of-the-century long underwear. His men were lifeguards and football players, Native Americans and Pilgrims, knights and soldiers, society men in tails, and sock models bending over in their underwear, all somehow combining a very 1920s elegance with a sweaty and flamboyant physicality. While his women were doe-eyed and soignée in the ideal manner of the time, his men were all large, angular, and athletic, either posed like classical statues or springing into action, their butts and crotches framed and centered with hilarious consistency.

This broad-shouldered, heavy-browed, perpetually sweaty version of masculinity would be picked up by other queer artists of the twentieth century, expanded upon, codified as purely sexual, and made more extreme with the changing of the times. But when you look at twentieth-century queer male erotic artwork, it's extremely easy to draw a line starting with J. C. Leyendecker's work in the first third of it.

Leyendecker mentored and inspired Norman Rockwell, who succeeded him as the cover artist of *The Saturday Evening Post* by the mid-1930s (and would serve as one of his pallbearers). Rockwell went on to a career so iconic, he's often considered the greatest American illustrator of all time. And yet, he spent his entire career clearly having been inspired by Leyendecker, with similar themes and compositions playing out in some of his most famous works for decades after his mentor's death—stripped of any queer sensibilities or innate love of the male body, of course. Still, despite the occasionally curious similarities, nothing could further define the differences between the two artists' outlooks than their respective iconic Thanksgiving-themed covers for the *Post*. Rockwell's 1943 illustration "Freedom from Want" is the better known, having been copied and parodied in countless films, TV shows, and advertisements. His early-twentieth-century version of a multigenerational family gathering around the table celebrating the most American of holidays is practically a visual synonym for "home and hearth" to several generations of Americans. Leyendecker's 1928 Thanksgiving cover for the *Post*, on the other hand, seems designed to get your pulse racing rather than inspire any feelings of harvest and hearth. Instead of a family around the table, the cover features two broad-shouldered sweaty men staring directly into each other's eyes. One, a Pilgrim, who looks less like a pacifist religious zealot and more like someone who could tear a man apart with his bare—and enormous—hands; the other, a football player in a torn jersey, his sweaty chest no doubt heaving with autumnal visions of cornucopias, looks like he wants to rip that Pilgrim's stupid hat off his head and make out with him. Honestly, it's almost hilariously homoerotic, given the decidedly un-queer nature of the holiday—not to mention the readership of the *Post*. But we can't help thinking a whole tenth of a generation of teenage boys must have held on to that copy of the *Post* all the way through the 1930s, stored under countless mattresses and floorboards, a sacred snapshot of queer lust smack in the middle of Americana fueling who knows how many spank sessions and daydreams, stashed with some old Eugen Sandow postcards, probably.

Sandow and Leyendecker each had long-lasting effects on how queer men articulated and visualized their desires for the next century, perched as they were at the intersection of mainstream culture and queerness for most of their careers. If you know where to look, you can see exactly how both inspired generations of queer men.

So let's look.

The Relentless Desire of Bob Mizer

In November 1951, three months after Charles Beach burned J. C. Leyendecker's private papers after his funeral, a young gay photographer and fitness enthusiast (or at least supporter of *other* fitness enthusiasts) named Bob Mizer, having already formed the Athletic Model Guild (AMG), launched its accompanying magazine, *Physique Pictorial*, thereby birthing the modern physique magazine industry. With names like *Physical Culture*, *The Young Physique*, and *Body Beautiful*, physique mags featured young men in posing straps, briefs, or thongs, greased up and flexing in a variety of testosterone-fueled scenarios. Part of the reason gay, bi, and queer men fetishized the superfit to such an extent is because for the longest time, "physical culture" magazines were the only mainstream entry available into a life of admiring the naked male form. Obscenity laws of the midtwentieth century allowed for the distribution of imagery featuring naked women (hence *Playboy*, which launched to tremendous, culture-shifting success in 1953), but anything featuring naked men was illegal and extremely difficult to come by, and carried heavy penalties for anyone caught distributing it, not to mention deep shame for any male caught owning it. For a gay man in the 1950s and 1960s, these precursors to the men's fitness magazines (and full-blown porn) of today were the best and sometimes only way for them to . . . *express their queerness*, let's say.

"It is an assault to the dignity of man and his creator to treat any portion of the body as something shameful and disgusting," Bob Mizer wrote in a *Physique Pictorial* editorial in 1965. In the magazine's long run, Mizer suffered the slings and arrows of a society and legal system that constantly looked for ways to shut his burgeoning operation down, and he found himself facing obscenity charges and accusations of operating a prostitution ring more than once throughout his long career. But he remained deeply committed to the passion he developed going back to his boyhood: photographing as many beautiful men in as little clothing as he could possibly get away with. This was no mere fetish, but a life's calling. Mizer could have happily taken as many nudie pictures of men as he liked and fulfilled his own desires, but he felt a need and a drive to fight for the right to *display* his desires, to reach out to other men with the same desires, and to form bonds with them. The Pit Crew, working their briefs and flexing their butts just like the physique models of yore, represent not just the history of queer male desire but how the need to express that desire helped form a community.

Mizer, for his part, *literally* formed a community. Buying up the properties surrounding his mother's downtown Los Angeles home after she died in the early 1960s (and after she'd spent years supporting and aiding him in his semi-nude-modeling entrepreneurial efforts), Mizer secured a physique modeling compound around himself—a series of connected properties in which he lived and worked. He also provided housing for the rotating roster of young men—some homeless, some out of the military, some who were runaways, and some who just liked the money—who modeled for him in mesh thongs, cowboy getups, Roman centurion costumes, and any other scenario that he could dream up. Bob saw himself as a moral guide to these men, adopting a paternal or taskmaster role, even if he occasionally slept with some of them. He also curated a menagerie of animals (useful in various themed photoshoots) from monkeys to peacocks, wandering the grounds. And a somewhat low-rent, totally gay Playboy mansion, with Bob as the Hugh Hefner figure, cowboys instead of bunnies, and the whole operation constantly having to fight off harassment from the police and the post office over obscenity laws.

Still, for decades, young men lounged around the AMG compound pool, waiting to be called up to smile for the cameras and, whether knowingly or not (and plenty of them knew), offering queer boys all over the country a glimpse of the kind of life—the kind of *man*—they could have. It's been estimated that the Athletic Model Guild and Mizer himself photographed over ten thousand men (including future governor of California Arnold Schwarzenegger in 1975) in more than a million images during the magazine's four-decade run.

For an enterprise that could come off terribly seedy to outsiders, run by a man who might have come across with a bit of sexual obsession fueling his work, AMG and Bob Mizer himself had a profound influence on the culture. He inspired queer artists like David Hockney, who claimed Mizer's vision of a smiling, muscular, sexually free Los Angeles drew him there from his native Great Britain and inspired several of his works. Robert Mapplethorpe, whose own explorations of his queer sexual obsessions and male bodies in his photography of the 1970s and 1980s became the stuff of legends (and inspired his own set of obscenity trials), claimed Mizer as an inspiration, as did the seminal queer erotic artist known as Tom of Finland. Mapplethorpe and Tom of Finland would take the pre-porn sexual imagery of Mizer's work to further and further extremes of expression, challenging the culture's ideas about masculinity, queerness, desire, the definition of art, and whether there should be limits to self-expression. All that from Bob's massive collection of smiling, greased-up young men happily flexing in their thongs. And if inspiring some of the biggest and most controversial queer artists of the twentieth century wasn't enough of a legacy, Mizer's vision of cops and construction workers, centurions and soldiers, cowboys and bikers (all of whom usually lacked either a top or a bottom to their outfit) codified queer desire into a set of archetypes that had massive influence on how gay and queer men saw themselves and that continue to resonate today.

From Smiling Pop Stars to the Man in the Polyester Suit

If you want to travel the queer cultural and erotic history road from Bob Mizer to Robert Mapplethorpe, you have to make a long stop at George Quaintance's place first. It's a little artist's studio called Rancho Siesta, just outside Phoenix, where he and his succession of Latino lovers and partners helped define male queer desires through art and modeling. Quaintance, born in Virginia in 1902, was something of an early-twentieth-century übergay who studied art, dance, and hairstyling, becoming adept at all three. That would all be impressive if not notable, except his artistic endeavors wound up becoming iconic to entire generations of queer men. Picking up the brushes J. C. Leyendecker had laid down, Quaintance expressed his queerness through a succession of legendary erotic male art pieces, made famous because Bob Mizer commissioned many of them for *Physique Pictorial*—including the cover of its inaugural issue. Like Mizer, Quaintance had a particular fascination with uniforms and archetypes, the role-playing of masculinity. His glamorous, gently smiling, perfectly muscular, and largely undressed men were Roman soldiers, cowboys, matadors, Mexican ranchers, and Aztec princes, mostly.

Like Leyendecker's idealized figures, Quaintance's men were shiny, masculine, and very much of their time. The bulk of his male erotic artwork reflects the aesthetics of the 1940s and 1950s, when it was produced. His men tended to look like the crooners and pop stars of the postwar to pre-Beatles period, such as Elvis and Ricky Nelson—sexy for the period but hopelessly clean-cut today, their sleek pompadours always looking slightly ridiculous in Roman bath and prairie campfire settings. But they had flawlessly muscular and hairless bodies, always shiny and squeaky-looking, with a predilection for hanging around innocently with other squeaky men who, like them, had a tendency to remove their pants at every opportunity.

Unlike Leyendecker, whose work was strictly for mainstream audiences, Quaintance painted and sketched for gay men like himself, which meant the erotic undertones could become a lot less subtle. Showing the D was still out of the question, but George made sure that nothing more than a well-placed boot or even a horse's mane flowing in the wind obscured the full picture, as if you would get a glimpse of the forbidden if you just stared at it long enough. Like Leyendecker, he was known to use his lovers as models for many of his men.

Quaintance died of a heart attack in 1957, over a decade before the obscenity laws in the United States would start getting struck down, but he'd already paved the way for other men to make sure that happened. His influence lived on well past his life span, and in ways he couldn't have foreseen, providing inspiration for other queer artists throughout the decades, such as legendary French gay multimedia artists and couple Pierre et Gilles, whose highly stylized photographic work celebrates a similarly iconographic, almost smoothly ceramic form of hypermasculinity rendered in a kitschy hyperreality. More generally, Quaintance's Native American, cowboy, and Roman gladiator imagery became closely identified with gay male desire and found its representation in everything from gay dressing norms (like the late-1970s clone phenomenon) to gladiator B movies of the 1960s (another very popular form of pre-porn entertainment to queer men) to legendary disco group the Village People.

But the most direct descendant of Quaintance's work is unquestionably Finnish artist Touko Laaksonen, the man who became known (thanks to Bob Mizer, who coined the name) as Tom of Finland, whose legendary career launched in the late 1950s, right around the time of Quaintance's death. To discuss the effect this artist had on queer male identity in the twentieth century would take a book three times the size of this one, so massive is his footprint on the culture. Suffice it to say, his hugely muscular, impossibly square-jawed men with nipples the size of teacup saucers and erections the dimensions of an average-size man's arm exploded the queer male consciousness (not to mention its collective id) when the last of the US obscenity laws regarding the depiction of male nudity were struck down by the end of the 1960s. Up until then, Laaksonen's explicit work wasn't available in this country, but he'd already been providing toned-down, less pornographic illustrations for Bob Mizer's *Physique Pictorial* since the late 1950s.

Like J. C. Leyendecker, Laaksonen was an accomplished illustrator; he got his start in advertising in his native Finland. After World War II, which introduced him to his lifelong fetishistic obsession with uniforms (including some fascistic imagery that popped up in his erotica throughout his life), Laaksonen started sketching his male sex fantasy figures, largely sticking to the smooth muscularity envisioned by George Quaintance, along with the archetypal role-playing embodied in Bob Mizer's work. He had less use for cowboy imagery than his American forebears, but Tom of Finland's jaw-dropping eroticism almost singlehandedly established permanent social and style norms for gay and queer men through his fetishistic fascination with military men, policemen, lumberjacks, and bikers. To this day, it's unlikely that you *wouldn't* encounter some version of the looks he established in his work in gay male social spaces.

And finally, to close out this quintet of queer male artists who defined gay male desire, there's the legendary late-twentieth-century photographer Robert Mapplethorpe, whose work photographing his own fetishes and desires helped redefine modern art in the closing days of the century. "Sex is, for me, probably the most important thing in life," he once said. And while his portrait work, including his iconic photos of one-time girlfriend Patti Smith, and his still-life work, including some of the most erotic flowers seen since Georgia O'Keeffe laid down her brushes, gained him much critical praise (and money), it was his pictures of naked men and close-ups of their genitalia that secured him a single-name level of fame and turned it into a synonym for queer male sexual desire. Like

Laaksonen's, his contributions to the culture are so large and well documented that we would be doing them a disservice here if we tried to encapsulate them. But Mapplethorpe's work makes a particularly good way to close out this part of the discussion because it didn't operate or have the same effects of the work of Mizer, Quaintance, and Laaksonen, who told gay men who they wanted to be and who they wanted to do.

When we talk about Mapplethorpe's contribution to the culture, we mean the contribution to the dominant, mainstream one. His work didn't establish queer male desires; it displayed already existing ones in a shockingly personal and uncomfortably public way. He made the fact of his own personal desires explicit in the work rather than dancing around it, none more so than his 1978 self-portrait, which depicts him bent over, in a pair of leather chaps, with the handle of a bullwhip inserted in his anus. This was no fantasy illustration or demurely smiling muscleboy in a thong. Mapplethorpe's art picked up on all the themes in the work of Mizer, Quaintance, and Laaksonen, all the barriers they broke down, inserted him directly into it, and then thrust it all out into the world of art galleries and art critics. It was the ultimate piercing of the barrier between the world of queer desire and the mainstream world that circulated around it.

There's something incredibly satisfying about the circularity of that journey, the way it started with J. C. Leyendecker subtly and slyly putting his desires into the mainstream, followed by a succession of men working underground to make those desires more explicit and more acceptable, and finally culminating with a queer artist pushing all that explicitness from the underground and out into the mainstream. Mapplethorpe's iconic 1980 photograph *Man in Polyester Suit* (the title of which is accurate, even if it leaves out the central aspect: the large black penis of Mapplethorpe's lover Milton Moore hanging out of said suit) sold for $478,000 in 2015. That's the journey. From the smooth, white, demure, soap-ad sexual desire of J. C. Leyendecker to the dick-out blackness and high art of Robert Mapplethorpe, all in the space of less than a century, all driven by queer men who needed to use their art to get their desires out in front of the world.

Sapphic Sisters of the Dime Novel Rack

This next song is for the ladies in the room.

This chapter necessarily focuses on male-oriented erotica in queer culture because of its clear connections to the Pit Crew, but there's a universality to how queer erotica was expressed back in the days when it was dangerous to express it, and while there isn't much lesbian culture to be found in the bulge-filled posing straps of male erotica, it takes only a tiny leap to connect the burgeoning midcentury expressions of queer male erotica with the lesbian pulp fiction phenomenon happening at the exact same time. While they were packaged with attention-getting titles like *The Third Sex*, *Women's Barracks*, and *The Girls in 3-B*, many of the lesbian pulp novels of the era—those actually written by women—were more focused on romantic issues or universal problems of desire, secrets, and infidelity. This isn't to suggest that queer women of the time didn't have a preference for more erotic or pornographic expressions. Legendary fetish queen of the 1950s Bettie Page, whose work regularly featured spanking and bondage scenes with women, didn't become a lesbian icon because of her way with a folk

song, after all. There were certainly women in the 1950s and
1960s producing raunchy artwork and photographs for their
own pleasure or that of their sisters, but raunch wasn't going to
be the gateway for queer women in the same way it was for
queer men, possibly because the existence of mainstream
female-centered pornography for straight men made the has-
sles of producing lesbian-specific content too much for any
Mizer-like impresario to rise up and fill the void. While it
wouldn't have necessarily been a breeze for a woman to procure
the kinds of nudie magazines and postcards available and marketed to men, it was out there and could be passed around or
stumbled upon if a lesbian, bi, or queer woman of the time
wanted it. But it wasn't for them and it wasn't of them. The idea
of any woman launching a for-profit lesbian-targeted erotic industry in the 1950s, when most banks wouldn't allow them to
open a checking account without a man's permission, is sadly
absurd. No, the expression of lesbian desire in the mainstream
was going to have to come through another channel, one just as
camouflaged as the physique mags their queer brothers were
pumping out.

Like the male erotica giants of queer culture, the lesbian pulp
novels of the fifties and sixties represent that very queer need to
push the truth of your desires and identity out into the world, to
express it through the only art you know, whether that's photography, painting, or writing, to a world not only unreceptive but
outright hostile to it. Because of fear on the publishers' part of
obscenity laws forbidding any work that promotes homosexuality, these books ended unhappily for many of the main characters, until actual queer women started writing the books and
their focus defiantly shifted.

Ann Bannon was the pen name of Ann Weldy, whose novels

were so popular with queer women for decades that she's often credited with creating or articulating lesbian archetypes, including what is considered for many the ultimate butch lesbian archetype character, Beebo Brinker. With evocative titles like *Odd Girl Out*, *Journey to a Woman*, and *Women in the Shadows*, Bannon's books defied the norm for the lesbian pulp fiction genre by depicting lesbian relationships as warm, healthy, loving, and, most important, fulfilling instead of harmful. Just as the queer men were off playing cowboys and cops using the tools of art and photography and the arena of physique culture, queer women were quietly using the tools and arena of cheap pulp fiction to define their desires, their roles, their aspirations, and themselves. Weldy was a typical (on the surface, at least) middle-class housewife of the 1950s, who wrote her way through five legendary novels, trying to come to terms with her own desires and to will into existence the kind of life she wanted and the kind of women she wanted in it. She gave up her work in the genre and stayed in her marriage for almost three decades, got a degree in linguistics, and became a college professor, before a rerelease of her titles in the early 1980s shocked her into the discovery that her long-ago books were considered generational classics and she embraced her status as a pioneer in lesbian literature and identity.

In 1952, under the pen name Claire Morgan, celebrated novelist Patricia Highsmith wrote *The Price of Salt*, largely considered either a more highbrow version of the pulp lesbian novel or even the highest version, depending on who you ask. The story of shopgirl Therese Belivet's relationship with coolly intriguing suburban wife and mother Carol Aird was born out of Highsmith's own experiences, particularly the infatuation she had for a woman who came into Bloomingdale's in the late 1940s to buy a doll. Highsmith was working there at the time to help pay for the therapist who was helping her deal with her same-sex urges, and it's possible that very connection is what spurred her creative obsession to develop it into a full-blown novel. Like Ann Weldy, Highsmith resisted taking public credit for the book for decades, even when asked outright by the many literary detectives and interviewers who figured it out. It's interesting how both of these women came to this form of expression based entirely on their own hidden desires, put them on the page, and then tried to walk away from them for major chunks of their lives. Both eventually embraced their past work and came to understand its importance to other women, but it's tragic that they lived in times that made it extremely difficult for them to enjoy or even take credit for it.

The Price of Salt was made into a film directed by Todd Haynes in 2015, *Carol*, starring Cate Blanchett and Rooney Mara, playing out many of the themes of midcentury lesbian literature: complex middle-class lives full of desire and shame, an older mentor figure and a younger naïf, the disapproval of men and authority figures, white middle-class concerns about propriety versus truthful self-expression. Haynes said that the near-total mystery of lesbian lives was partially what drove the novel to greatness, allowing Highsmith to educate as much as express. Her novel and his film of it took underground queer expression and elevated it to high art, much like . . . well, everyone else mentioned in this book, we suppose. Queer culture is the result of queer artists and visionaries leading their lives, figuring it out, reaching out to each other, and expressing their desires, including the desire to enact social change. What started out as a cheap form of titillation for straight men utilizing the lives and bodies of queer women wound up a celebrated and beloved art form responsible for awakening those asleep and broadening the perspectives of queer women who wanted to find out more.

The majority of the lesbian pulp fiction books were written for men, by men, in the manner of all female-centered erotica and pornography. Not to put too fine a point on it, but this tends to make a really good example of how privilege works, even at its most base level. Thanks to the invention of photography and the rise of cheap printing in the nineteenth century, any adult heterosexual male could easily procure pornography and other forms of adult entertainment that catered to his tastes, while any form of it that catered to anyone *other* than straight men was considered indecent if not downright satanic. It wouldn't be fair or correct to liken these books to pornography, however. They wouldn't have even qualified as bodice rippers, but like Bob Mizer and Robert Mapplethorpe, whose work is now celebrated as art rather than derided as pornography, Patricia Highsmith, Ann Weldy, and many other queer female writers of the mid-twentieth century are legendary figures in queer women's lit who used the format of drugstore dime paperbacks to push their desires and aspirations through the barrier and out into the world, for like-minded women to find it—and each other. They were a secret community speaking in code using the detritus of the patriarchy.

The Backroom and Bathhouse Betties of Drag

This is getting somewhat far afield of the world of drag entertainment, so allow us to bring it all back around again. This image of gay male desire we're talking about—the ripped, muscular, youthful, hairless male body in a pair of briefs—was as much a part of queer social life as drag shows, and the two have always stood more or less side by side in queer entertainment. If a young queer man of the mid-twentieth century wanted a night of entertainment that catered to him and was lucky enough to live in a county, town, or city where such things either were allowed or went unenforced, going to a nightclub with drag entertainment and scantily dressed chorus or go-go boys was his best bet from the 1940s through the 1960s. For many queer folks, their introduction to drag went hand in hand with their introduction to the gay male obsession with the male body, because both existed for the longest time as the only open expressions of queerness one could find. A traditional heterosexually oriented burlesque show offers pretty much all the same things a drag show does with the bonus of serving sex appeal to its straight male audience members. Having go-go boys or half-naked chorus boys in drag and gay nightclub entertainment is simply the same urges and dynamics playing out for queer male audiences.

This book is necessarily focused on the big names and the game changers of queer cultural history, but we'd like to take a minute to celebrate those queens who didn't get to play Vegas or Broadway or in a massive drag entertainment revue. The vast majority of drag entertainers in the pre-Stonewall days, when both homosexuality and cross-dressing were outlawed activities, did their work entertaining their brothers and sisters in tiny underground queer spaces. These are the queens of the backrooms and bathhouses, the queens of the twentieth century who plied their trade up and down this great land of ours, surrounded by men in jockstraps on stages the size of a diner booth.

They didn't get to play glittering revues or in front of celebrity audiences or anywhere near a TV studio. These queens sang and told jokes in places where men sought out other men for more than drinks and dancing, sometimes in settings that were either clothing optional or strictly towel only. With bawdy jokes, non-stop patter, and the occasional torch song, they gave queer men a soundtrack for their debauchery, if not their freedom. This social dynamic was a consequence of how and where gay, bi, or same-sex-attracted men could gather and express themselves. And this wasn't just in the pre-Stonewall days of the 1960s—even today, there are small towns and rural communities where local drag queens sing and joke their hearts out next to male dancing enter-tainment at the local one-stop shop of queerness, an oasis where queer desire and queer-specific entertainment can coexist safely. Looking through old gay magazines and newspapers of the 1970s and up through today, you can find an avalanche of ads for local entertainment featuring drag queens posing alongside muscular boys in skimpy costumes.

This isn't to suggest that the big cities lacked such arrange-ments, of course. The absolutely legendary Continental Baths in the Ansonia Hotel (1968–1975) in New York offered multiple floors of queer male entertainment and pleasure seeking, from cabaret shows to salons to discos and, of course, to the baths and private rooms where men who sought sex with men could retire briefly from all that exhausting entertainment. Icon-to-the-gays Bette Midler got her start with a cabaret act at the Continental, featuring Barry Manilow as her accompanist on the piano. She's always been open and proud of her time at the baths and titled her 1998 album *Bathhouse Betty* to honor her time singing, joking, and basically doing her version of drag to a houseful of semi-naked men. In this way, Midler can be com-pared to the camp queens like Mae West and Jayne Mansfield, who routinely featured skimpily dressed bodybuilders in their stage shows and public appearances of the 1960s—a trick they more than likely picked up from the very drag revues that tended to spoof them.

Drag Race likes to celebrate the careers of world-famous queens who travel the globe entertaining their fans, but for the past century, the vast majority of drag entertainers were largely confined to working their own community's bars, and if they were well-enough established, they could travel up and down their area of the country, hitting the gay bar circuit and landing on Fire Island or in San Francisco, Palm Springs, Key West, New Orleans, or Provincetown for the summer. Most of these queens didn't become legends in the grand sense of the word; they may not have always had the polish or stunning collection of costumes of their more accomplished sisters, but these queens were often long-standing members of their local communities, sometimes for their entire lives. Pretty much every single gay community in the country has someone who can tell a story about some legendary drag queen's legendary funeral, when everyone came out to honor a local entertainer who had devoted their life to entertaining their queer family, between acts of gyrating young men in jockstraps or briefs. They got old onstage while their go-go dancers remained ever youthful.

Abs and Butches:
Your Gateways to Queerness

The Pit Crew represents that past, that history, that connection, but it doesn't represent the be-all and end-all of male beauty, no tea, no shade. Queer life isn't about pursuing or exalting the physically perfect, let alone about narrowing the definitions of it to simple archetypes. But we'd argue that a repressive and oppressive society is going to ensure that the most sexually oppressed people of all are going to have the most complicated route to their own sexual expression. Straight, cisgender people never have to "come to terms" with essential factors of themselves the way queer folks do. Some queer folks need those archetypes—whether we're talking about a muscled cowboy or a butch lesbian—in order to navigate their way to an acceptance of their desires and identity.

This isn't to suggest that all same-sex-attracted men ever had a uniform set of desires. When we talk about LGBTQ culture, we talk about those parts of the vast spectrum of LGBTQ life that bubbled up to prominence—the values, aesthetics, practices, slang, and ideas that are, if not shared by most people in a community, at least the most discussed or spotlighted in that community. There was never a time when all—or even the majority of—queer men were uniformly attracted to muscular men. There was never a time when all queer women fell into either the butch or femme category. But these images and aspirations achieved central status in queer life because they were the ones able to pierce the barrier of repression so that other forms of expression could follow. You could get pictures of mostly naked men into the hands of men who desired such things by wrapping them in a veneer of masculinity-enforcing "physical culture." You could get deep, soulful explorations of lesbian lives and dreams into the hands of women by pretending you were writing a steamy pulp novel for straight men to read one-handed.

When queerness was outlawed and feminism was considered a hilarious curiosity, sometimes the best route for expressing queer- or women-centered ideas was through the massive plat-forms open to male consumers. Think of Gloria Steinem going undercover as a bunny at a Playboy Club in 1963 to write about the experience from a feminist perspective, resulting in the most famous exposé of the magazine ever written. That was gender and sexual espionage. If you pretended that your audience was straight men, you could get your defiance through the barriers. What is all this outlaw erotic expression ultimately, if not hope for a confirmation that you are not alone and the pursuit of a connection with like-minded others?

Think of the Pit Crew as the end result of that struggle to express queer desire, from Bob Mizer's mesh thongs and posing suits to Tom of Finland's log-size erections to Mapplethorpe sticking a bullwhip up his ass for a self-portrait and in the process redefining high art. In the end, all that boundary pushing, social change, and legal trouble allowed for something like the Pit Crew to exist on an Emmy Award–winning TV show with-out anyone so much as batting an eye when they bend over for the camera with a wink and a smile.

But no bullwhip.

History lesson:
The Village People

The briefly popular and long-term legendary 1970s disco group the Village People were costumed as representations of several decades of gay male erotic imagery arising out of the work of Bob Mizer, Tom of Finland, George Quaintance, and other queer artists: the cop, the cowboy, the construction worker, the Native American, the leather guy, and the G.I.

Their songs celebrated gay freedom and debauchery by hiding them in catchy tunes and easy-to-mimic dance routines, such that roughly half the wedding receptions in America held in the past forty years have featured America's clueless aunts and uncles line-dancing to a song about gay sex at the YMCA. Oh, they've always been coy about the meaning of songs like "YMCA," "Macho Man," and "Go West," but every queer man in America knew exactly what those songs and images were about. Once again, queer desire pierces the barriers of expression by speaking in code and wrapping itself in the most mainstream and heterosexual of traditions.

History lesson:
The Castro Clone

In response to decades of male erotic artists defining the perfect male figure, gay men of the late 1970s, the first generation to live and socialize freely without fear of being jailed for it, codified the first real across-the-board trend for the increasingly visible community: the Castro clone look. The term has nothing to do with science fiction and everything to do with the kind of rigid conformity you could find in the mostly white gay male social scene of the time. The look, which was popularized in the exploding queer scene of San Francisco's Castro district: close-cropped hair (this at a time when mainstream male pop stars had gorgeously blow-dried lion manes), sideburns, a mustache, a tight plaid flannel shirt or tight T-shirt, tight jeans, boots, and an optional leather jacket depending on weather. Basically a sexy lumberjack or sexy biker costume. There are countless pictures of Pride parades taken at the height of the seventies gay cultural moment where the street is a scene furiously dotted with white men all dressed the exact same way, sporting the same haircut, plaid shirt, and facial hair. The clone look was both extremely influential (some variation of it has existed in gay male social fashion and erotic art in every decade since) and easily derided by the vast majority of gay men who weren't interested in maintaining the rigid conformity or were automatically excluded from it by virtue of being any kind of gay man other than a fit white one. The very term describing it is meant to automatically criticize it. The clone look doesn't have the same power or hold over queer men that it once did, but it sprang up as the first style trend of openly gay men in large part because Bob Mizer, Tom of Finland, and George Quaintance had already spent a couple of decades hammering that very image home to their appreciative audiences.

Chapter 7

The Category Is . . . Serving Sickening Lewks!

*C*ome *through*, queens!

Of all the aspects of *Drag Race* that pay tribute to queer culture and drag history, none are so obvious and direct as the runway portion of each episode. The influences of the runway are easy to parse but impossible to separate from each other because every runway portion of a *Drag Race* episode represents or pays direct homage to three distinct strains of drag influences and styles. First and most clear: From the announcement of the category by RuPaul in the vein and sometimes phrasing of legendary ball announcer Junior Labeija to the catcalling from the judges, the references to ball culture and *Paris Is Burning* are clear and direct. Equally as clear an inspiration in each episode's catwalk promenade is the long history of drag pageants, which expect and promote the kind of high-glamour, realness-serving drag that Ru and the judges tend to support as well as the kind of poise and presentation skills *Drag Race* tends to reward. But if the format echoes drag balls and the presentation style brings drag pageants to mind, there's a third influence, one that's much more about the look, not at all about the poise or presentation skills, and it draws on Ru's own earliest experiences in drag: the Club Kid aesthetic.

The sort of thematic umbrella over all three of these influences, implied by the presence of the runway and as a reference to Ru's breakthrough 1993 hit, "Supermodel (You Better Work)," is his lifelong obsession with the world of high fashion. Similar to his relationship with pop culture, Ru has an encyclopedic knowledge of fashion history. Amid all the bad puns and shticky jokes the judges make during a queen's runway walk, Ru is still the one most likely to reference an iconic fashion look or designer in her remarks.

The judging panel on *Drag Race* evolved over the show's first decade, but it always made sure to keep a fashion expert on it. In the initial seasons, fashion journalist Merle Ginsberg handled the co-judging, along with former *Project Runway* finalist and independent fashion designer Santino Rice. When Michelle Visage came along, she brought a more showbiz point of view, as well as a closer tie to the drag balls, since she'd spent her youth walking the balls and then touring as part of the eighties girl group Seduction. Carson Kressley came onto the panel and brought with him his years of experience as a stylist for major fashion houses as well as his experience as a fashion commentator and even pageant judge.

The judging criteria have also shifted on *Drag Race* over time, not just because the judging lineup changed but also because the culture did. In the earliest days of the show, "realness" in the conventional, *Paris Is Burning*–inspired, gender-illusion sense was much more of a consideration, and anyone who didn't look entirely female got criticized for serving "boy in a dress." Early winners like BeBe Zahara Benet, Tyra Sanchez, and Raja gave the impression that the show specifically favored realness-serving high-fashion glamour queens. Over time, with winning queens like Jinkx Monsoon, Sharon Needles, Alaska

Thunderfuck, Trixie Mattel, and Bianca Del Rio, the show embraced broader forms of drag. Comedy queens were celebrated, and freaky queens like Sharon and Acid Betty were given a bit more leeway to express themselves (although they might disagree with that assessment).

When Merle and Santino were flanking Ru, the critiques were also far more strictly fashion based and interested in matters of taste (believe it or not), fit, and proportion, in line with the show's early-season direction to model itself on *America's Next Top Model* and *Project Runway.* There was a greater focus on femininity and on applying conventional rules of style and presentation to the queens. As the judging panel shifted toward Michelle, Carson, and Ross, so did the criteria and focus of the critiques. At the same time, the show went from airing on Logo TV to reaching a much bigger and broader audience on VH1, taking its early-season aesthetic from greasy lenses and poor lighting to high definition.

And in the manner of all successful reality shows, once the popularity kicked in, a much more competitive style of queen started showing up, with trunks of high-end costumes and couture. With the playing field leveled up, the culture's idea of gender identity and gender presentation changing, and the harsh reality of high definition setting in, the costumes got much grander, and the critiques focused less on realness and "serving fish" (a now rarely used term) and far more on variety, personal expression, impeccable detailing, and show business appeal. In other words, they went from a fashion-based critique to applying a set of criteria far closer to the ones used in the pageant world. *Drag Race* went on a journey as the culture—specifically queer culture—changed beneath its well-heeled feet. Now the criteria tend to ask the queens to show variety in their looks and to push themselves out of their comfort zones. Pageant queens are asked to serve up edgy looks, freak queens are asked to serve up beauty, Club Kid queens are asked to show more technical skills like contouring their faces or padding their bodies, and so on. The point in later seasons of *Drag Race* has been to ask the queens not to stick to one kind of drag, but to push themselves to offer as many kinds as they can manage.

The struggle for *Drag Race* to embrace broader forms of drag and different kinds of drag queens (including transgender queens) is pretty reflective of the history of drag balls and drag pageants, which originated from largely the same idea: queer folks presenting, representing, and defining themselves apart from mainstream ideas of comportment and gender, while undergoing an evolving acceptance of all the forms of queerness. The balls have evolved tremendously over time, largely progressing from a white-only social practice to one strictly representative of people of color and a longtime corner of the culture that welcomed, elevated, and celebrated transgender women. The pageant world, by its nature, has been slower to accept broader definitions of presentation and has come in for criticism over this fact in recent years. To this day, the broadening of criteria to include transgender women and contestants who have undergone cosmetic surgery "below the neck" is a continuing conversation surrounding some of the largest and most prestigious drag pageants, which still tend to adhere to a fairly traditional form of cisgender male, body-mod-free drag just as mainstream beauty pageants for women tend to adhere to a mainstream and conservative version of female beauty. As much as it plays with reality TV tropes and pulls from ball culture, in the end, every season of *Drag Race* is essentially a pageant. Note that they don't give the winner a trophy at the season finale, as drag balls normally do; they crown her with a massive pageant-style crown, give her a scepter, and ask her to walk the stage like Miss America. Or more accurately, Miss Gay America.

Norma Kristie, Queen of America

In 1972, a self-described "country bumpkin queen" from Arkansas named Norman Jones borrowed a dress to compete in the first Miss Gay America pageant and, to her complete shock, won the thing. A savvy operator and quick learner, she wound up buying the pageant, and for the next three decades she helped define mainstream drag at a singular level unseen until RuPaul essentially took over the job with the premiere of *Drag Race*. All this while also fighting back evangelical preachers and the Ku Klux Klan in his extremely conservative community, opening a string of bars and social spaces for local queer folks bereft of nightlife options, and rallying his fellow drag queens to band together and support the very community he practically founded through the worst years of the AIDS crisis.

Born in 1947 in a shack in rural Arkansas, Norman Jones knew from a young age that he had feelings for boys he wasn't supposed to have. Growing up in a religious family in a rural setting at the midcentury, he largely kept his feelings to himself until he graduated from high school in 1964 and promptly flunked out of Ouachita Baptist University. Fearing the draft during the height of the Vietnam War, he joined the navy and wound up stationed at Bethesda Naval Hospital, barely a hop and skip from the gay bars of Washington, D.C., where his true education in gay nightlife began. Norman hadn't had any exposure to socializing with queer men on this level before. It would change the entire direction of his life.

After getting out of the military, he returned home to Hot Springs, missing the freedom and sense of community he'd found in the gay bars of D.C. He eventually found a local gay watering hole, but he had to deal with members of the community occasionally coming by and shooting up the place—sometimes while he was inside. Still, he kept going back and eventually became close friends with a drag queen who went by the name of Tuna Starr. Tuna mentored Norman, more or less becoming his drag mother for a time.

Norma relentlessly promoted the Miss Gay America pageant for several years after her win, eventually taking ownership in 1975 and going all in to promote and elevate it as the premiere drag and gay cultural event of the year. With a preference for realness-serving queens and old-school beauty pageant hair and makeup, the Miss Gay America pageant under Norma's leadership promoted and articulated a long-lasting and highly influential form of glamour and drag presentation that still resonates today and can be seen on the *Drag Race* catwalk modeled by queens like Latrice, Trinity the Tuck, Alyssa Edwards, Naysha Lopez, Coco Montrese, and many others. One of the more common forms of shade thrown at the pageant queens on *Drag Race* is that they can "only" look stunning and beautiful, but the pageant system—especially the Miss Gay America event—asks for a grueling set of requirements and talent displays that makes the vast majority of the *Drag Race* challenges look like amateur night by comparison. Michelle Visage has noted that pageant queens are extremely focused, driven, and performance oriented in a way that Club Kids generally aren't, which may explain why they tend to do well in the competition.

Norma was a local legend in Little Rock as well, turning herself into quite the gay nightlife impresario, opening several clubs that became community mainstays and spending decades fighting off threats and protests from the Klan and local rowdy boys. In the 1980s, as AIDS swept through queer communities and devastated them, Norma helped form the Helping People with AIDS group with fellow queens and members of the community. At the height of the crisis, when her friends were dropping left and right, she did everything in her power to secure them meds, food, housing, support, and a base level of dignity. Norma ruled as a highly influential queen on both the national and local levels, defining modern pageant drag and holding a community together through some of its toughest times.

Like the world and art of drag itself, the arena of drag pageantry has changed and shifted over time. There are ongoing arguments regarding the inclusion of transgender women and the acceptance of beauty standards outside the conventional pageant queen look, such as visible tattoos or other forms of body modification including breast implants and plastic surgery. Norma sold the pageant in 2005, but Miss Gay America still has strict rules about its contestants being male, non–surgically altered, and traditional in comportment and experience. While there's plenty of reason to question these criteria, the Miss Gay America pageant and Norma Kristie are unquestionable legends in queer cultural history and the elevation of drag from the shadows into the spotlight during the twentieth century.

170 LEGENDARY CHILDREN

Bring It to the Ball

To paraphrase the legendary Venus Xtravaganza, You want to talk about ball culture? Let's talk about ball culture. Because you can't talk about *Drag Race* without talking about ball culture, especially the runway portion.

In the late 1980s, a white lesbian documentary filmmaker named Jennie Livingston undertook the task of documenting the vibrant, defiant, and poignant world of the Harlem ball scene, at a time when it was being ravaged by AIDS in communities beset by crime, poverty, and the crack epidemic. The resulting film, *Paris Is Burning*, became a worldwide, award-winning success of such long standing that it has defined the general public's understanding of the ball scene and inspired the current fictional television series based on this time and place—*Pose*, produced by gay television überproducer Ryan Murphy. It made legends out of many of its subjects—not just Dorian Corey and Venus Xtravaganza, but Pepper LaBeija, Willi Ninja, Octavia St. Laurent, Angie Xtravaganza, and Freddie Pendavis.

It did not, however, make any of them rich. Willi Ninja launched a successful career as a dancer and choreographer, helped tremendously by Madonna's appropriative 1990 hit based on the ball scene, "Vogue." He toured as one of her backup dancers for years along with Jose Xtravaganza and used that as a springboard for a well-regarded career in dance until he died of AIDS complications in 2006. But most of the rest of the featured cast of the film struggled, with many dying young and not seeing any significant change in their lives after becoming icons.

Livingston has come in for some criticism over the years.

Some felt she exploited her subjects and some felt she took a colonialist point of view that rendered the ball scene far more tragic and poignant in tone than the defiant act of celebration and competition that it always was. Without so much as implying a rebuttal to any of those criticisms, the film still stands as an intensely focused look at a slice of the culture almost entirely ignored at the time. It didn't make any of its subjects' lives markedly better on its own; but as a document of the culture, *Paris Is Burning* still inspires celebration and examination more than a generation later. The 2016 documentary *Kiki* looks at the same ball scene in the next generation, from the perspectives of people inside it. It makes a perfect companion piece to Livingston's revolutionary documentary, showing in tandem how the ball scene has changed and how the people who keep it alive see and understand it versus how a person from the outside once viewed it.

Michelle Visage has her roots in the 1980s New York ball scene, getting her early training and introduction to the art of voguing and walking the balls by legendary choreographer Willi Ninja. She was the first cisgender woman to walk for the balls and was affiliated with the House of Magnifique. After joining the eighties girl group Seduction, she can be seen voguing in their 1989 video for their hit "It Takes Two," a full year before Madonna released her "Vogue" video. She has quite literally walked the walk, giving her runway critiques the weight of experience.

But all this has much deeper roots than *Paris Is Burning*; the history of ball culture is one that displays and elucidates the shifting definitions of queer identity over that time, not to mention the shifting racial makeup of the ball scene.

The Harlem balls are one of the oldest LGBTQ social

traditions in the United States, going back to the mid- to late nineteenth century. The first gay masquerade ball in Harlem was reported in 1869. The ball scene was originally established by white gay men, who largely controlled it for its first half century of existence. To no one's surprise in retrospect, the ball scene was slow to allow black participants and attendees, a practice that broke down during the social high of the Harlem Renaissance when queer people of color began participating in the ball season (and mainstream nightlife) in greater numbers. The first all-black ball was put together in 1962 by Marcel Christian, who later became a member of the House of LaBeija, which is perhaps not surprising given the house's seminal role in re-centering the balls for people of color.

This dynamic of white gay men and white drag queens controlling the levers of queer social life and culture also played out in the gay pageant scene, which shouldn't be surprising since the balls and pageants were largely born of the same type of event in their earliest years, with pageants breaking off into a different formalized approach. The balls originally stuck with a sort of "debutante's coming out" model of social event while the pageants borrowed from—what else?—beauty pageants. Since both of these heterosexual and cisgender social forms elevated and celebrated a strictly white form of female beauty, it's perhaps no surprise that the same prejudices played out in both scenes. This is, of course, exactly what prompted Crystal LaBeija to walk off the stage of the Miss All-American Camp pageant in 1967 and make cinematic and queer history in *The Queen*, when she thought the judges favored white contestants. Crystal's defiance ultimately led her to found the first of the ball houses and effectively yanked the ball scene completely away from any communities other than queer communities of color.

People tend to think of the ball scene as a drag scene, but that was never strictly the case and is even less so in the modern day. Unequivocally queer and centered on the identities and experiences of black and Latinx artists, the modern drag ball, much like its earliest forebears, is about high forms of presentation first, with drag as only one component of the scene. But whether we're talking about queens in gowns, transgender women in dance costumes, or queer men in high fashion or outrageously eye-popping creations of color and sparkle, the ball scene or kiki scene is about queer people of color expressing their beauty, their desires, and their realities. Note that the great houses of ball culture have a tradition of naming themselves after iconic fashion houses. Note also that the primary dance form arising out of ball culture was named after *Vogue*, the world's number one fashion magazine. What began as a form of display and presentation has morphed into an art form, a competitive dance, and a tool for enacting social justice and fostering community, from the drag balls of the Harlem Renaissance to Crystal LaBeija breaking from the white-oriented pageant system to the modern kiki scene, providing community, family, and opportunity for queer and transgender people of color. Walking the balls is no longer about how you look or even how you present but how you *represent*.

The connection between ball culture and the world of fashion is as strong as the one between ball culture and the world of drag. It all overlaps and it all comes down to the same idea, voiced best in the 2016 documentary *Kiki* by one of the modern ball scene's most important players, Twiggy Pucci Garçon, founder of the Opulent Haus of PUCCI: "When people step onto the ballroom floor, they're not just competing in a category. They're telling their story. Someone who walks is telling you 'I am beautiful.'"

Tracey Norman's Journey from the Runway to the Ball and Back

It wasn't always nice and it was never easy.

Tracey Norman was a stunning African American model in the 1970s who posed in front of legendary fashion photographer Irving Penn's lens, wound up on the cover of Italian *Vogue*, walked the Paris showrooms of Balenciaga, and launched into a steady and quickly escalating career for brands like Clairol, Ultra Sheen, and Avon and magazines like *Essence* and *Harper's Bazaar*. She was also a transgender woman, a fact of her identity she kept to herself in order to continue to work as a model. It worked for a time, but she spent every day of her working life wondering if that was going to be the day her truth was discovered. Black models in high fashion were rare enough in the 1970s, with only a handful of them—such as Iman, Beverly Johnson, and Pat Cleveland—achieving any prominence. For any black woman to make a name for herself in the fashion world at that time was extraordinary. For a black transgender woman, it was more akin to miraculous.

Born in 1952 and raised in Newark, New Jersey, Tracey spent a good portion of her childhood observing the tension and arguments between her parents over her feminine presentation. Her father tried toughening her up with boxing gloves and other forms of socially appreciated masculinity, but Tracey couldn't be boxed out of her identity. Eventually her father disappeared from her life, leaving Tracey with her mother, who literally greeted the news of her truth with open arms when Tracey came out on the day of her high school graduation. Feminine presenting by her very nature, Tracey had only female friends growing up, who shielded her from bullying and pushed her into pursuing modeling. She would lie her way into fashion shows by telling them she was a design student and stand in the back, watching how the models moved and posed, educating herself. In 1975, on a tip, she found herself walking into the Pierre hotel in New York behind a gaggle of well-known black models who were there to be looked over by Irving Penn and the editor of Italian *Vogue* for a future cover. Summoning her courage, Tracey entered the interview space and gave her name, fueled largely by a desire to avoid sex work, which she felt was her only other option as a transgender woman. Penn and the Italian *Vogue* editor were smitten by her poise and gag-worthy set of cheekbones. They hired her on the spot for a two-day shoot in Milan for fifteen hundred dollars a day.

After that, she secured an agent, and the work started rolling in steadily. Clairol shot her in the mid-1970s; for more than six years, her face graced the drugstores of America as the one modeling Clairol color number 512, Dark Auburn.

But the truth eventually came out when a photographer's assistant on an *Essence* magazine shoot in 1980 recognized her from her old neighborhood in Newark and informed the magazine's editor, who ended the shoot on the spot. The modeling opportunities ceased immediately and, in Tracey's words, "the doors closed." Though she knew why, no one in fashion would come right out and tell her. Frustrated and a little humiliated, she left New York and moved to Paris, where she modeled in the

Balenciaga showroom and eventually started picking up a few other gigs here and there in Europe. She made what she later characterized as the mistake of coming home to New York to see if she could continue her momentum and pick up work again on her home turf. But the world of fashion in the 1980s wasn't ready for a black, openly transgender woman to be associated with their brands. The work—and her remaining money—dried up. She wound up working in Times Square in a transgender burlesque show, but her need to serve sickening lewks to the world was still great; she decided to grab herself a gown and walk the balls. She didn't win a trophy on her first try because she didn't have an evening bag, but the experience lit a fire in her and she became a prominent and popular figure on the ball scene, joining the House of Africa and eventually rising in the ranks to become mother of the house.

She was a legendary figure to people who knew of her history in the fashion world, and a profile on the *New York* magazine fashion blog *The Cut* in 2015 returned her to a spotlight large enough to gain the attention of Clairol once again, who read her story and immediately moved to hire her back as a brand model for the Nice'n Easy "Color as Real as You Are" ad campaign in 2016, at the age of sixty-five. Tracey Norman paid the kinds of prices in her life and career that would ultimately help break down the barriers so that the idea of a transgender model working in high fashion isn't just accepted now but rapidly approaching normal. Of all things, the copy for her Nice'n Easy campaign summed up Tracey's journey best: "She's back. She's beautiful. And she's every bit her real self."

Tracey Africa still walks the balls, though.

Party Hard: The Club Kids

"In the '90s, the Club Kids changed drag forever.
They had an influence on, like, every type of drag;
beauty drag, pageant drag—it all has,
I think, felt the legacy of the Club Kids."

Sasha Velour, Club Kid–inspired runway, season 9

At exactly the same time Jennie Livingston was shooting Pepper LaBeija walking the drag balls uptown for *Paris Is Burning* in the late 1980s, a much more well-covered group of queer kids and their friends were taking over the nightlife scene downtown and having just as seismic an effect on the culture.

The Club Kid movement began in the New York club scene of the 1980s and early 1990s, with young queer kids like James St. James and Michael Alig, who came to the city to escape the boring conformity of their white middle- and upper-class upbringings. Creative, wild, and more than a little bratty, Alig and St. James hit the scene like a bomb exploding, throwing increasingly successful parties at clubs all over town (and sometimes just at a subway station or McDonald's or Dunkin' Donuts, with almost no warning or planning), picking up followers and acolytes to follow their brand of drag-inspired nightlife style and total sybaritic abandon. The Club Kid scene was a response in part to the sudden death of Andy Warhol in 1987, which left a massive hole in a New York nightlife scene that was still searching for the next Studio 54, seven years after that legendary queer-friendly night spot was shuttered for income tax evasion. It launched an extreme and outrageous presentation aesthetic that stole from punk, new wave, goth, and drag, heavily utilizing makeup, wigs, hair dye, and outrageous clothing that ranged from raver wear to reappropriated prom dresses to assless sailor uniforms. RuPaul partied on the Club Kid scene and got most of her early nightlife and drag experience in it. She was crowned Queen of Manhattan in 1989 as a leader of the scene. At the time, talk shows like *Geraldo* and *The Phil Donahue Show* loved to invite the major names of the Club Kid movement (including Alig and St. James) to shock the daytime audiences tuning in. Ru made one of her first television appearances on an episode of *Geraldo* in 1990 wherein she deployed her signature phrase "Everybody say love" on the audience and informed America that she'd dropped out of society since Reagan had been elected. The goal of Club Kids was to be shocking but also beautiful in a way that they chose to define for themselves.

The Club Kids took over New York nightlife for nearly a decade, inspiring other Club Kid cliques in major cities around the world and giving birth to several unforgettable cultural figures, from RuPaul himself; transgender model and performer Amanda Lepore; Lady Bunny; nightclub impresario Susanne Bartsch; singer Nina Hagen; Richie Rich, who would go on to cofound the turn-of-the-century bad-boy fashion line Heatherette; actress Lisa Edelstein; season 6 *Drag Race* contestant Vivacious (she of Ornacia, the extra head fame); Patricia Field, fashion designer and costume designer for *Sex and the City*; artist and jewelry designer Walt Cassidy; Kabuki Starshine, one of the most sought-after makeup artists in the fashion industry; and Desi Santiago, who is also one of the most sought-after people in the fashion industry—in his case, for designing stunning runway sets for Marc Jacobs and Opening Ceremony, among others. Gay nightlife columnist Michael Musto spent years documenting and commenting upon the Club Kids phenomenon, going on to his own legendary career as a journalist, cultural critic, and author.

The Unavoidable Part of the Club Kid Story

In 1996, the Club Kid world saw the beginning of its end as a cultural moment when Michael Alig and his roommate Robert "Freeze" Riggs murdered fellow Club Kid Angel Melendez and spent several drug-fueled weeks attempting to dispose of his body (ultimately unsuccessfully) in a grisly and disturbing manner. Eventually, both would be arrested and sent to jail, sending the press into a frenzy of recriminating and tut-tutting over Generation X and how it was full of nothing but layabouts, perverts, and murderers. You know—the usual response whenever someone from an upcoming generation does something terrible.

But the shocking and brutal murder of Angel Melendez is one of those events—like Gene Malin's car crash signaling the end of the Pansy Craze—that tend to put a too-neat closure on something that defines them in retrospect, in a way of looking at it that is perhaps not the most accurate. It's pretty much impossible to write about or discuss the Club Kid phenomenon without mentioning the Melendez murder, but it's also an over-referenced event that shouldn't necessarily be seen as central to the meaning of the moment. Critics of the Club Kids—and of central figures like Alig especially—would argue that their debauchery and the elevation of bratty, drug-addicted attention seekers points to the murder of Melendez as an inevitability arising out of a social movement that was inherently self-centered, unconcerned with social norms, and tainted with an apocalyptic sense of 1980s-style narcissism. This is pretty much the exact argument people made when they declared the disastrous 1969 Rolling Stones concert at a music festival at the Altamont Speedway, which left several people dead, the death of the baby boomer countercultural movement. It's facile and premature in its death-of-the-movement announcements.

The point of the Club Kid scene wasn't drug-inspired nihilism and it certainly wasn't murder; the point was to embrace all types of people—queer, straight, bi, trans, and drag queens—in an unceasing desire to party away the apocalyptic 1980s and blandly conformist 1990s. The point is that it inspired artists, designers, performers, and writers for decades because it centered on the ideas that beauty could be *anything*, that art could be *anywhere*, and that parties, fashion, and self-expression were the height of human existence.

There are plenty of people and events you can point to and declare as the reason why the Club Kid movement happened, but one of its clearest and most obvious heroes wasn't a kid at the height of this moment and wasn't even in New York. Leigh Bowery was personally invited by Michael Alig to come perform at one of their parties and the legendary ground-breaking drag performer happily took the opportunity to spread his madness on yet another continent.

Leigh Bowery, the Boy from Sunshine

"Rather than, say, doing a painting on canvas or sculpting
in clay, I put all these ideas onto myself."

Leigh Bowery, in an early 1990s interview

How to explain Leigh Bowery? Let's try this:

A larger-than-life fashion designer/performance artist/drag
queen/cultural anarchist/nightclub impresario who dominated
the London nightlife of the 1980s, helped inspire the Club Kid
nightlife movement of the 1990s, and continues to have long-
lasting effects on the worlds of drag, fashion, and underground
nightlife decades after his death from AIDS complications.

Nah. That barely covers it.

Born in an Australian town called Sunshine to a supportive
and indulgent family, Leigh was expressive and artistic practically from toddlerhood, and from the moment he could articulate such things, he knew he was going to leave Sunshine for a
big city where he could make a splash and express himself in the
manner he wanted. He flew to London to study fashion, wound
up working in a Burger King, and practically ran screaming into
the night when they offered him a job as a manager. This was
not the plan for Leigh.

He became a figure on the early 1980s London New Romantic nightlife scene and a friend of Boy George. New Romantic
style played with absurdity, glamour, and aspects of drag (hence
Boy George's classic look), but that wasn't enough for Leigh, and
he began creating more and more outrageous ensembles to present himself on the nightlife scene. Wearing wigs and makeup
and items that could be called dresses, he had a drag-inspired

aesthetic that was shot through a punk lens, with a complete disregard for gender presentation in the conventional sense. Leigh was interested in using the body as a canvas and using fashion and drag to distort that canvas as much as possible. Typical of the thinking among boundary-pushing types of the time, he felt that culture was approaching an end point where there would be nothing left to explore or challenge. "I think the only modern thing left to exaggerate is the body," he said. In the early 1980s London fashion and club scene, Leigh stood out, as one critic put it, "like an erection in a convent."

He was a fashion designer who served as his own muse, his own model, his own customer. He didn't really want other people wearing his designs and made very few attempts to sell them. Boy George mentioned that Leigh responded with disgust at the thought of selling his fashion. When he looked at conventional art shows or fashion pieces, he would ask, "Where's the poison?" His goal, outside of the purity of his self-expression, wasn't merely to shock but to challenge, to make uncomfortable, and ultimately to change. "That'll spook them," he'd say about a new look or design. And spook them he did, distorting his shape by taping his belly up to form a pair of breasts, drawing a massive pair of scary-clown lips, dripping paint down his face from his bald crown, shoving himself into latex and wearing an oversize dress with a harness underneath that secured his performing partner (and eventual wife, Nicola Bateman) upside down so that he could portray the act of giving birth to her as she ripped her way through the crotch of his latex bodysuit onstage midway through the performance.

Yes. Leigh was like *that*. "I certainly hope to stimulate people," he said of his work, "and if they're shocked, that's fine as well."

He opened Taboo nightclub in London in 1985 because as he put it, "The social side of a fashion designer is very, very important." Taboo became a legendary hot spot almost immediately, fueled entirely by its proprietor's jaw-dropping sense of presentation and how it can be melded to practically any other form of expression. "It's performance, it's music, it's fashion, it's art—all of those things I've always liked," he said of the club. In bizarre full-body latex body suits and full-face mask topped off by a ponytail (to describe just one look), he towered over the dance floor at Taboo, a spectacularly weird Gulliver to a club full of tweaking Lilliputians, and yet in reality, he was only about six feet tall. His drag, his art, and his personality made him seem larger, scarier, more threatening and imposing than he actually was. Even the famous naked portraits by English painter Lucian Freud (one of which hangs in the National Gallery in London) depict him as a mountainous figure, while the photographs of his sessions with Freud show him to be chubby at most.

Leigh Bowery was like a slow-motion fashion explosion that is still blooming outward a quarter century after his 1994 death. Anytime you see a queen with a paint-drip wig or a model with a huge misshapen mouth, you're seeing Leigh's ongoing influence.

If anything, the fashion of the past decade has paid more of an homage to Leigh than the fashion of the decade after his death. This would probably have been of no surprise to him, since he was aware that the culture hadn't caught up to his vision yet. Alexander McQueen, John Galliano, Vivienne Westwood, Jean Paul Gaultier, and Rick Owens have dipped into the Bowery waters to inform and inspire their own work. From the jewel-encrusted full-face masks of McQueen, to the upside-down birthing harnesses that walked Rick Owens's spring 2016 runway, to the full-body coverings and face masks of Moschino spring 2019, to the crystal-embellished face masks of Gucci fall 2019, to the oversize lips, misshapen head coverings, and body-distorting dresses of McQueen fall 2019, these aren't allusions to Bowery's aesthetic but open homages by designers who speak of his designs with an awe and reverence that belies the years passed since he left.

In 2002, *Taboo*—a musical about the club, the New Romantic movement, Leigh Bowery, and Boy George—debuted on the West End, written by Charles Busch, with lyrics by Boy George. Over its West End run, brief Broadway run in 2004, and revival in 2012, the show and cast members picked up Olivier Awards, Tony Awards, Drama Desk Awards, and a Theatre World Award, all of which comprise far more formal acclaim than Leigh ever saw during his life, even if the art world understood he was a visionary. Isn't that the way with boundary-pushing people whose entire lives serve as art? They rarely live to see the boundaries actually move from all their pushing.

How Do I Look?

From Harlem speakeasies to the nightclubs of 1980s and '90s New York and London, queer folks have a long and well-established history of presentation, costume, and fashion, using all of them to create and define personae and make statements about who they are and how they relate to the world around them. Drag is not always about being pretty or shocking or chic. It's not always just about gender modes or paradigm challenging or shattering the binary. But one thing drag is, in all its many beautiful and horrifying forms, is look-based. You've gotta have a look, honey; whether that look is country queen or horror queen or big girl or pageant or genderfuck, every drag queen, the minute she becomes a drag queen, starts working on her look and how she's going to present herself. In fact, she never really stops. Pageant queens and Club Kids and ball queens, no matter how much they may bicker and put each other down, are all in the same business: using drag to serve stunning, jaw-dropping lewks.

But in a much broader sense, the runway portion of *Drag Race* and all its inspirations are an example of how queer presentation is so highly valued and such an important part of queer identity. Whether gay, lesbian, transgender, genderqueer, or bi, once a queer person comes out and declares their identity openly, there is almost always a follow-up question centering around how they intend to present themselves. Sometimes it's a question of how they intend to seek out romantic or sexual partners and sometimes it's a question of how they are going to express their true gender and sometimes it's a question of how to define their gender identity because it doesn't fit on the binary. For many, perhaps even most queer folks, this question isn't necessarily an important consideration for their sense of self, but on a community and cultural level, the need for queer folks to signal their identity visually, to adopt a mode of dress or manner of presentation, is endemic to their queer experience.

Queerness asks for, if not demands, a level of presentation higher than that of straight or cisgender folks, who don't, after all, have to come out about their straightness or cisness. There's no reveal, so there's no need to present. Queer folks never stop coming out, which means the desire or need to present as queer always exists in our lives in ways big and small. This may be why industries like fashion, beauty, and the performing arts seem to attract a higher percentage of queer folks.

Twinks, bears, butches, femmes, straight-acting, nonbinary, transmasculine, or genderqueer; drag kings, leather daddies, or dykes on bikes—people of the LGBTQ community feel a pressure to declare visually who we are in a way straight folks never really do, or at least, not in the same way. The fact is, queer folks have always been presenting and representing a series of sickening lewks that defined them and help define their culture, ultimately changing the culture around them.

Now walk that runway, darling. Serve it like the world is waiting for it.

Herstory Lesson:
The 1990s: Drag's Previous Golden Age

Paris Is Burning, Madonna's "Vogue," the Club Kid scene, and RuPaul's smash hit "Supermodel (You Better Work)" all hit the culture at roughly the same time. Legendary drag queens and performers like Charles Busch, Lady Bunny, Candis Cayne, Lypsinka, Kevin Aviance, Jackie Beat, Varla Jean Merman, and Joey Arias were making huge splashes in cabaret, theater, and nightclubs. *The Adventures of Priscilla, Queen of the Desert* was an international movie hit that won an Oscar for costume design—all based on classic drag queen aesthetics. The American copycat film *To Wong Foo, Thanks for Everything! Julie Newmar* starred two of the biggest action movie heroes of the decade, Wesley Snipes and Patrick Swayze, happily queering it up (to varying success). Wigstock was an annual event in New York founded in the late 1980s by Lady Bunny that eventually became a popular and award-winning documentary in 1995.

The Lady Chablis portrayed herself in the movie adaptation of *Midnight in the Garden of Good and Evil*, and k.d. lang posed for *Vanity Fair* in male drag in a barber chair while supermodel Cindy Crawford applied shaving cream to her face.

The AIDS crisis was still in full swing for most of this period, but a lot of this big, draggy energy hitting the mainstream all at once was largely a response to the decade-long trauma of the crisis and the utter devastation it visited upon the queer community, queer art, and queer performance. Some saw the nineties queer moment, with its attendant focus on drag, nightlife, and gym culture, as a sort of sublimation of the gay sex drive into other more colorful forms of expression. This is probably a bit too simple, since there was never any indication, despite a lot of opining in both the gay and mainstream press, that people stopped having sex in response to AIDS. But communities and venues based entirely around sex-seeking were less popular than they once were, and many cities, including New York, made a big show of closing down bathhouses, cracking down on public cruising spots, and slapping fines on queer spaces where sexual activity was known to happen. In New York, Mayor Rudolph Giuliani swept into office on an aggressive "quality of life" campaign that sought to turn the devastated infrastructure and high crime of the city into a playground for investors and the wealthy. (Spoiler: He succeeded.)

The big queer response of the nineties wasn't because queer folks weren't having sex but because the dominant culture decided that after a decade of doing nothing while unimaginable numbers of them suffered and died, their spaces and practices were unbecoming. The nineties golden age of drag was a fuck-you to the dying of Reaganism, a fuck-you to Giuliani's aggressive landscaping of New York City, and a fuck-you to the don't-ask-don't-tell triangulating moderation of the Clinton era. By the end of the decade, conformity won out, with white cisgender upper-class gays represented by Ellen DeGeneres's coming out and the smash network television hit *Will & Grace*. In the wake of the medical breakthrough of protease inhibitors, which drastically slowed the death rate among HIV-positive patients, the community turned its collective political attention toward marriage, military service, and adoption rights. The drag moment ended and RuPaul started the twenty-first century at a fairly low point in her career. She has noted in countless interviews that in the first decade of the century, celebrated mainstream drag performances were being presented by largely straight male comedians like Tyler Perry (Madea), Martin Lawrence (Sheneneh Jenkins), and Marlon and Shawn Wayans, in their 2004 film, *White Chicks*. As Ru noted in a 2012 interview, looking back to this period, "Drag had really fallen into the gutter and nobody really cared about it so much." This was the world that saw the debut episode of *RuPaul's Drag Race* in 2009, which changed the modern idea of drag—as well as the profession of drag, the world of drag, and the careers of more than 120 drag queens and counting.

Chapter 8

Mouthing Off: The History
of Lip-Syncing

ome queens become legends over a lifetime and some become legends in the space of a minute.

At the 2001 Miss Gay Black America pageant, as the opening notes of Bonnie Tyler's classic 1984 hit from the *Footloose* soundtrack "Holding Out for a Hero" played over the waiting crowd, a dancer in a sleeveless sequined Superman outfit shielded his eyes and scanned the waiting crowd, setting the stage for what has been called the greatest drag queen entrance of all time. Just as the song intro reached its crescendo and Bonnie Tyler's raspy voice screamed of her search for the perfect man, an ambitious, focused, and clearly hellaciously talented queen by the name of Tandi Iman Dupree wowed the crowd, made herstory, and passed into legend by unexpectedly dropping from the ceiling and landing in a perfect split timed to the first syllable. The crowd roared and Miss Dupree, in a fringed Wonder Woman costume, went on to give them five minutes of stunningly choreographed and perfectly executed lip syncing, the likes of which would have had Ru and Michelle weeping. Four years later she would be dead from AIDS complications, her dreams of becoming the greatest pageant queen in herstory denied her. She would have passed into whispered legend among her drag comrades, the story of her iconic performance retold year after year until it either faded or warped into unrecognizability, but in a twist that reveals just how much modern forms of media and social media have forever altered the drag world, a video of her performance wound up on YouTube, where it has been watched more than two million times— an audience Tandi herself might never have dreamed of. Willam, who revealed in his web series *Beatdown* that this was the first video he saw that made him realize how amazing drag can be, said of Tandi Iman Dupree's legendary performance, "This bitch doesn't just pick the apples, she fucking plows the field the apples were planted in."

A drag lip sync is about providing those unforgettable moments, and some of the best uses of the lip-sync format, like Tandi Iman Dupree's, offer something most singers could not manage while singing. The point is to lean into the artifice while still making it appear seamlessly real. When you produce that perfect lip-sync moment—and you're lucky enough that someone recorded it (as someone always is today)—you can secure your own legendary status with one perfectly executed drop to the floor. The lip sync is the ultimate form of drag expression because beauty and art being wrung out of artifice is at the very heart of drag.

This idea of lip-syncing as a format for jaw-dropping drag moments is at the heart of the Lip Sync for Your Life showdown that ends every episode of *Drag Race* and seals the fate of the two queens standing before Ru. To force two queens to lip-sync simultaneously to determine their fate, after having gone through a usually exhausting set of challenges, is perfectly executed reality show drama crossed with queer sensibilities—and it's not a coincidence that some of the show's best moments tend to come from this feature.

A good lip sync isn't merely about artifice, however. A talented lip-sync artist will find and express their own truth, separate from the original vocal artist's intent. A truly *masterful* lip-sync artist will remix the emotions of a song, filter them through their own character and life experiences, punctuate them with exaggerated flourishes that almost act like a conductor's movements, and play with the audience's emotions and expectations like a virtuoso. It's like a remix without actually remixing. As we've tried to show throughout this book, drag is often about repurposing or remixing from the dominant culture. Whether it's delivering a pastiche of Hollywood tropes or commenting on more important matters with political parody, whether it's serving realness or skewering social norms, the art of drag is constantly taking something "normal" and making it something . . . else.

The Qualities of a Killer Lip Sync

The first truly epic Lip Sync for Your Life occurred in the fifth episode of the first season of *Drag Race*, when BeBe Zahara Benet faced off against Ongina lip-syncing Britney Spears's "Stronger." Both performances were so grandly executed and laden with meaning (Ongina had revealed her HIV status in a tearful meltdown the previous episode) that they left the judging panel stunned and Ru walked off set to compose herself. This was the first time two queens understood what the lip-sync challenge could be, understood that the show's focus on vulnerability and sincerity wasn't just reality TV babble.

But if you want to talk about legendary lip syncs on *Drag Race*, Latrice Royale's face-off against Kenya Michaels in season 4 passed into the annals of high drag almost immediately and to this day tends to appear at or near the top of most listings of the best lip syncs in *Drag Race* herstory. What makes Latrice's performance of Aretha Franklin's "(You Make Me Feel Like) A Natural Woman" so iconic is not just the stunning depth of emotion she brought to the performance—enough to get most of the judging panel to cry. It wasn't just how she used the natural shape of her body combined with acting and mimicry to get the audience to see her as a pregnant woman singing to her unborn child. It was how the performance represented the end point of drag's evolution over the past century. Here was a plus-size black man mimicking a pregnant woman and lip-syncing a popular song. Fifty years earlier, it would have been seen as a raunchy comedy act, the performance would have likely had more than a bit of a misogynistic undertone to it, and instead of being received as high art by a tearful audience, it would have been derided as cheap entertainment from a talentless person off the street who didn't know how to sing. No, really. We'll show you those receipts in a minute. For now, we want to highlight some more high-drama moments in *Drag Race* lip-syncing herstory.

Every queen who finds herself lip-syncing for her life on *Drag Race* wants to prove her worth and bury that other bitch, but no two ever wanted to reach those goals more desperately than Alyssa Edwards and Coco Montrese. In season 4, they brought a ton of emotional baggage with them to sit neatly alongside all their costume trunks. Alyssa had been crowned Miss Gay America and Coco was her first runner-up. For reasons that aren't particularly clear, Alyssa was forced to give up her crown and Coco took over the title. There was resentment on both sides and a history of shade-throwing that had escalated into real anger toward each other and had overtaken the Werk Room with shouted and shaded confrontations. These two queens had *had* it—*officially*—with each other and each wanted the other one out of her line of sight and stripped from the competition. And *that's* why the show forcing them to lip-sync Paula Abdul's "Cold Hearted" in order to send the other one home was like the freaking *Apocalypse Now* of lip syncs. It wasn't so much the performances themselves that made it so dramatic—although they were both on fire and the song could not have been more perfectly chosen for the showdown—it was how weighted with emotion, grudges, and questions of self-worth they were.

But anger and maternal love aren't the only emotions available to interpret, and sometimes a lip sync on *Drag Race* becomes elevated simply through the sheer joy of watching a queen really nail the hell out of a song, like DiDa Ritz firing off the nearly impossible lyrics of "This Will Be (An Everlasting Love)" right in front of its singer, Natalie Cole, who was brought to cheers and YAASes at the sight because she was so swept up in the emotion of watching a queen interpret her song with such life and precision. Latrice, who knows a few things about an epic lip sync, rightly said of this moment, "That is high drag at its finest."

Those are some of the most fun lip syncs to watch on *Drag Race*, when a performer gets so worked up through the power or emotion of the performance that it elevates them. This is when it truly becomes magic—when the artifice and the improvisation build and rise on a wave of confidence. Put in concrete terms, there is simply nothing like watching Peppermint dressed as Madonna in her "Material Girl" video, in the iconic pink gown Marilyn Monroe wore to sing "Diamonds Are a Girl's Best Friend" in *Gentlemen Prefer Blondes* over a half century earlier, perfectly miming a shotgun blast timed to the beat of Madonna's "Music" and aimed at the floundering Cynthia Lee Fontaine. Precision, improvisation, a remixing of the meaning of the song—and all while paying homage to *two* of the most iconic blondes of all time as a transgender woman of color. There are so many layers to that, so many aspects working both on and beneath the surface of the performance to turn it into something viscerally exciting to watch. It's the very definition of slaying the lip sync.

Like Peppermint's shotgun blast, Kameron Michaels and Eureka's facing off in season 10 to Patti LaBelle's "New Attitude" and going into simultaneous impromptu side-by-side jump splits so perfectly timed you'd think they'd spent weeks rehearsing it is a specific type of drama that arises out of the lip-sync challenge— a more kinetic, body-based kind, the kind that Tandi Iman Dupree pulled off so brilliantly. Those sorts of sublime moments of interpretation are what make the lip-sync challenge so exciting— and in the case of Eureka and Kameron, got Ru to take the highly unusual step of not sending anyone home.

From wig snatches to dips to "Swiffering the floor with [one's] taint," in the immortal phrasing of Willam, to "pounding my vagina into the stage so hard the building shakes," to borrow Katya's, the lip syncs on *Drag Race* tend to center an increasingly acrobatic and melodramatic style, imbuing a half-century-old tradition in drag with more meaning and dramatic stakes than anyone could have predicted, let alone imagined, in the hazy, back-of-the-bar days when lip sync and drag were introduced to each other.

But before we talk about how lip-syncing became a tradition in drag, we have to take a moment to look at how it developed in mainstream culture. Why? Say it with us now:

Drag is all about repurposing mainstream culture into something uniquely queer.

Also because the story of lip-syncing in all its forms makes a perfect jumping-off point to discuss issues of artifice and realness as they're defined in both the queer world and the mainstream one, and to point out the bigotry, classism, homophobia, and transphobia underlying lip sync's elevation as a drag art form.

Yes. All of *that*.

A Short History of the Non-Drag Lip Sync

In 1929, MGM studios was about to make history by releasing its first sound picture and the first in what would become an iconic and genre-defining string of musicals. The film was called *The Broadway Melody* and it was historic in a whole bunch of other ways as well. It had what some film historians have called the first clear and obvious-to-the-audience portrayal of a gay male character: a costume designer, complete with lisp and obvious-at-the-time references to lavender, which was a slang allusion to homosexuality. It was also the first film utilizing the songwriting and musical talents of composer Arthur Freed and the first MGM film to utilize a Technicolor sequence, shot for the big production number for Freed's song "Wedding of the Painted Doll," which leads us to the film's most important innovation. MGM execs weren't happy with how the footage and sound from the "Painted Doll" number was coming across but they didn't want to scrap such an ambitious number, with the potential to dazzle audiences with not just the novelty of sound but also the total shock of Technicolor. The studio's sound supervisor, Douglas Shearer, made what would seem like a no-brainer suggestion to any of us, but was a total game changer and a boldly modern way of understanding the medium of film. He suggested that instead of simultaneously recording the sound while shooting the performers, they should not record sound at all and have the singers and dancers perform to a prerecorded track of the song. In other words, he invented the lip-synced musical performance. His simple but brilliant innovation not only saved the number, it may have helped snag the film the first Best Picture Oscar ever awarded to a musical, and it established the industry standard for filmed musical numbers to this day. Arthur Freed would eventually be named a producer at MGM and go on to head his own eponymous department, the Freed Unit, which turned out an astonishing string of legendary movie musicals from the 1930s all the way through the 1950s. They were all legendary productions in their own way, but the most famous and well-regarded of them all was 1952's *Singin' in the Rain*, with a plot that hinges largely on . . . the development of lip-syncing in the early days of sound movies, which brings this little origin story neatly full circle for us.

But lip-syncing wasn't a development that was going to stay limited to the movies, what with television just sitting there by the 1950s. An instant novelty that very quickly became a major trend and then a total game changer for the culture by the end of its first decade, TV was a medium that was largely considered a lesser form than that of theater and motion pictures in its early years, which is partially why so much of early television was turned over to attempts at placing well-acted theatrical productions and full-blown live variety shows in the living rooms of America. There was an instant need and desire in the television industry to prove its artistic worth, which may be why, despite the vast array of musical entertainment options in the first decade of TV, lip-syncing wasn't a common practice on the medium in its early years. It was the series of seismic changes in popular music during the 1960s that got TV as a medium to embrace it. But first, let's have a cocktail.

In the early 1960s, a device for exhibiting early precursors to music videos called Scopitone was installed in hundreds of cocktail lounges and nightclubs throughout America. In essence, they were a jukebox that played filmed or videotaped singers lip-syncing to their hits in usually highly stylized settings on a screen mounted to the top of the unit. They never quite became the explosive new medium that television did, nor did they ever break out of a relatively limited market. But for most of that decade, dozens of pop music acts filmed some form of theatrical, lip-synced performance, most of which still survive today, some of which actually passed into legend. Nancy Sinatra's 1966 Scopitone short for "These Boots Are Made for Walkin'" is legitimately a classic and wound up getting rediscovered in the 1990s when it went into heavy rotation on VH1. Debbie Reynolds's short of "If I Had a Hammer" went on to become something of a modern camp classic when it was rediscovered in the YouTube age, if only for her total unsuitability to the material and the incongruously glamorous staging, which had her descending an enormous space-age suspended staircase in a cocktail dress, heels, and bouffant hairdo while perkily doing her best to let us know she's planning on hammering for justice all over this land.

The point of this happy diversion: Pop music of the sixties lent itself to lip-syncing for reasons of style and performance aesthetics (it allowed for a lot more dancing by the lead singer mid-song), and to a lesser extent, in response to a wave of untrained singers whose style fit the times taking over the charts. Scopitones were an early method of normalizing lip-syncing as something that can be appreciated in forms other than a classic movie musical. Highly popular television shows of the late 1960s and early '70s like *The Monkees* and *The Partridge Family* portrayed "live" performances in-story each episode where the entire cast was lip-syncing. At the same time, pop music showcases like *American Bandstand* and *Soul Train* featured weekly appearances of some of the biggest pop stars of the day, pretending to sing their songs into prop mics while teenagers got their groove on, completely unfussed by the artifice so long as it had a good beat and they could dance to it.

In 1981, MTV was launched and the slow normalization of lip-syncing popular music in staged settings or in front of a televised audience achieved full saturation. Music videos indulged in the artifice of lip-syncing in a way previous forms didn't try, sometimes making the artificial aspect of the performance the entire point of the music video. Gay singer George Michael may have taken the form to its lip-syncing heights with his 1990 video for "Freedom! '90," which featured a string of the most iconic supermodels of the era lip-syncing to his voice.

All these forms of mainstream lip-syncing—classic Hollywood musicals, Scopitone shorts and music videos, variety show performances and sitcoms, even the Macy's Thanksgiving Day

Parade—normalized the idea of lip-syncing as a performing style in the mainstream. There have been times over the years when audiences and the public reacted negatively to singers making live appearances and lip-syncing the words, the most famous in recent years being the performance of the national anthem by Beyoncé at President Obama's 2012 inauguration, a charge she and her team vehemently denied. The only times it was ever seen as a serious scandal was when a singer was discovered to be lip-syncing to someone else's voice. That is a level of artifice the mainstream public doesn't like, and there is usually a significant backlash, to such an extent that it ruined the careers of 1980s pop group Milli Vanilli and at roughly the same time landed the producers of C+C Music Factory in court because Martha Wash (late of Sylvester's backup singers Two Tons O' Fun and her own group, the Weather Girls) sued them for depicting another woman mouthing her iconic vocals ("*Everybody dance now!*") in the music video for "Gonna Make You Sweat." The case settled out of court and Martha Wash was given more prominent credit going forward. But the point was clear: The public doesn't like "fake" lip-syncing, which is, of course, exactly what drag lip-syncing is.

So Why Did Drag Queens Start Lip-Syncing?

Like so many aspects of queer culture, the roots of lip-syncing specifically as a form of drag entertainment are not particularly well documented. We can tell roughly when the practice started on a professional level. If nothing else, we have the development of sound recording and its climb toward ubiquity to give us a rough guide. And there are reasons of money, harassment, and bigotry that can be highlighted as the cause of lip-syncing's prominence in the drag oeuvre. There are approximate dates to circle on history's calendar and rough outlines as to why, but there is no "pioneer" of the origins of lip-syncing in drag. There is no one queen or even one dozen queens you can point to and say, "There she is. There's the queen who put on a dress and a record and called it an act first." This isn't exactly surprising since, as we've mentioned, so much of twentieth-century pre-Stonewall queer culture developed in the away spaces and undergrounds of the United States—and there were no historians on hand to record most of it.

For most of the early to mid-twentieth century, public transvestitism and cross-dressing was against the law in one form or another and varied from county to county, metro area to metro area, making the working life of a traveling drag queen a never-ending litany of stressful situations. Working queens and their establishments had to figure out ways around the police raids and harassment. They didn't always succeed, of course, and plenty of drag queens and performing transgender women had police records for plying their trade or living their truths. A result of this constant threat to establishments that hosted drag shows was a collective reluctance on the part of many musicians to play such venues. The tendency of the culture to accept queer performing and then reject it based on the shifting sands of politics and social mores was highlighted by the rise and fall of the Pansy Craze, the literally violent rejection of disco, and the petering out of the grand 1990s drag moment outlined in previous chapters.

After World War II, drag performing spaces and revues like Finocchio's in San Francisco, the Garden of Allah in Seattle, and the traveling Jewel Box Revue offered high-end female impersonation entertainment to largely straight audiences who were willing to loosen up just a little, what with having survived a Great Depression and a World War. But as the 1950s advanced and McCarthyism took hold as a political movement and social phenomenon, all sorts of backlashes occurred up and down the culture as a paranoid form of conformity became increasingly common and sought to stamp out social heresy. In short, it got harder and harder to put on a drag show in an America that just wanted everyone to act "normal" and was willing to penalize those who didn't. In 1956, Seattle's legendary Garden of Allah, often cited as the first openly gay-owned establishment for gay customers, had to close after many years of providing the best in drag entertainment because the local musicians guild started charging more and more expensive rates to play there, eventually exerting enough economic pressure on the club to ultimately shut it down. It was in this atmosphere that lip-syncing acts became much more prominent in the drag world. Lip-syncing, like so many queer forms of art and expression, arose directly out of and in response to oppression, bigotry, and harassment.

For many years, "record acts" were seen as the lowest, most amateur form of drag there is. Queens who spent years perfecting their female vocalization skills sneered at lip-sync acts for having no talent and artistry and faking the effect without working for it. This wasn't mere drag classism on display— although it's safe to say that's part of it. Lip-syncing's sharp rise in the late 1950s brought about a drastic change in the world of drag, allowing for many performers with little or no training in performing arts to take the stage and fake their hearts out.

In lesbian anthropologist Esther Newton's revolutionary 1972 book about her study of drag queens, *Mother Camp*, the queens she interviewed are quite clear in their sentiments regarding record acts, noting that such shows are cheap to produce because the queens involved are paid much less than other performers. As she was told by one queen, in a commonly expressed sentiment in the profession, "Anybody can mouth a record."

But the queens who launched and popularized this type of performance were doing it for reasons of class, gender presentation, and practicality. First, lip-syncing to a popular female vocalist served as another tool for a female impersonator to help them nail the illusion, just like corsets, wigs, and padding. They weren't lip-syncing to Elvis and the Beatles, after all. The early years of drag lip-syncing were more about big-voiced cabaret and torch singers, whose dramatic vocal styles lent themselves to broad movements and theatrical interpretations—often to deliberately humorous effect.

Second, even before musicians guilds and the cops made it harder to mount live drag shows in more glamourous big-city venues, the tiny underground gay bars and queer house parties in a small town somewhere in the first half of the twentieth century weren't going to be providing their local drag artisans any musical accompaniment even if they wanted it. Putting on a record—or playing a jukebox—was sometimes all a gay bar or watering hole could offer a queen intent on lip-syncing her way to scattered applause. For this reason alone, we think it's fair to say that some form of drag lip-syncing was happening in tiny gay bars and far-from-the-city queer gathering spaces with little to no options for live entertainment well before the rise of the practice professionally by the late 1950s and early '60s.

House parties were common queer gathering spaces from the Victorian era straight through to Stonewall, and they were frequently the only places transgender and queer folks could express themselves in their communities. There isn't exactly a ton of material left that documents these common social gatherings—everyone attending was breaking the law in one form or another—but private photographic stashes over the years have consistently shown a strong drag element in queer house parties. Since there's really no point in having a house party without a record player to keep the crowd jumping (live music might get the police called in for noise violations), that combination of elements—a loose and safe space with drag queens, assorted queer folks, music, alcohol, and possibly party drugs—means there were probably plenty of drag queens lip-syncing to applause from their peers going back to the 1930s. They just weren't professionals or well known outside their social circles. This is conjecture, but ask yourself: Have you *ever* been to a house party where someone didn't lip-sync to the music once it got good or they got a buzz on?

Comedy Lip Syncs

But not all early professional lip-syncing was set to music. For a time, the more popular of the record acts in 1960s drag mouthed the words to comedy routines by popular female stand-up comics like Phyllis Diller, whose classic look incorporating wild hair, tons of eyeliner, opera gloves, feathers, and a cigarette holder was about as close to comedy drag as any female performer came in the midsixties, making her a very popular choice of female impersonators. In *Mother Camp*, Esther Newton describes how the queen performing such an act would often use her body and props to impart dirtier or raunchier connotations to the female comics' jokes, noting how a "typical ploy" of such acts was to "draw attention to the genital area" when the subject of falling in love is worked into a joke and to hold up bottles of lubricant or condoms at inappropriate times. Another common form of recording-based comedy was to perform a torchy heartbreak song while done up in drag as a pregnant "fallen woman" figure, often ending with a baby doll falling out from under the queen's skirt by song's end. Hey, remember when we said Latrice Royale's beautiful portrayal of a mother-to-be lip-syncing Aretha Franklin to her unborn child represented how far the art of drag had progressed in the past half century? There you go—from a cheap gag making fun of women to a pure expression of maternal love and longing, utilizing exactly the same technique to different effects and at vastly different times.

In Pudgy Roberts's 1967 *Female Impersonator's Handbook*, the ol' gal had a few things to impart on the matter of "comic pantomiming" in her typical blunt manner:

Within the field of pantomime, there has sprung into some prominence a type of comedian known as the record comic. (Lately, this is also being done with the glamorous type impersonators, but should, by professional standards, be only for comedy.) As the name implies, phonograph or taped recordings form the basis of his work. A popular comical recording is played offstage while the impersonator silently mouths the lyrics, accompanying them with a pantomime burlesquing of their meaning. This may be a satisfactory means by which a budding comic may make his first venture. However, it should not continue into his professional career as live entertaining puts him in the professional bracket.

Two things about all that: Despite Pudgy's implication that lip-syncing was purely for amateurs—which was the conventional thinking at the time and still has some resonance today—spoken-word lip syncs have always been an important subset of the form to this day. Second, Pudgy was correct to call it a pantomime, suggesting something that is rarely expressed about lip-syncing: that its best renditions and executions constitute an advanced and highly meticulous form of mime.

Going back to the vaudeville era of the nineteenth century, there were drag performers like Julian Eltinge who provided their audiences an evening of song and theatrical performance. The history of drag, as we hope we've proven by now, is one loaded with talented performers and artists of all types—actors, singers, dancers, impressionists, and comics. There have been drag jugglers, magicians, strippers, and fire breathers. If there's a thing that can be done onstage that people will pay to see, a drag queen has done it.

From that perspective, it might be understandable why lip-syncing was looked down on by performing queens. But without besmirching the memories of so many of our queer drag grandmothers and aunties, they weren't seeing it in quite the same way as we do today—and we don't mean that they should have recognized lip-syncing as the art form we recognize it as now. Modern lip-syncing is far more performance oriented, utilizing much better equipment than an old 78 LP on a midcentury record player's speaker. No, the difference is that those queens of previous generations didn't necessarily focus on *drag itself* as an art form. And by that we mean that anyone who gets up in drag is practicing the specific art form of drag. What they do while they're onstage determines what type of queen they are and how well they can do whatever it is they do.

A lip-syncing queen is performing her art, which is the art of being a lip-syncing queen. Some drag queens chose lip-syncing as part of their act not because they can't do anything else but because it was the form of drag that most inspired them. Providing the illusion of a woman's vocals coming out of a man's mouth is, to many queens, no different than contouring her face and putting on a wig to provide the illusion. And one drag artist in particular is credited with elevating the lip sync to previously unconsidered and unimagined levels, forever banishing any idea that a lip-syncing queen is practicing a lower form of drag.

Lypsinka's Wild-Eyed Women on the Verge

Lypsinka, the legendary drag creation of musical performer John Epperson, became synonymous with the art of lip-syncing not just because of her name but because of her meticulously lip-synced performances using songs and dialogue from iconic cabaret acts, films, and television shows of the twentieth century, often moving wildly from voice to voice, song to song, and phrase to phrase at breakneck speed, creating an experience that became a scathing commentary on the mediated image of the twentieth-century woman. His characters are brimming with a kind of broad-grinned, wild-eyed midcentury cabaret or TV hostess glamour and lust for life, but they're also a taut and brittle wire, ready to snap, answering an endless array of ringing phones. To see some of his early New York bar performances in the 1980s is to see the entire reason for lip-syncing—small spaces, no sound equipment or musicians, just a boy in drag, serving up high glamour and female illusion on a stage not much larger than a cafeteria table. He didn't invent lip-syncing as a component of drag, nor was he the first to turn it into art, but he's the most well-known purveyor of the form and he championed and exemplified the idea of the drag performer as legitimate artist. Before Lypsinka, lip-syncing was viewed as a cheap form of drag. After her, it's considered not only a respectable type of performance but a form of expression that can approach high artistic status.

Despite his clear love of silver-screen divas, Epperson's primary inspirations were cabaret performers like Dolores Gray and Kay Thompson, both midcentury singers with big personalities and big voices. The inspiration for her high-fashion retro look came from legendary midcentury fashion models Dovima and Veruschka, who also inspired Lypsinka's name. Capable of lip-syncing a midcentury chanteuse with verve, style, and precision while performing perfect stage choreography and even making mid-song costume changes, Lypsinka was perhaps more well known for her spoken-word lip syncs—and rightly so. In them, his divas give increasingly hysterical monologues, often shouting snippets into a succession of ringing (but nonexistent, because Epperson is extremely gifted at mime) telephones, their rage, fear, and pain escalating to a primal female scream. The singing portions of her lip sync are served up with brio and bravado, like a belting song-and-dance diva from Hollywood's golden age, all broad gestures, cocked hips, three-quarter-turn foot placement, and smiles to the back row.

John Epperson has said that Lypsinka was created as a sort of avatar of his own rage and trauma, growing up in Hazlehurst, Mississippi, as a sensitive, expressive gay boy, constantly belittled and bullied by the surrounding community. He felt like an outsider in his own family because of his love of show business, something no one around him seemed to share. He spoke of being spanked for mimicking Natalie Wood in the film *Gypsy* as a child. He's called Lypsinka a firebrand and "red-headed monster," alluding to the idea that she is full of rage but also brimming with confidence. There aren't many ways you can claim a connection between the two because you won't find two drag artists further apart in style, but Epperson's Lypsinka was very much like the alter ego of sensitive, bullied Glenn Milstead, a.k.a. Divine. Both channeled and performed rage through the art of drag but came about it in such different ways. Epperson has called his performances artificial and distancing to the audience. By leaning into the mimicry and artifice, Lypsinka is able to cycle through as many as forty different female voices in one show and still manage to convey a coherent image of one woman, struggling against outside forces and constantly ringing telephones—and often failing to hold herself together.

Lypsinka modeled, walked runways, acted in theater and film, wrote plays and performed cabaret, played the big venues and the tiny gay bars, and occasionally offered impeccable drag impersonations of Joan Crawford and other leading ladies. She did all these things while elevating and centering the art of lip-syncing. In many ways, despite John Epperson's dislike of the term, Lypsinka can be considered *the* überdrag queen of the late twentieth and early twenty-first centuries, combining high style, musical talent, acting, dancing, celebrity impersonation, and lip-syncing all in the same fascinatingly glamorous and captivating figure. Very few drag performers have straddled so many different strains of drag and excelled at them to her level—not Ru, not Divine, not Lady Bunny, not Jim Bailey or Charles Pierce, not Leigh Bowery or Julian Eltinge. Lypsinka has been lauded as a great artist for several decades but, perhaps owing to her own reluctance regarding the term, she never truly got her due as a legendary figure in the development of modern drag queens.

Sasha Velour has cited Lypsinka as one of her greatest influences, which should be clear to anyone who saw her season 10 finale lip-sync performance of Whitney Houston's "So Emotional," in which she brought the crowd to an ecstatic standing ovation by pulling off her wig in a tremulous fit of what looked like very Lypsinka-esque rage only to have red rose petals fall out from underneath, like some romantic, slow-motion spray of blood. Sasha has gone on since her win to prove herself to be a worthy successor to Lypsinka (who, it should be said, isn't going anywhere anytime soon), with such projects as her long-running *Nightgowns* revue in Brooklyn, for which Lypsinka has performed, and her 2019 show *Smoke & Mirrors*, which revealed the artistry and sophistication of her lip-sync performances. Sasha Velour has credited Lypsinka with inventing modern drag, and that's not hyperbole on her part. Lypsinka encompassed all the parts of modern drag in her work and then elevated them to a higher status. We were wrong to say earlier that there were no pioneers of lip-syncing. It just took about twenty-five years after the form became de rigueur in drag for someone like Lypsinka to come along and turn it into art.

The Tea On:

Priscilla, Queen of the Lip Sync

The 1994 Australian film *The Adventures of Priscilla, Queen of the Desert*, which was, the screen credits informed us, "Filmed in Dragarama," was the watershed moment in pop culture when the public was exposed to world-class drag lip-syncing performances on a much broader scale than ever before. An international critical and box office hit that secured an Academy Award for costume design, the film was part of that 1990s drag moment mentioned in the previous chapter and could rightly be considered one of the main drivers of it. People who had never even entertained the idea of attending a drag show came away from the film with a fairly accurate view of what most of them entail in the gay bar and nightclub scene. As lead character Tick put it when asked what it is he and his fellow queens do for a living, "We dress up in women's clothes and parade around mouthing the words to other people's songs."

The story of three drag queens stuck in the Australian outback and trying to find their way back to a civilization that kept throwing up signals that they weren't welcome could have been a depressing slog of a story as the original AIDS crisis was winding down except for two factors: a wittily funny script (with some elements of early-nineties racism and transphobia, to be fair) and a bunch of hilariously entertaining lip-sync performances. These scenes demonstrated how a lip sync could be both expressive and funny at the same time, something that Ru often looks for in a performance. In the film, they also express character and underline story points, not just by displaying the skill they each have as lip-sync performers but in the choice of material they lip-sync and when.

The opening scene of the film has a bored and disdainful Mitzi and Felicia barely making it through a lip sync of the 1980s unintentional camp classic "I've Never Been to Me," by Charlene, complete with a baby prop they wind up dropping and kicking off the stage. The song, a somewhat awful lament about a woman looking back on her life with regret, set the tone and themes of the film, which puts all three main characters through their paces in order to face up to the decisions they've made (including parenthood) and the people they've become. In one of the film's more heartening scenes, the queens' lip sync of Gloria Gaynor's disco anthem "I Will Survive" allows the indigenous people watching their performance with some puzzlement to bridge the divide and join in, with chants, harmonizing, and didgeridoos added to the mix. In this context, the artifice of the lip sync brought two extremely different groups of people together in joy and self-expression.

Midway through the film, just before she heads out into the night to pick up some rough trade and winds up getting beaten, Felicia perfectly lip-syncs Patti Page's lyrics "I don't care if the sun don't shine / I get my lovin' in the evening time," foreshadowing her own disastrous search for loving in the evening time. Just before the trio's first performance in the Hot Springs casino that spurred their journey on, Bernadette receives a bouquet of roses from her admirer and realizes that she has fallen in love for the first time in her life. Cut to her onstage in an eye-popping lewk, opening her mouth so that CeCe Peniston's "Finally" can come forth and explain her emotional state.

After lead character Mitzi has accepted parenthood by agreeing to raise her son, and her frenemy Felicia has been rescued from a nearly brutal gay bashing, they return home, to the same stage where they kicked a baby doll in boredom, to joyfully lip-sync ABBA's "Mamma Mia" to the film's only depiction of an appreciative audience. *The Adventures of Priscilla, Queen of the Desert* didn't just expose drag lip-syncing to its widest audience to date, it also schooled them on the ways in which a lip sync can be a viable expressive form that filters emotional states into performing artistry.

The Tea On:

The Hierarchy of Drag

Many of the drag performers we've mentioned in this book insisted on being called something other than a drag queen. We're not here to judge them; we're just pointing out that the world of drag performing has always arranged itself hierarchically in one way or another. Theater artists like Charles Ludlam and Charles Busch openly denied the term for their work. Celebrity female impersonators like Charles Pierce and Jim Bailey preferred to call themselves actors or impressionists rather than drag queens. Lypsinka alter ego John Epperson considers the term disparaging and prefers to be called a "surrealist."

When you read firsthand accounts of pre-Stonewall drag queens, such as in Pudgy Roberts's *Female Impersonators Handbook*, Esther Newton's anthropological examination *Mother Camp*, or *Femme Mimics* magazine, it's difficult not to come away with the distinct impression that *drag queen* was often seen as a disparaging term to the professional female impersonator of that time because it was more accurately used for what some professional queens called "street fairies." This term appears to describe transgender women who were possibly sex workers, people who "stay in drag" all day, walking the streets in women's clothing, something many female impersonators of the time considered totally anathema to the idea of being a professional female impersonator in the first place. Newton's book in particular underlines a certain level of disdain and embarrassment on the part of the professionals at the very idea of stepping outside the confines of a performing venue or bar in drag.

Modern drag has its hierarchies and pecking orders still, and there are plenty of modern entertainers and performers who utilize the tropes and aesthetic of drag but refuse to call themselves drag queens. These days, the demarcation line between drag queens and those who do the same job but don't want to claim the term has little to do with gender identity or class and more to do with perceived artistic value or demonstrated economic value—that is, drag artists in the theatrical and cabaret traditions or gender illusionists and female impersonators working high-end entertainment venues such as those found in Las Vegas. The implication these days is that a "drag queen" is someone who performs in gay venues, while a performing artist who utilizes drag but prefers a different term performs in mainstream spaces. This is not written in stone, however. Then again, these sorts of "not our kind" designations never really are.

Drag Race has engendered (no pun intended) a broader acceptance of the term by drag performers; but even now, and probably forevermore, self-identified drag queens tend to separate themselves according to which genre of drag they work in. As we noted in the previous chapter, pageant queens, ball queens, and Club Kid queens can be somewhat tribal in the ways they delineate the differences among themselves. In literature and interviews of the pre-Stonewall era, there was a constant need for "glamour queens" to separate themselves from "comedy queens," a dynamic we still see play out on *Drag*

Race. In the present drag world, there are plenty of working—and in many cases very popular and well-known—queens who make a point of announcing that they're not a *Drag Race* queen and they don't do the kind of drag you see on the show. For all her support of it and her friendship with Ru, Lady Bunny is very clear and open about how she sees *Drag Race* as a corner of drag culture and history, not the be-all and end-all of the art.

These classifications and separations of various forms of drag artistry have been at the center of drag since its inception as a queer art form, and show no signs of dissipating even as the art has achieved previously unheard-of prominence in the culture. The history of this sort of thing is rife with classism and sometimes transphobia, but those aren't necessarily the main reasons why drag is so hierarchical; they're just some of the tools used to separate some forms of drag from others. Why do drag performers see the need to define themselves apart from other drag performers? Because it was an outlaw form of expression for most of its history, arising out of oppression. Any drag performer who managed to carve out a living for herself in that world was naturally going to be incredibly protective of her space and her standing. And let's face it, being kind of bitchy about other drag queens is pretty much essential to the culture of drag. Despite all the demarcation lines and classifications, there's no real history of serious enmity between various drag camps; there's just a deep-seated need to define oneself, which is, when you get right down to it, what drag is all about.

Chapter 9

Untucking the Queer Family

I t's a common scene on *Untucked!*, the *Drag Race* behind-the-scenes companion series that usually airs after each episode. While Ru and the judges deliberate on the fates of that week's greater and lesser efforts, the queens are invited to unwind and untuck at a designating untucking spot. Whether it takes place in the Gold Bar, the Interior Illusions Lounge, or just backstage, the queens kick off their shoes and loosen their corsets post-challenge, letting the opinions and occasionally the shade fly, when suddenly a video monitor clicks on with a message from someone's husband or boyfriend, parents or friends, and the mood in the room changes.

All the shade and the competitive nastiness gets dropped immediately out of respect to the tearful queen listening to her loved one's words. Ru has often joked that *Drag Race* is about bringing families together, but the show truly does make a point to center the idea of queer families—specifically the families queer people create around themselves.

It could be Nina Bo'nina Brown's mother telling her to win because she's been making a mess of her bathroom for years or Farrah Moan's mom talking with pride about how she played with Barbies and faced off against town bullies or Laganja

Estranja's mom apologizing for not reaching out and promising that she still loves her. It could be Bianca receiving a glitter-filled note from her friend's daughter Lola, addressed to "Roy Lady," or maybe it's Trixie Mattel sending a message of support to her old friend Kim Chi (who wasn't out to her family). It could be Ginger Minj's husband sending his love, prompting a tearful Ginger to say to the faces of her tear-streaked sisters, "I did not have a very good life until I met that man," or it could be Chi Chi DeVayne's mother admitting that she didn't know what to make of her growing up but is proud of her, prompting Chi Chi to say through tears, "Y'all just don't know."

But these queens, they know. They *all* know.

It's fair to say, based on a towering archive of anecdotal evidence, that in the performing community you're likely to find a higher-than-average number of people who sought careers in performing spurred on by a lack of support in family life. It's even more fair to say, based on a towering archive of statistical evidence about LGBTQ people and their families, that number is even higher among the drag community. Queer people have always, as a group, struggled with the rejection of their families, and *Drag Race* has made it a point to not only showcase that fact, but to show how queer people deal with said rejection. The "message from home" is a reality TV trope of such commonality that it's seen as a cliché by many seasoned viewers at this point; but *Drag Race*, because of its largely unstated commitment to portraying and highlighting all the nuances and aspects of queer life, has turned it into something more meaningful and emotional. There's no better illustration of that than the way all the queens will suddenly drop any fights, arguments, or reading sessions when someone's family comes into the picture. There's a time and a place for a queen to read another queen, but every queen knows you don't do it while her mama's talking.

In a season 5 episode of *Untucked!*, the queens are all sitting around, reading and throwing shade at Alyssa Edwards, as the queens were wont to do at the time. When they receive a mysterious note telling one queen she'll always be "Daddy's Little Girl," Alyssa, already exhausted from defending herself against the other bitches, snorts that there's no way the message is referring to her because of her nearly nonexistent relationship with her father. Sure enough, a video monitor clicks on and to Alyssa's clear shock, her father appears with a tearful message expressing profound regret for all the ways he's failed his son by not accepting him or by punishing him for not being something he never could be. It ended with him practically sobbing on the words "God sent me a gift and it was you." There were, as to be expected, a mile of mascara tracks running down the faces of those queens by the end, all of whom forgot they were supposed to be ragging on Alyssa's back rolls. Detox summed it up the best, on behalf of so many LGBTQ people: "I know so many of us have been dying for our parents to say that to us."

Like Ru's oft-referenced "teach the children" phrase that pops up with the same regularity, her line about the show bringing families together is meant to be both tongue-in-cheek and deadly serious at the same time. Ru really does want *Drag Race* to teach young people about the world of drag and the lives of its queens. More directly, the show has devised challenges and scenarios specifically to showcase the bonds that families have with their queer members and to showcase how queer people construct families around themselves. "As gay people," Ru has said many a time, "we get to create our own families." The backstage portion of *Drag Race* has served as a showcase of the broad array of family options available in queer life, and when the queens aren't talking about or listening to messages from their families of origin, they're revealing the stories of the family members they chose and formed around themselves.

Call Me Mother

"When someone has rejection from their mother and father, their family . . . When they get out into the world, they search. They search for someone to fill that void."

Pepper LaBeija, mother of the legendary House of LaBeija, in Paris Is Burning

The tradition of drag mothers, like virtually all drag traditions, isn't something to be pinned down to one person or moment in history. It's fair to say that Crystal LaBeija is easily designated as the first person in the ball scene to formalize the title for herself and her house when she formed the legendary House of LaBeija after years of being passed over or ignored in white-dominated balls and pageants. It's fair to say that the ball tradition of houses with mothers, fathers, and other parental figures arose from Crystal's act of formalization and is the one aspect of queer culture most responsible for the proliferation of the drag mother figure in popular culture. But the general relationship of more experienced drag queens and transgender women mentoring younger ones predates Crystal's first declaration in the 1970s. Like the lip-syncing tradition in drag, we suggest that it's more than likely that some form of mentor-mentee/parent-child relationship has been a part of queer drag since its inception in the late nineteenth century. Performing and theatrical communities are rife with this sort of relationship in any case, but when you add the outlaw elements of queerness and cross-dressing, there is even more reason for queen mothers and queen daughters to form bonds.

The drag mother role was certainly formalized and popularized through the ball scene, from Crystal onward, encompassing countless drag queens, their titular houses, and their own legendary children, but drag mother figures are as old as drag itself. Vaudevillian drag acts emphasized "crone" or "wench" figures, with the former often being portrayed by mature or plus-size men in order to convey a matronly style. Julian Eltinge played more than a few matron figures in his career, especially as he got older. For an aging drag queen intent on continuing to perform, leaning into the motherhood persona was pretty much the only option available, and by the 1950s, plenty of queens who learned their trade during the 1920s Pansy Craze were continuing to get up in front of nightclub and gay bar audiences in plus-size dresses, feather boas, bouffants, and a sort of "red-hot mama" persona in order to do some stand-up, sing a song or two, and introduce the next, usually younger, act. The drag mother persona originated as a creature of the stage, born out of the aging drag performer's love of the art and a need to pay the bills.

In fact, the impetus of Crystal LaBeija's cinematic rage was herself following and upholding the tradition of maternal drag. Jack Doroshow was the narrator of the 1967 documentary *The Queen*, as well as the emcee and pageant organizer for the Miss All-American Camp Beauty Pageant of 1967 in her drag alter ego, Mother Flawless Sabrina. "I do this whole 'Bar Mitzvah mother' thing—you know, gaudy gowns, pushy," he narrates, explaining that a maternal figure makes it easier to wrangle the drag queens and keep them in line. "It's a good relationship with them because they don't fear me as competition." But the maternal persona of Sabrina eventually became much more than an act for Doroshow, who spent over a decade organizing hundreds of drag pageants across the country, racking up nearly a hundred arrests over the years for public transvestitism. After retiring from the pageant business by the late 1960s, Sabrina went on to become an activist, first by spending years seeking to overturn every one of her arrests, which spurred her on to fight and protest those laws in the general sense. She moved into a more activist/art scene lifestyle and spent decades working for transgender rights and mentoring a succession of young queer and transgender people, becoming a truly flawless mother to them. Sabrina died in 2018, but her mentees and queer children work today maintaining the Mother Flawless Sabrina archive, which contains all her papers, correspondence, art, and activist work. What was once a saggy-breasted camp persona wound up becoming a life's direction. Mother Flawless Sabrina is considered a drag and transgender rights champion today rather than merely the queen who denied Crystal LaBeija her due.

Sometimes a drag queen becomes a mother to another queen because they've been cut off from their own family and are in dire need of some loving guidance and support. Other times, a drag queen becomes a mother because she sees potential in an up-and-coming queen and feels she can guide her to career excellence. In this way, drag mothers can serve as true maternal figures or they can serve as career mentors, but usually, they wind up straddling the line between them.

Drag Race has been on the air long enough that the drag daughters of earlier contestants have entered the competition, making it a multigenerational tradition among drag families, passed down from mother to daughter. Aquaria became Sharon Needles's daughter. Miz Cracker counts Bob the Drag Queen as her drag mother. Alyssa Edwards has seen her drag daughters Shangela, Laganja Estranja, and Plastique Tiara become part of the family. The Davenport drag family is well represented, from sisters Sahara and Kennedy to their drag nieces A'Keria Chanel and Honey Davenport, who is also Monét X Change's drag mother. Honestly, you need a chart at this point. *Drag Race* has pulled from all these queer family traditions to create its own tradition in drag families.

Family disenfranchisement and LGBTQ youth in crisis are still enormous issues today, but back in the pre- and early post-Stonewall days it was nearly a 100 percent, across-the-board given for any queer person attempting to live an out life. There was a time, not that long ago, when being out meant you basically couldn't remain a part of your family. When a civil rights flash point like the Stonewall Riots occurs, the results can be galvanizing not only for the people demanding their rights but for the people in their immediate circle to examine the ways in which they're impeding those rights. In other words, Stonewall didn't happen just to queer people. It happened to their families too.

Jeanne Manford, the Movement's Mother Superior

In December 1969, the Gay Activists Alliance (GAA) was formed in New York City. Part of a flurry of gay liberation groups formed in the months and years immediately following

the Stonewall Riots that summer, the GAA was an offshoot
of the Gay Liberation Front and initially coalesced in response
to the arrest of Sylvia Rivera as she was handing out gay liberation literature in Times Square. One of the earliest members of
the group was a young gay activist named Morty Manford. In
April 1972, the GAA staged a "zap" at New York's annual Inner
Circle dinner, an event hosted and attended by the New York
media elite. Zaps were a form of protest popular in the 1970s in
which activists suddenly and chaotically descended upon a
scene, disrupted it, and then dispersed as quickly as possible.
Precursors to today's flash mobs but considered much more
disruptive and threatening at a time when public protesting
had become common and occasionally violent, zaps were particularly useful in the burgeoning gay rights movement, because the earliest days had a focus on visibility and getting the
message out to gay people that it was time to come together.
Zaps were a way for queer activists to make a big public menace
of themselves just long enough to get press attention and then
duck back to relative safety and anonymity before the scene escalated. At the Inner Circle dinner, the GAA planned on handing out leaflets to the media to educate them on the rise of the
gay liberation movement, but they unexpectedly encountered
several labor union figures, one of whom got into an altercation
with Morty, throwing him down an escalator and repeatedly
punching and kicking him—all in full view of police officers,
who did nothing to intervene. Morty was rushed to the hospital
and the police eventually called his mother, Jeanne, to inform
her. The officer who called her made sure to let her know her
son was a homosexual, to which she replied, "I know. Why are
you bothering him?"

Jeanne Manford was a teacher in the New York public school

system, and a married mother of three. She'd lost her older son, Chuck, to a drug overdose in 1966, which may be one reason why she so fiercely stood by her surviving son. When Morty became politically active in the gay liberation movement, leading to several altercations with the police, she accepted the truth of his life and told him she supported him for who he was. This was such an unusual sentiment for a woman of her background and time to express that Morty didn't quite believe it himself. She got the chance to prove it to him in a manner the young activist could never have imagined. Unhappy with the police and media response to her son's beating, she wrote a letter to the *New York Post* a few weeks later, taking both to task, urging further action on her son's assault, and underlining her anger at the mistreatment of gay people and their misrepresentation in the media. The letter included the immortal and unforgettable line "I have a homosexual son and I love him."

The bravery of this public statement of support in 1972 is almost impossible to convey. We suppose one way to illustrate how unheard-of her sentiments were at the time is to point to the immediate press attention her letter generated, leading Jeanne to make countless appearances on television and in print interviews, always willing and ready to talk about the lives and struggles of gay people and the responsibility of their parents to show them love and support, often with her son Morty and her husband, Jules, by her side.

She became something of a celebrity in the nascent gay liberation movement of New York, and Morty invited her to walk in the 1972 Christopher Street Parade in June, the early precursor to today's Pride parades. She walked with Morty and the GAA, carrying a hand-lettered sign that read PARENTS OF GAYS: UNITE IN SUPPORT FOR OUR CHILDREN. It took the Manfords some time to realize that all the cheering on the sidelines of the parade was for Jeanne, a spontaneous and joyous outpouring of love from the queer community, delighted by the novel sight of a mother of their own walking proudly alongside her son. She met many well-wishers and grateful members of the community that day, earning an instantaneous status as an honorary mother to many of them. It was a role that immediately became more than symbolic. Her house in Flushing, Queens, soon became a place for gay and queer young people to stop by, knowing that she would welcome them, listen to them, feed them if they needed it, and even call their parents if they asked.

She and her husband conceived of a support group for parents of gays, which she christened, appropriately enough, Parents of Gays. They convened their first meeting in March 1973, less than a year after her first public declaration of support for her gay son—and the first public support of its kind anyone had ever seen. The first meeting of PoG had about twenty attendees, an encouraging number at a time when homosexuality was still listed as a mental health disorder by the American Psychiatric Association. The formation of the group inspired similar groups all over the country, and in less than a decade they were united under the newly formed Parents and Friends of Lesbians and Gays (PFLAG).

In the years since, PFLAG has become a worldwide organization, advocating on behalf of LGBTQ people everywhere and supporting their family members through outreach and education. Jeanne Manford's boldly simple declaration of love for her son, followed immediately by her committed actions toward educating the straight community and reaching out to the queer one, snowballed into a culture-changing phenomenon that transformed the way families of queer people responded to them, worked to oppose antigay crusades, fought to shine a light on the suicide rates of LGBTQ youth, and secured legislation to keep their queer children safe in their schools. Jeanne Manford's tremendous ability to love changed the world. Today there are over four hundred chapters and two hundred thousand PFLAG members in the United States alone, with affiliated or similar groups all over the world, taking inspiration from her fiercely unshakable love for her gay son.

Jules Manford died in 1982. Morty Manford graduated from Columbia Law School and went on to work for the Legal Aid Society and the New York attorney general's office. He died of AIDS complications in 1992. Jeanne lived for another twenty-one years, serving as grand marshal to several Pride parades and continuing to keep the flame of love and acceptance alive until she died in January 2013. President Obama posthumously bestowed the Presidential Citizens Medal on her a month later. In April 2014, almost exactly forty-two years after Morty's beating and his parents' rush to fight on his behalf, 171st Street between Thirty-third and Thirty-fifth avenues in Flushing Queens was renamed Jean, Jules, Morty Manford PFLAG Way. Their legacies and struggles continue to resonate among queer people and their families today. Every time you see some video or letter from a parent to their newly out queer or transgender child go viral, they are following directly in the pioneering footsteps of Jeanne Manford. "I was not the type of person who belonged to organizations," she would later say of her earlier life. "But I wasn't going to let anybody walk over Morty."

Morty Manford was clearly very lucky to have a mother like Jeanne, especially at a time when parental rejection of queer children was the default response. Just as *Drag Race* has made a point to show and highlight the biological family members and parents of queens who have accepted them and celebrated them, it has also made a point to show how queer people often construct their own families in response to the rejection of their families of origin.

This is not only a long tradition in LGBTQ life—for the longest time, it was the defining feature of it. And no period in the past century of queer history made that clearer than the AIDS crisis of the 1980s.

Ruth Coker Burks and the Angels of the Plague

In 1984, Ruth Coker Burks was a twenty-five-year-old single mother visiting a friend in the hospital in Hot Springs, Arkansas, when she noticed one of the patient room doors was covered in a plastic tarp and the nurses were making dark jokes about drawing straws to determine who would go next to check on the patient inside. The AIDS crisis had exploded, both in the numbers of the afflicted and the public consciousness, which responded with fear and paranoia about the disease at a time of tremendous ignorance about its causes and raging homophobia in the face of a community in crisis. Ruth sensed this was what was playing out in front of her, and she decided to push aside the plastic tarp and visit the patient inside herself.

She met a clearly dying young man, wasting away alone. As she chatted with him, he said he would like to see his mother one more time before the end. When Ruth confronted the snickering nurses outside, who were appalled that she even entered the room and interacted with him, they told her that his mother had no interest in seeing him again. Ruth wouldn't accept this and demanded the woman's number, which appeared to be relatively easy to get since the nurses didn't really see the young man as a person, let alone someone whose personal information shouldn't be shared with strangers. Ruth called the woman that night but was met with only anger and shouted prayers about hell and brimstone in response to her pleas for the woman to come and say good-bye to her son. Dejected, Ruth went back to the hospital the next day to deliver the sad news to her new friend. When she entered his room, he lit up.

"Oh, Mama," he said in the throes of end-stage dementia. "I knew you'd come."

"I'm here, honey," she said as she rushed to his side and grasped his hand, skin-to-skin. "I'm here." She sat with him for thirteen hours, giving him the family he so desperately needed as she saw him off on his journey, whispering assurances of love and never letting go of his hand. Since no one would claim his body, she took it upon herself to have him cremated, put his remains in a chipped cookie jar, and then buried him with her bare hands in her family cemetery because she couldn't find a funeral director who would do the job or a cemetery that would take the body.

That moment of devastating kindness and bravery put Ruth on a long journey ushering dozens of men to their deaths with dignity and a hand to hold. When no one else would take their bodies, she buried them in her family's cemetery, which just so happened to have over 250 empty plots available because Ruth's mother had bought every single one of them when she had a falling out with her brother and wanted to make sure his branch of the family would never be buried next to hers. From that one bit of (it has to be said, *shady as hell*) family squabbling came the final moment of dignity for over forty queer men who succumbed at the height of the plague and were left unclaimed by their families of origin.

For years and years, Ruth Coker Burks sat by their bedsides, took them to doctor's appointments, organized their meds, and did everything in her power to make their lives easier and just a little bit longer. She'd order a pizza and sit with them while they filled out their death certificates or wrote their obituaries. She even gave one dying young drag queen his life's wish of an elephant ride at the local zoo. Over time she aided more than a thousand people with HIV, in many cases adding months and years to their lives; in others, holding their hands, giving them love, and letting them know they'd have a place to rest among her kin. "Her boys," she called them. She eventually crossed paths with Norma Kristie, owner of the Miss Gay America pageant and Arkansas drag legend, who began putting together drag benefit shows to raise money for her work. The two of them worked together to secure medications, meals, housing, and support for the dying men in their community. Ruth's back-breaking, heartbreaking work went on for over a decade, until the development of drug cocktails slowed the progression of the AIDS crisis and there were no more desperate men clinging to her for support. She would eventually serve as the White House consultant on AIDS education for her childhood friend, President Bill Clinton. "If it hadn't been for the drag queens," she has said, "I don't know what we would have done."

Ruth Coker Burks was only one woman who managed to do incredible things, but the story of the AIDS crisis during the 1980s and 1990s is also the story of countless unnamed caregivers who tended to the needs of dying gay and queer men—many of them their queer and lesbian sisters in the community—pulling together to raise funds, prepare funerals, organize meds, and feed, house, and raise the spirits of the dying.

There's Barbara Vick, who founded the Blood Sisters of San Diego, a group of over two hundred lesbians who gathered to donate blood to gay men struggling with HIV in the 1980s. Because gay men were barred from donating blood to help their afflicted brothers, these women stepped up to become family to them, literal blood sisters. Many of them were at first reluctant to have anything to do with gay men, evincing a split prevalent in the LGBTQ community by the 1980s, which arose partially out of the decade-long tendency for the gay liberation movement to center on the voices and perspectives of cisgender white gay men, and partially out of the concurrent rise of the women's liberation movement.

There's Dr. Kristen Ries, who, along with a physician's assistant named Maggie Snyder, established Salt Lake City's only AIDS clinic in the 1980s because the community, both religious and secular, had left the city's HIV patients with nowhere to go, no hospital or doctor willing to treat them. Ries and Snyder devised a form of palliative care that centered on human touch and hugging because the mostly queer men coming to see them felt ashamed and dirty. For well over a decade, Dr. Ries and P.A. Snyder saw thousands and thousands of Utah's AIDS patients, advising them, listening to them, and holding their hands at a time when there was little in the way of treatment and nothing in the way of social or familial support. Kristen and Maggie bonded so tightly over their work that they became life partners and eventually spouses, forming their own family unit out of years of being kin to those left behind.

There are hundreds of stories about the legendary caregivers during the AIDS crisis—the lesbians who rose up in sisterhood with their gay brothers, donated blood, delivered meals, and shuttled men to their doctor's appointments; the gay besties and girlfriends who held their hands and called their parents when it was time; the drag queens who performed benefit after benefit, raising funds and awareness throughout the community; and the enraged and loudmouthed political activists who formed groups like ACT UP and took to the streets to shame the straight world and demand action.

In LGBTQ communities all over the world, queer people came together in a time of crisis to huddle and provide aid and protection, support and affection, anger and activism. If Stonewall pissed us off, AIDS made us aware of our responsibilities to each other as a community—and as a family.

Hector Xtravaganza, Grandfather of the Ballroom

On December 30, 2018, the Instagram account for the legendary House of Xtravaganza announced the family's loss. "It is with profound sadness the House of Xtravaganza family announce the passing of our beloved Grandfather Hector. He was a friend to everyone he met, a source of inspiration for all who knew him, and a cornerstone of our House family." There followed a public outpouring of grief and memorials on a level nearly unheard of for a member of the ball community, a testament to Hector's work and life, as well as a testament to the house itself, a sprawling, multiracial, multigenerational family that had just celebrated its thirty-fifth anniversary and thrived under the paternal guidance of this legendary figure of the ballroom. "Blood does not a family make," Hector was fond of saying. It was clear that these were not mere words to him but his entire life's work and philosophy.

The House of Xtravaganza was founded in 1982 by original house mother Angie Xtravaganza. Angie is seen near the end of *Paris Is Burning*, talking with sadness about the murder of her "number one daughter of the house," Venus. Prior to the formal founding of her house, Angie was already acting like a surrogate mother to the queer kids of color who regularly hung out at the Christopher Street Pier, even though, in her midteens, she wasn't any older than most of them. But part of her transition to living as a woman meant, for Angie, a natural evolution toward a more overtly maternal way of relating to the world. Around 1980, she met Hector Crespo, a hard case who had been living more or less on the streets since his early teens, trying to get as far away as possible from the memories of a hellish home life and his own mother kicking him out when she found out he was gay. Hector had already attended his first ball in 1979, at the invitation of none other than Dorian Corey, who he referred to as his "gay auntie," but a life of rejection and the stress of living on the streets had left him pretty messed up; he'd already tried to kill himself a couple of times by the time he met Angie. Even though he was at least a few years older than she was, she took him under her wing and helped him clean himself up. When she founded her own house a few years later, Hector was there, a child of her family since its founding. Angie died of AIDS complications in 1993 before reaching her thirtieth birthday, but her own legendary children kept her house and her legacy alive, Hector foremost among them, as the newly recognized father of the house.

The House of Xtravaganza was the first predominantly Latinx house in the ball community, which had, since Crystal LaBeija's founding of her eponymous house in the 1970s, been a space and a culture designed for mostly black queer and transgender people to congregate, commune, and compete. Over the years it has become one of the more iconic of the legendary houses, partly due to its pioneering Latinx membership, but also because several of its members became legends in their own rights. Angie and Venus Xtravaganza both became famous through their memorable appearances in *Paris Is Burning*; Hector and Jose Gutierez Xtravaganza became early legends in the art of voguing.

Hector devoted himself to reaching out to queer and transgender youth on the streets, just as Angie had for him, establishing himself as an icon of the ball community as well as a father and later grandfather (to which he ascended when Jose Xtravaganza succeeded him as house father in 2003) to countless queer people of color who needed help and support. "This family is more real to me than my biological family," he said in an interview not long before he died. An activist and artist, he taught and judged voguing competitions all over the world, dressed the windows at Bloomingdale's, coached and mentored countless people in the ball community, and, of course, walked and vogued his way into legend. Forever living up to his family name, he served up style and flair and passion for life, personally inspiring thousands. He continued to walk the balls his whole life. "I'm still moist," he'd say, taunting his youngers and children to just try to do a better set of moves than his.

A facilitator and mentor, a father and grandfather, an artist, visionary, and pioneer, Hector Xtravaganza represented the very best of the ball community: acceptance, family, artistry, and fierceness. When asked what it felt like to vogue at a Berlin voguing competition in 2012, he answered in terms of family: "The only way I can say it is I just feel like a damn-ass, good-ass Xtravaganza."

The House of Xtravaganza, like all the legendary houses of the ballroom scene, welcomed the forgotten and cast-aside members of their community, saving or changing countless lives for the better, putting queer Latinx people on a path of self-expression and self-acceptance, with unshakable family support promised to them for life—and through nearly four decades of that work, Hector Xtravaganza proudly and ceaselessly cast his arms wide, sometimes to strike a pose and sometimes to embrace a new child of the family.

Herstory Lesson:
The AIDS Quilt

The AIDS crisis of the 1980s and 1990s devastated queer communities and left a scar on LGBTQ history a mile long and a mile deep. Queer people at the time saw their years of post-Stonewall freedom of expression met with a stone-faced lack of concern from the mainstream when the LGBTQ community needed them most. The result, especially among the activist class, was twofold: an incandescent queer rage and a bone-deep understanding that the queer community needed to rely on itself and come together as a family more than ever.

In November 1985, gay activist Cleve Jones was leading a memorial march and candlelight vigil in the memory of legendary gay rights activist and politician Harvey Milk and Mayor

George Moscone. Both men were murdered in 1978 in a crime
that shocked the country and turned Milk into an iconic figure
in the gay rights movement. Jones, a colleague and friend of
Harvey Milk's, had led the memorial march every year since.
This particular year, the march happened just as the news hit
that a thousand San Francisco residents had died from AIDS.
Distraught by this news and the public's indifference to the devastation happening around them, Jones asked the people in the
crowd to write down the names of those they had lost on their
placards and signs. At the end of the march, those names were
taped to walls of the San Francisco Federal Building, which
made a particularly suitable backdrop for the horrifying mosaic
of names, given the nearly total lack of response to the crisis
from the government. This was the same year that President
Ronald Reagan deigned to utter the word *AIDS* in public for the
first time, having waited until more than twelve thousand
Americans had died of the disease before acknowledging its
existence.

Cleve Jones noted the stunned reaction of the crowd at the
overwhelming display of the dead and noted to himself that it
looked like a quilt. As he told it later, many times over the years
(as one does when one witnesses something legendary being
born), he then closed his eyes and saw a vision of a giant quilt
memorializing the dead and covering the National Mall in Washington, D.C., the ultimate fuck-you to the federal government's
infuriating lack of concern. One of the people in the crowd that
night was a young woman, a self-described party girl and "wild
child" named Gert McMullin, who loved to party in the gay bars
and nightclubs with her friends—until they all started dying at a
rapid clip, leaving her not just in mourning but consumed with
rage, needing an outlet and desperately casting about looking

for one. In retrospect, it feels like she and Cleve Jones were bound to come together sooner rather than later—and that's exactly what happened. Between the two of them and a small group of early volunteers, the NAMES Project Memorial Quilt was born. Working out of a small storefront in San Francisco, Gert McMullin and other volunteers compiled information, reached out to the community, and sewed until their fingers bled, as what became colloquially known as the AIDS Quilt began literally taking shape. Gert would eventually make more than 130 panels of the quilt herself, each one in memory of a friend gone. Cleve Jones realized his vision in 1987 when the quilt was displayed on the National Mall the first of several times over the years. To this day, three-by-six-foot panels are continually added to the quilt, which has over forty-eight thousand of them, memorializing over ninety-four thousand of the dead.

Conceiving of a giant quilt might seem, from several decades out, like an odd way to react to a mass death event like the AIDS crisis, but the AIDS Quilt not only helped family and friends of the dead express their grief and memorialize their fallen, it helped the larger LGBTQ community to come together around a powerful symbol of comfort, warmth, and a sense of being home. What could possibly be cozier than a quilt encompassing the entire queer family?

Much like the Stonewall Riots, the effects of the AIDS crisis of the 1980s are still being felt today as marginalized communities continue to struggle with HIV. To date, over seven hundred thousand Americans have died from the disease. The initial crisis acted as an ignition agent for the modern gay political movement as queer men and women, little more than a decade after Stonewall and the birth of the gay rights movement, came face-to-face not only with a devastating plague but with the realization that the larger community could shun and ignore them so easily and without hesitation.

The AIDS crisis was a tragedy regardless of the nature of the people it took, but there was a special poignance not only because it hit the disenfranchised and powerless so hard but also because it caused long-lasting damage to the queer community and the mainstream culture as a whole, considering that entire generations of performers, designers, authors, and artists were wiped out. Queer men and women have always been drawn to the expressive arts, and the loss of countless thousands of talented people working to create the culture left it bereft of the kind of wildly energetic queer art that characterized the twentieth century up until its last decade and a half. This loss galvanized the queer community like never before or since, and much of what constitutes the modern queer family was solidified in the years the family was most threatened and felt most abandoned. Isn't that the way with all families? When they go through a trial, they either fall apart or pull the string encircling them tighter.

The Tea On:

Drag Makeover Challenges: Building a Family Through Drag

"We choose our own families." Time and time again over the course of the show's history, Ru has stated this point. In fact, he has stated it so often and with such vehemence that it seems to us it's up there with "If you can't love yourself, how in the hell you gonna love somebody else?" and "We're all born naked and the rest is drag," forming a sort of triptych of his most closely held beliefs about the transformative and empowering nature of drag. Like so many of Ru's ideas about drag, along with *Drag Race*'s unstated role as a museum of queer cultural life, several aspects of the show revolve directly around this point.

The *Untucked!* episodes that feature family messages highlight the queer family dynamic, but the once-a-season drag makeover challenges actually make the queer family dynamic manifest through the art of drag. In these challenges competing queens are assigned a person who has never done drag before—often a straight man—and the queens are tasked with turning them into a drag sister, mother, or daughter. In the end, they are judged on how well a "family resemblance" is achieved through the use of makeup, wigs, and costuming, as well as how the two queens relate to each other onstage. It's a challenge that asks queens to make someone into a family member, complete with a family resemblance. It's making Ru's belief about queer families take physical form using drag as both a tool and a metaphor for family bonds. If the Werk Room is about doing the work of being a queer person in the world, then the makeover challenges and *Untucked!* reveals are about living your queer life the best way you can, whether that's in the arms of your parents, your spouse, your best friends, or your drag sisters.

The queens have been asked to make over a group of female martial artists, social media influencers, and the cast of *Little Women: LA*; they've taught gay military veterans, straight jocks, and senior citizen gay activists how to walk in heels and flip their hair like a diva. They've turned straight grooms into blushing brides, kiki'd with members of the *Drag Race* crew as they taught them to tuck and werk, and even made over their own sisters and family members in their drag image—all the while bonding and sharing, learning and teaching. You know, family stuff. When *RuPaul's Drag Race* debuted in 2009, gay couples could not get legal recognition for their marriages in the United States. Almost ten years to the day from the show's debut, *Drag Race All Stars* season 4 featured the honest-to–Supreme Court husbands of several queens in that season's family makeover challenge, underlining just how much had changed for the queer family in the span of the show.

The early family challenges seemed to deliberately play into some stereotypes, like lecherous mature gay men or total bro jocks. Over time, they served to bridge a gay-straight divide and open up discussions about gay marriage and queer families. Through humorous scenes of straight men learning to wear heels, corsets, and wigs, and cringing through a tucking tutorial, the show is using drag itself as a metaphor for family ties. Or put more succinctly (by Ru, of course) during season 9's Crew Better Work challenge, "The family that drags together slays together."

Chapter 10

The Ministry of Drag

You know, people always come to me, "Girl, why you take drag so seriously? You're not curing cancer." No, but I'm making it easier for people to live with.

Ginger Minj at the makeup mirror, season 7

*D*rag Race season 4 alum Kenya Michaels was performing her set at a local gay bar on Latin Night and the club was packed with Latinx LGBTQ folks and their friends, who were all feeling what Miss Michaels was serving in her white bodysuit, cha-cha heels, and Beyoncé wig. Finishing her lip-syncing and dancing set, a sweaty and out-of-breath Kenya took her bows to the cheering crowd, blew them kisses, waved good night, and headed back to the portion of the club that served as her dressing room. That's when the guy with the semiautomatic rifle opened fire on the crowd that had just applauded her. It was June 12, 2016, this was the Pulse nightclub in Orlando, and forty-nine queer and queer-friendly people were killed as one man's rage was once again turned toward the disenfranchised and unleashed on them while at their most vulnerable. Kenya hid during the shooting and later posted on Instagram of her emotional devastation and of the many friends killed that night: "My heart is broke. They took everything from me."

It's not surprising that a drag queen was at the single worst instance of anti-LGBTQ violence in history. A drag queen threw her shot glass at the bar mirror at Stonewall and screamed for her civil rights. Drag queens twirled and joked and lip-synced their way through the AIDS crisis, raising money and awareness and pulling the community together. Drag queens marched for marriage, screamed for the right of their queer siblings to serve in the military, and danced their joy for half a century on enough Pride floats to make it to the moon and back if you stacked them end to end. Drag queens and kings have been at the center of queer life and present at every single battle and celebration in the past century of queer history. When they weren't the soldiers on the front line, they were the queer fife and drum corps, keeping time and urging the community to continue pressing on.

Drag Race initially offered and defined drag as a way of making sense of the world and challenging its assumptions, but over time, Ru started talking about drag as a tool to *change* the world, a person at a time, a family at a time, a country at a time. Part of the reason the show was ripe for success from the start was that it debuted at the beginning of the Obama era, when inclusivity and LGBTQ recognition seemed to be at an all-time high. Part of the reason the show has become more political over time can be traced to the sudden political shift that occurred with the Trump presidency. This is not the stretch it might sound like. RuPaul was loudly and proudly devoted to celebrating the Obamas and all the possibilities they represented (going so far as to pose for a composite portrait as both Michelle and Barack when he was first elected in 2008) and has become a vehemently vocal anti-Trump voice in the past few years, openly advocating drag and self-expression as ways of combating political oppression. Does this seem like a realistic goal or an achievable one, to think you can change the course of history by promoting drag? Maybe not. But ten years ago, the idea that a reality show about drag queens sandwiched between lube and HIV meds ads on a mostly unwatched cable network catering to a fairly small demographic would win Emmys and make stars out of its contestants while changing basic ideas about gender, LGBTQ life, and expression the world over seemed downright laughable—so maybe we should all give Ru a little benefit of the doubt on this one.

In its earliest form, *Drag Race* was as close as any television show ever got to depicting life inside a gay bar. Over time, as it highlighted queer families and told queer stories and confronted queer issues, it expanded outward. With the shift in the culture toward acceptance of gay marriage rights, the rise of the transgender community as a political force, and the culture-wide questioning of the gender binary that all occurred during the run of the show, Ru has adopted a phrasing about drag that highlights its political as well as personally transformative value: "the ministry of drag," which indicates how far the show has come from its dirty little poorly lit drag revue days on Logo. The focus now is on overcoming adversity, on drag as an act of personal and cultural triumph, on drag as a political statement, if not an outright call to revolution. "Drag doesn't change who you are," Ru noted during an *All Stars* season 4 judging session. "It reveals who you are." Ru's belief in the revelatory power of drag on both a personal and political level is, like so much of the show, born out of actual figures and events in queer cultural and political history. The most glaring and obvious example of drag's spiritual potential can be found in one of the oldest and largest drag organizations in the world—and it all started with *The Sound of Music.*

The Spiritual Joy of the Sisters of Perpetual Indulgence

The Sisters of Perpetual Indulgence are a queer anarcho-political street-theater-oriented order of activist drag nuns who have been "promulgating universal joy and expiating stigmatic guilt" in accordance with their sacred vows since 1979.

Yes, really.

The genesis of the order is shrouded in legend, but it goes something like this: A young gay man named Kenneth Bunch was living in Cedar Rapids, Iowa, in the late 1970s. He was an actor with a low-budget community theater group mounting a production of *The Sound of Music.* Kenneth hit up a local convent for some habits and veils for the production and the sisters, no doubt charmed by the wholesomeness of the request, were only too happy to help out. Legend doesn't record if the production about the plucky Austrian nun who found romance was ever actually pulled off, only that Kenneth kept the box of habits and that it wound up making the trip with him when he moved to San Francisco soon thereafter. On Easter Sunday 1979, Kenneth and two friends decided they were bored by the stultifying queer conformity of the Castro clone era, pulled out Kenneth's box of nun's habits, got themselves all dolled up, and headed to the local nude beach—as one does when one is queer and bored and thinks the world could use an enema. These three men, along with a fourth cofounder, came up with the idea of an order of queer nuns, and promptly took their monastic names as Sister Vicious Power Hungry Bitch, Sister Missionary Position, Sister Hysterectoria-Agnes, and Reverend Mother and established the Sisters of Perpetual Indulgence.

The early group was something of an offshoot of the Radical Faeries and found a good deal of its early membership among that tribe of queers. The Radical Faeries were founded in the late 1970s by Harry Hay, legendary early pioneer of gay rights, who felt that the movement had become far too assimilationist. The Radical Faeries rejected heteronormativity and celebrated a countercultural pansexual and pangender queerness that was decades ahead of its time. Their insistence on radical gender politics, freethinking, and the liberal use of glitter for self-expression made the Radical Faeries a perfect recruiting ground for the order.

Dressed in habits and elaborate wimples based on those of Belgian nuns, paired with a ton of face paint, glitter, baubles, and jewelry, the Sisters of Perpetual Indulgence are sacred clowns of drag, using the trappings of Catholic female spirituality to forge their own mission, their own spiritual calling, and their own traditions. The order is no joke. In fact, many of the sisters don't like to be called drag queens at all because they see themselves as nuns following a stated mission of serving the community both spiritually and politically. Applicants must go through a process mirroring that of many Catholic nun orders, moving from aspirant to postulant to novitiate as they formalize their calling and pass a series of tests and tasks. What makes them interesting is how engaged they are with the community at large, not just the LGBTQ parts of it. They have marched, protested, and advocated for such causes as safe-sex education, HIV/AIDS research, "no nukes," pot legalization, breast cancer research, LGBTQ youth issues, and safer streets. Co-founder

Sister Vicious Power Hungry Bitch described the order's sense of spirituality in a video produced by the order in the early 1990s: "We recognize that there is grace in this life and there is power, and there is something that creates, generates, moves, and sustains everything. I feel that as long as I hold myself before whatever that is, then the grace can flow through me to do whatever needs to be done." What's most notable here are the final six words: "do whatever needs to be done." The sisters aren't here just to perform or poke at norms, although that's clearly a huge part of their philosophy. They have a calling, and every sister who declares herself is expected to fulfill that calling, to herself and to her community.

On Easter Sunday 2019, the San Francisco chapter of the Sisters of Perpetual Indulgence celebrated forty years of anarcho-queer spirituality by once again holding their legendary Hunky Jesus contest in Dolores Park, to an appreciative crowd of thousands. Today, the order is worldwide, with over six hundred sisters administering the work of the order in countries all over the world.

The sisters are part of a long San Francisco tradition of politically active, issues-focused drag that seeks to affect the culture, whether we're talking about the Cockettes and their glitter-bombed anarchist hippie drag or the Empress of San Francisco herself, blazing trails and opening doors for countless LGBTQ folks.

José Sarria, Absolute Empress of Drag

José Sarria worked at the legendary San Francisco queer café the Black Cat in the 1950s as a waiter and, later—because like any queen worth her glitter, José couldn't keep his mouth shut while working and soon became known for his singing voice—as an opera-singing drag queen. José was born in San Francisco in 1922 and, to hear him tell it, never really had to come out of the closet because he was never really in it. He lived his life openly—even while serving in the army during World War II, when all hands were needed and the fact of his open gayness mattered less than the fact that he was willing to serve.

After he came back from the war and started gaining a reputation as a local drag queen of some talent and flair, he became known and billed as "the Nightingale of Montgomery Street," famous among the queens and queers of the time for his practice of leading everyone out of the bar at closing time, singing a parody of "God Save the Queen" reworded as "God Save Us Nelly Queens." Bear in mind just how incredibly restrictive and conformist the 1950s were and how bold it was to round up a bunch of queer folks to literally sing out their queerness into the night. More pointedly, José led the song while directing the group to sing it to the men being held at the roundhouse across the street, locked up for cruising. That is some seriously fabulous defiance.

In 1960, he jumped feet-first into politics, first by forming the League for Civil Education, which he launched to combat the laws that made it illegal for bars and restaurants to serve alcohol to queer people. He was the first openly gay candidate to run for office in the United States, making a run for the San Francisco Board of Supervisors in 1961, in response to ongoing police harassment of the gay community. He didn't win, but he garnered enough votes, press, and visibility to change San Francisco politics for good, ensuring from that day forward that the gay community was itself a voting bloc and constituency whose voices deserved a hearing and whose needs deserved consideration. It was a huge step, and for most people, that would be enough of a legend to hang your name on, but José was just getting started.

In 1965, after being awarded a crown as queen of the Beaux Arts Ball, José declared himself "Her Royal Majesty, Empress of San Francisco, José I, The Widow Norton." That latter part of her title was a reference to the legendary nineteenth-century San Francisco character Joshua Norton, who similarly declared his de facto royal status in 1859 as the Emperor Norton. From that initial inspiration, José went on to form his own court, awarding titles of nobility to its members and dubbed it, naturally enough, the Imperial Court of San Francisco. Not just a form of queer socializing or cosplay, the Imperial Court of San Francisco was civic minded, raising money for LGBTQ organizations and groups through—what else?—drag shows.

As you might imagine, the idea of drag queens and queer folks modeling themselves on the grand royal courts of Europe was too delicious to remain within the confines of San Francisco. Imperial Courts started springing up in other cities, and within a decade of the San Francisco court's founding, the International Imperial Court System was established, bringing together chapters in cities all over the world, dedicated to raising funds and awareness of LGBTQ causes and giving queer folks and drag queens a way of bonding together and using their fabulousness to help change the world. Today with over sixty-five chapters worldwide, the International Imperial Court System stands as one of the oldest and largest LGBTQ organizations in existence.

The Absolute Empress José Sarria died in 2013 at the age of ninety, having achieved legendary status through her groundbreaking political and organizing work. She is buried in a plot next to the Emperor Norton.

The Upcoming Legendary Children

As *Drag Race* and its host rack up Emmy wins, the alumna queens walk the runways and red carpets of the world, record albums, shoot movies, star on Broadway, and guest-star on television shows; as the world of drag becomes more mainstream by the minute, the next decade of *Drag Race* could be even more game changing than the first. Even better, there are already scores of queens and queer folks out there doing the work of changing the world for the better—often using drag as the tool to do it. These are the upcoming legendary children.

In 2017, Daniel Vais, a London choreographer working with a company for dancers with Down syndrome called Culture Device Dance Project, was scouting performance spaces with a member of the group when they came upon a drag show mid-performance. The dancer with Vais, a young woman named Sarah Gordy, was the first person with Down syndrome to be awarded an MBE by the Queen, an award typically presented to people who have achieved high status in the arts. She was delighted by the drag show, which inspired Vais on the spot to introduce her fellow Culture Device performers to drag. And thus the performance group known as Drag Syndrome was formed. Initially consisting of a half dozen or so enthusiastic performers with Down syndrome, the group immediately took on new recruits after its first performance in March 2018 to a sold-out crowd at a queer performance space in East London. Vais is very clear that the group is not a charity but an honest appreciation for the art of drag, opening it up to a group of people uniquely suited to interpreting its skewed take on the world. With members of the group taking inspiration from *The Rocky Horror Picture Show*, *The Adventures of Priscilla, Queen of the Desert*, and yes, *RuPaul's Drag Race*, they are upholding some of the oldest traditions of drag, consulting its holy texts, and moving the form forward.

A Texas drag queen named Beatrix Lestrange rallied a half dozen of her drag sisters in February 2019 and headed to Brownsville to stage a protest at the border of the United States and Mexico, which had become a hot-button political issue thanks to the efforts of the Trump administration. Beatrix and her posse of queens went to the border specifically to raise money and awareness for their sisters and other members of the LGBTQ immigrant community in the best way they knew how: by putting on a drag show, right there at the border. A few months earlier, a group of LGBTQ asylum seekers had broken off from a migrant caravan, fearful of mistreatment and violence in the group. Around the same time, a transgender woman from Honduras named Roxsana Hernandez died while in the custody of the United States Immigration and Customs Enforcement agency. Beatrix and her sisters performed for the small crowd and raised over six hundred dollars for RAICES, a nonprofit organization that provides legal services to immigrants. "The vision was to perform in front of this wall, and project our beauty, and our glamour, and our empowerment against this symbol that stands for hate, racism, and xenophobia," she said to the press.

The performer known as Desmond Is Amazing is something no drag queen or female impersonator could ever have conceived of for . . . well, the entire history of drag performing: a drag queen who is a child—literally one of the legendary children. Born just two years before *Drag Race* debuted, Desmond says his earliest memories revolve around the show, which fascinated and dazzled him pretty much since he learned to walk and talk. His parents suspected he might be gay from toddlerhood and encouraged Desmond to express himself in any way he saw fit, with no gender-based boundaries applied to him—not just as a way of accepting himself but as a tool for navigating life as a person on the autism spectrum. He supposedly came out by the time he entered kindergarten, and he started teaching himself the art of drag—with all the alumnae of *Drag Race* plus Ru herself as the best teachers any little drag-interested boy could hope for. He has performed in the New York Pride parade, appeared in Jinkx Monsoon's video for her song "The Bacon Shake," walked New York Fashion Week runways, appeared in *Vogue*—and suffered the slings and arrows of people and politicians who have accused his parents of child abuse and likened his interest in drag to child pornography. He remains unbowed and amazing, serving as an LGBTQ youth ambassador and activist and establishing the first drag house for children: the Haus of Amazing. It's perhaps not surprising that someone who has accomplished so much before even hitting puberty also has a motto by which he lives his life. It's even less surprising what that motto is, given how he's living it: "Be yourself, always."

Panti Bliss is the most popular drag queen in all of Ireland. That might be considered accomplishment enough, but she is also widely beloved for her political advocacy and the sharp wit she employs to get her points across about LGBTQ equality. "My job as a drag queen is to sort of commentate from the fringes, to stand on the outside looking in, shouting abuse," she explains in the 2017 documentary *The Queen of Ireland*. "I'm a clown, I'm a fool, I'm a court jester. And like the court jester of old it is my job to sometimes say the unsayable." And that she did, giving an impromptu speech at the Abbey Theatre in Dublin in 2014 that wound up going viral worldwide, in which she explained what it was like to grow up queer in a world loaded with homophobia, how damaging that is to queer people, and how much anger it has left in her after a lifetime of bearing that weight. RuPaul called it "one of the most powerful speeches I ever heard." Panti went on to become a gay activist and spokesperson for the LGBTQ community in Ireland, which was struggling in the twenty-first century to become a forward-looking, modern, and progressive country after centuries of conservative Catholic social mores dominating. She campaigned tirelessly to get gay marriage passed and argued passionately for why the country should do right by its gay and lesbian citizens, who were owed this base level of dignity. When the people of the Republic of Ireland voted to allow their gay and lesbian citizens full and equal rights of marriage in May 2015, Panti Bliss was heralded as a heroine to the community—a symbol of queer pride, drag fabulousness, and the power that can rise up when both are working together to foment change.

Indya Moore is a nonbinary transgender actor and model. Before they shot to stardom as a member of the cast of *Pose*, Ryan Murphy's television series about the Harlem ballroom community of the 1980s, they'd been kicked out of their parents' home, put in the foster care system, and dropped out of high school in response to relentless bullying. Strikingly beautiful and charismatic, they began modeling as a teenager, working with high-end brands such as Gucci and Dolce & Gabbana.

But they didn't love the fashion industry's take on body image and body positivity and didn't find the work fulfilling. Indya eventually crossed paths with Jose Xtravaganza and was a member of the legendary house for a time. Jose and Hector Xtravaganza were official consultants for *Pose*; it was through their connection with the show that Indya caught the eye of its producer, who cast them as a transgender sex worker and member of the fictional House of Evangelista, Angel Evangelista. *Pose* boasts the largest cast of transgender actors in the history of film and television, but even then, Indya managed to stand out, garnering critical acclaim for their portrayal of the young transgender girl just looking for love and a life to call her own. In 2019, Indya was named one of *Time* magazine's 100 Most Influential People, a tribute to their own work and talent, but also a sign of how far things have come for transgender and nonbinary representation in mainstream culture.

Fashion designers Phillipe Blond and his partner, David Blond, have taken genderqueer sparkle and sprinkled it all over the culture, thanks to their intense love of pop culture, fashion, and glamour. The Blonds, as they are known, trade in sparkly, glamorous, pop music–inspired fashion with Club Kid undertones and have outfitted Katy Perry, Beyoncé, Rihanna, Janelle Monáe, and Nicki Minaj for the stage and for the red carpet. To attend a Blonds runway show is to be treated to a parade of nonconformists, queers, downtown freaks, and celebrities. Unlike most shows at New York Fashion Week, theirs combines glamour, fashion, pop culture worship, and, most unique of all, fun. The centerpiece of every Blonds runway show is always Phillipe himself, who stomps down that catwalk in a pair of thigh-high stilettos, a face beat to the gods, and pin-straight blond hair trailing down to hit the back of his knees as he models his own creations. Long before the current drag moment happening in the culture, the Blonds used drag in their shows and in their aesthetic, reminding the fashion world that the two forms have always been intertwined.

Michell'e Michaels is a transgender woman who works as a performer, serves as mother of the legendary House of St. Laurent, and is answering the call of celebrity impersonation by wowing crowds with her Beyoncé lewks, moves, and impersonations as Miss Shalae. Queen Bey herself called out to Michell'e in the crowd at her historic Homecoming concert at Coachella in 2018, impressed that she was able to stunt her look from her concert a week before with such perfection and precision. This reminds us of moments in queer culture like Judy Garland hopping onstage to give Jim Bailey a hug while he was in Judy drag and Carol Channing noting at Charles Pierce's funeral that he did a better version of her than she did.

Marti Gould Cummings is a drag queen in New York who founded the group HK Dems to organize and rally voters in her Hell's Kitchen neighborhood. She has gone on to become a force in local politics with an eye toward national work and exposure. On a slightly less serious but just as high-impact note, a video of Marti lip-syncing "Baby Shark" to a little boy at a drag brunch went viral in March 2019—evidence of just how mainstream drag had become and with that mainstream position, how much more power drag now has to change the conversation.

Maebe A. Girl is a genderqueer nonbinary Los Angeles drag queen who was elected to the Silver Lake Neighborhood Council in April 2019, making them the very first drag queen to be elected to public office in the United States. Girl, who rose to political prominence by performing scathing impersonations of

Trump administration figures such as Betsy DeVos and Kelly-anne Conway at a Silver Lake weekly drag brunch (shades of the political underground films of the Cockettes), vowed to fight to "provide visibility for those that have historically been kept in the shadows of society" and expressed hope that they would inspire others to run for office. That same month, at the other end of the rainbow, South Bend, Indiana, mayor Pete Buttigieg announced his candidacy for the 2020 presidential election, making him the first openly gay candidate to formally run for the office and mount a nationwide campaign. The political work of the Absolute Empress José has been passed on to a new generation who are going to take it to a level she always knew would be achieved someday.

Kia LaBeija is an artist, queer woman of color, dancer, HIV activist, and mother of the iconic House of LaBeija, working to destigmatize HIV though photography, outreach, and voguing. Kia was literally born into the HIV-positive community and lost her mother to AIDS by the time she was thirteen years old. Educated at Juilliard and the New School, she vogued her way across the stage to accept her degree at her graduation from the latter. She was introduced to the balls in her college years and found solace, expression, and freedom there, among queer and HIV-positive people of color. Searching for something to replace the mother she'd lost to the plague, she found family, art, and identity in the ball scene. It's more than fitting that a woman like this—a woman of art and color, of dance and freedom, of beauty and defiance—would carry on the work and name of the legendary Crystal LaBeija, continuing Crystal's work of challenging the norms and restrictions of the LGBTQ community as it intersects with race and gender expression.

Current superstar transgender models like Hari Nef and

Andreja Pejić are signing historic contracts with beauty and fashion companies and sashaying down the runways of the world with a ferocity and power that calls back to Tracey Norman and her trailblazing work as a successful transgender model of the 1970s—without having to hide their truth or live in fear of being clocked, like she did. Popular singers like Big Freedia and Kim Petras are continuing the non-gender-conforming and trans queer music traditions that Jackie Shane, Sylvester, and countless other forebears and legends established, but with a freedom of expression (not to mention a freedom to live their lives openly and truthfully) that so many who came before them never had.

We note all these current and future legends not merely to celebrate the mainstreaming of queer drag and the elevation of transgender and nonbinary people in the culture, but to show how they walk in the high-heeled footsteps of those who struggled, suffered, and fought before them, building on and benefiting from the work they did. Mainstream sensibilities should never, in our opinion, be seen as the ultimate end goal of the LGBTQ community. We should always push for equality and tolerance, but we must continue to celebrate our outlaws and envelope pushers. We should still give people in the LGBTQ community plenty of space to be weird, or shocking, or freakish if they want to be. The history of the LGBTQ rights movement is one that centered the mainstream over the margins, and that was an early mistake that took many years to address and course-correct. We are a happily married white gay male couple who are about as mainstream as the modern LGBTQ community can get, but we would never advocate our own lives as the model upon which all queer lives should be based, nor should anyone else. The folks in this book were legends, heroes, and

rebels who literally changed the culture if not the world by defiantly living their truths, truths that were seen as shocking, un-
natural, and disturbing at the time. We should not reward their
bravery by insisting on a straight-and-narrow image of queerness that none of them ever subscribed to.

Right now, LGBTQ rights are threatened all over the globe,
including in the United States. Transgender women face enormous risks of violence; transgender women of color face the
highest risks of all. The HIV epidemic is still taking lives. Transgender people are barred from serving in the military, and
LGBTQ folks can still be fired from their jobs or denied housing
for who they are. Queer folks of all stripes are still at higher risk
of violence, depression, and suicide than the general public.
Queer and trans youth are mercilessly bullied in their schools
and communities. It is still, despite all the strides made, a hard-
ass job being a queer person out in the world. We still need
legends to stand up, declare themselves with purpose and fierceness, and, if need be, fight like hell for themselves and their
queer families.

If there's one thing we wanted to get across to you with this
book it's this: You stand in history. Smack-dab in the middle of
it. You are not at the end of it and you are not at the beginning
of it. No one ever is. You exist on an ever-shifting spectrum of
light that bends and changes and morphs underneath your feet.
Yes, it's true, legends once walked the earth. They still do.

Maybe you're one of them.

Suggestions for
Further Exploration

The following list is merely a starting point to deepen the understanding of topics raised and people highlighted in the book. Some of these items offer further material such as film, photos, or video to supplement the points raised in the book; some build on those points and take them further.

Films and Documentaries

The following are all available on streaming services or for individual rental online.

- *Paris Is Burning* (1990), directed by Jennie Livingston. The seminal drag ball documentary that introduced the world to voguing, shade, reading, and the lives of LGBTQ people of color at a time of social devastation due to the AIDS and crack epidemics.
- *Screaming Queens: The Riot at Compton's Cafeteria* (2005), directed by Susan Stryker and Victor Silverman. Detailing the Compton's Cafeteria riot of 1966, the film provides a very good illustration of the lives of "street queens" and transgender women in the days before Stonewall, touching on the illegality of their very existence at the time, as well as police harassment and the total lack of opportunities.
- *The Queen* (1968), directed by Frank Simon. A snapshot of drag pageants of the mid-1960s, inadvertently highlighting their

tendency to ignore queens of color, setting off Crystal LaBeija's legendary read. Also of interest: the hotel room scenes of young gay men in a pre-Stonewall era talking about many of the goals the gay rights movement would wind up pursuing, such as marriage equality and military service rights.

- *Tricia's Wedding* (1971), directed by Milton Miron. The Cockettes starred in this underground film, which serves as a prime example of the kind of parodic drag that arose out of trash cinema and underground theater of the 1960s and 1970s.
- *Pink Flamingos* (1972) and *Female Trouble* (1974), directed by John Waters and starring Divine. Legendary classics of underground trash cinema with a queer bent.
- *The Legend of Leigh Bowery* (2002), directed by Charles Atlas. Not just a profile of the legendary performance artist and designer but a snapshot of the New Romantic scene of the 1980s, which spawned the career of Boy George (also in the film) and inspired the Club Kids a decade later. Also serves as an illustration of how the art of drag can be pushed to further and further extremes to change the culture.
- *The Queen of Ireland* (2015), directed by Conor Horgan. A profile of Panti Bliss, the drag queen who fought for gay marriage rights in Ireland and became a heroine to the nation and an example of the power of drag to effect change.
- *Vegas in Space* (1991), directed by Phillip R. Ford. A high-camp science fiction spoof with some of the most jaw-dropping drag ever captured on film. It has inspired the modern evolution of the drag aesthetic and serves as a perfect companion to any *Drag Race* sketch comedy challenge, showing where it all comes from.

YouTube

- Sylvia Rivera's "Y'all better quiet down" speech in 1973 at the Christopher Street Parade. An example of Rivera's uncompromising personality as well as the sneering complacency of the gay community at the time.
- Jim Bailey's 1970 performance on *The Ed Sullivan Show* as Judy Garland (compare to Judy Garland's original performance of "The Man That Got Away" in 1954's *A Star Is Born*), highlighting the meticulousness of Bailey's impersonation as well as the somewhat

unusual spectacle of a full drag performance being broadcast into an unsuspecting America's living rooms one year post-Stonewall.

- Jackie Shane's 1965 performance of "Walking the Dog" on Canadian television in what we'd call genderqueer or nonbinary drag today. This at a time when the vast majority of viewers would have seen her as a man with a serious psychological issue. The bravery and poise is astounding.
- Lypsinka's 1991 short film *Anything Goes*, which captures the aesthetic of the "drag moment" of the 1990s and represents the act of drag lip-syncing at the highest levels of artistry.
- James St. James's "Daily Freak Show" episode 223, September 2012. Former Club Kid St. James interviews punk icon Jayne County on the set of Sharon Needles's video. Jayne talks about her time during Stonewall and in the underground scene of New York and London in the 1970s.
- Ballroom Throwbacks Television (https://www.youtube.com/user/BALLROOMTHROWBACKS/videos). A huge archive of ball and kiki scene videos spanning the twenty-first century, offering a much-needed update from inside the modern ball scene.
- The New York Club Kids appearances on *The Phil Donahue Show* and *Geraldo* circa 1990. Highlights the sometimes-sophomoric need of Club Kids to be shocking, as well as the middle American response of the time, which was to be shocked.

Online Archives

- Queer Music Heritage (www.queermusicheritage.com) has a stunning collection of musical recordings by queer and non-gender-conforming artists going back to the 1920s, as well as an exhaustively curated collection of digitized drag revue program booklets, advertising, performer interviews, and publicity materials dating back to before World War II. Thousands of publicity photos of long-forgotten drag queens and drag kings, representing a perfect overview of how the aesthetics of drag have changed over the decades.
- Digital Transgender Archive (www.digitaltransgenderarchive.net). A massive searchable database that includes thousands of materials documenting the lives and practices of drag queens and transgender figures both famous and long forgotten. You can find digital

copies of 1960s and '70s magazines *Femme Mimics* and *Drag*, as well as programs and advertisements for drag shows spanning the entire length of the twentieth century.

- Bob Mizer Foundation (http://bobmizer.org/). An archive of the work of queer erotic photographer Bob Mizer, including his writings on self-expression and obscenity.
- David de Alba's Theatrical Arts & Tributes (http://www.david -de-alba.com/). David was a working female impersonator for many years in the Jewel Box Revue and at Finocchio's in San Francisco in the 1960s. The site contains materials and photographs documenting both his career and the careers of many of his contemporaries and forebears, with rare (if amateur in tone) interviews with several performers you can't find anywhere else.

Articles and Essays

- "From *Paris Is Burning* to *Pose*: The House of Xtravaganza," by Michael Bullock, *The Cut* (blog), *New York*, October 26, 2018, https://www.thecut.com/2018/10/the-house-of-xtravaganza -at-35.html.
- "Throwing Shade: How Black Women Use Humor on Social Media to Deflect Pain," by Tameka Bradley Hobbs, http://www.forhar riet.com/2015/04/throwing-shade-how-black-women-use.html. Highlights and explains how shade arises out of marginalization and specifically African American cultural and humor traditions.
- "A Bit of Woman in Every Man: Creating Queer Community in Female Impersonation," by Mara Dauphin, *Valley Humanities Review* (Spring 2012). Further information on how drag and female impersonation revues in the twentieth century created queer-only backstage spaces while performing for mixed audiences.
- "Forbidden Love," by Margaret Talbot, *The New Yorker*, November 22, 2015, https://www.newyorker.com/magazine/2015/11/30/for bidden-love. A further exploration of the lesbian pulp fiction phenomenon and the social and legal restrictions placed on queer women of the mid-twentieth century, preventing them from expressing their desire openly.
- "Before Rockwell, a Gay Artist Defined the Perfect American Male," by Hunter Oatman-Stanford, *Collectors Weekly*, August 28, 2012,

https://www.collectorsweekly.com/articles/the-perfect-american
-male. Visual samples of J. C. Leyendecker's erotic queer artwork
that flew under the radar of the mainstream public and inspired
the greatest American illustrator of all time, the decidedly straight
Norman Rockwell.

- "The Great Blues Singer Gladys Bentley Broke All the Rules," by
Haleema Shah, Smithsonian.com, March 14, 2019, https://www
.smithsonianmag.com/smithsonian-institution/great-blues-singer
-gladys-bentley-broke-rules-180971708/. Pictures and video of the
seminal drag king performer of the 1920s and a deeper exploration
of her life.

Books

- *Queers in History: The Comprehensive Encyclopedia of Histori-
cal Gays, Lesbians, and Bisexuals*, by Keith Stern (Dallas: Ben-
Bella Books, 2009).
- *Transgender History: The Roots of Today's Revolution*, 2nd ed.,
by Susan Stryker (New York: Seal Press, 2017).
- *The Right Side of History: 100 Years of LGBTQI Activism*, by
Adrian Brooks (New York: Cleis Press, 2015).
- *Transgender Warriors*, by Leslie Feinberg (Boston: Beacon Press,
1996).
- *Beefcake: The Muscle Magazines of America 1950–1970*, by F. Val-
entine Hooven III (Cologne, Ger.: Taschen, 1995).
- *Out of the Past: Gay and Lesbian History from 1869 to the Pres-
ent*, by Neil Miller (New York: Vintage, 1995).

Acknowledgments

Because we'd never be able to live with ourselves if we pretended this all sprang forth from our brows fully formed, we must recognize and thank our agent, Monika Verma, for her incredible patience with us as well as for lighting a fire under us with one simple question: "Hey, why don't you guys write a book about *RuPaul's Drag Race*?" Further thanks and recognition must be paid to our editor at Penguin Classics, Elda Rotor, who saw a germ of a good idea in our initial proposal and gently nudged us into the direction that ultimately became this book. There are also countless queer historians, essayists, and journalists whose work over the years inspired or directed our research, foremost among them JD Doyle and his Queer Music Heritage site, as well as Hugh Ryan, Horacio Silva, and Mikelle Street, whose work documenting drag, LGBTQ, and ball culture kept popping up in our research over and over again, guiding and informing us. Our friends and families have been incredibly patient with us, forgiving us for our absences and indulging us when they finally saw us and we couldn't stop talking about this book. To the Bitter Kittens, the most devoted readers of our blog and listeners of our podcast, who also cheered us on and patiently waited for us to return to them, full of opinions. Special thanks to "Frankie" Brodsky. And finally, to RuPaul, Michelle Visage, Ross Mathews, Carson Kressley, and the entire alumnae cast of *RuPaul's Drag Race*, thank you for entertaining, enlightening, and inspiring. We hope you all continue to teach the children and walk them in nature forever.

Index

Note: Instances of "*DR*" refer to *Drag Race*.